ARCHIE

RICHARD H. GOLDWATER

VP/MANAGING EDITOR
VICTOR GORELICK

VP/DIRECTOR OF CIRCULATION
FRED MAUSSER

EDITOR
NELSON RIBEIRO

ART DIRECTOR
JOE PEP

COVER ART
STAN GOLDBERG
BOB SMITH

ARCHIE'S CAMP TALES,
Volume 1, 2007. Printed in Canada.
Published by Archie Comic Publications, Inc.,
325 Fayette Avenue, Mamaroneck, New York 10543-2318.
Archie characters created by John L. Goldwater; the likenesses of the
Archie characters were created by Bob Montana. The individual
characters' names and likenesses are the exclusive trademarks of
Archie Comic Publications, Inc. All stories previously
published and copyrighted by Archie Comic Publications, Inc.
(or its predecessors) in magazine form in
1966-2003. This compilation copyright © 2007
Archie Comic Publications, Inc. All rights reserved.
Nothing may be reprinted in whole or part
without written permission from
Archie Comic Publications, Inc.

ISBN-13: 978-1-879794-23-8
ISBN-10: 1-879794-23-3

www.archiecomics.com

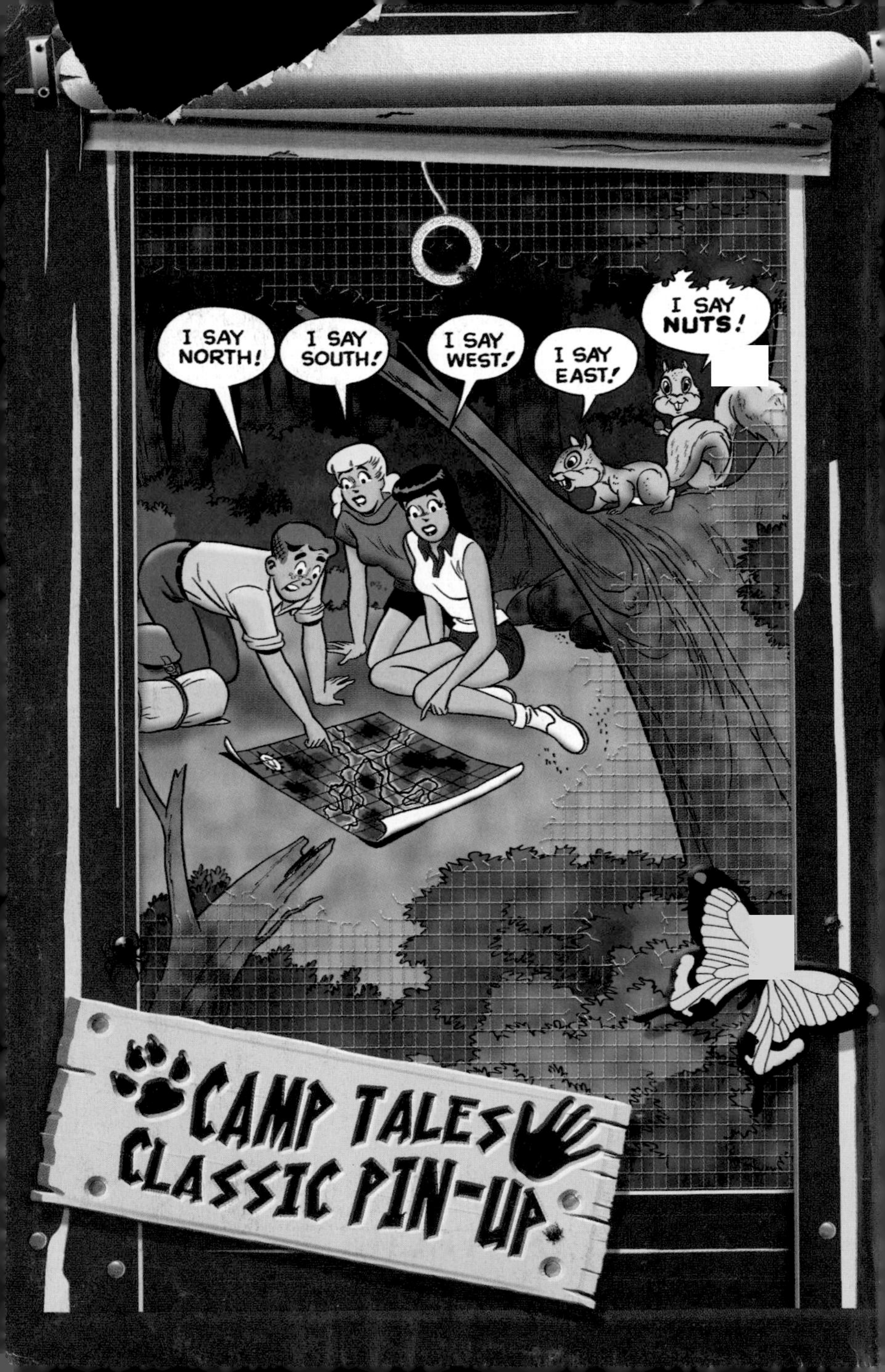
I SAY NORTH!
I SAY SOUTH!
I SAY WEST!
I SAY EAST!
I SAY NUTS!
CAMP TALES
CLASSIC PIN-UP

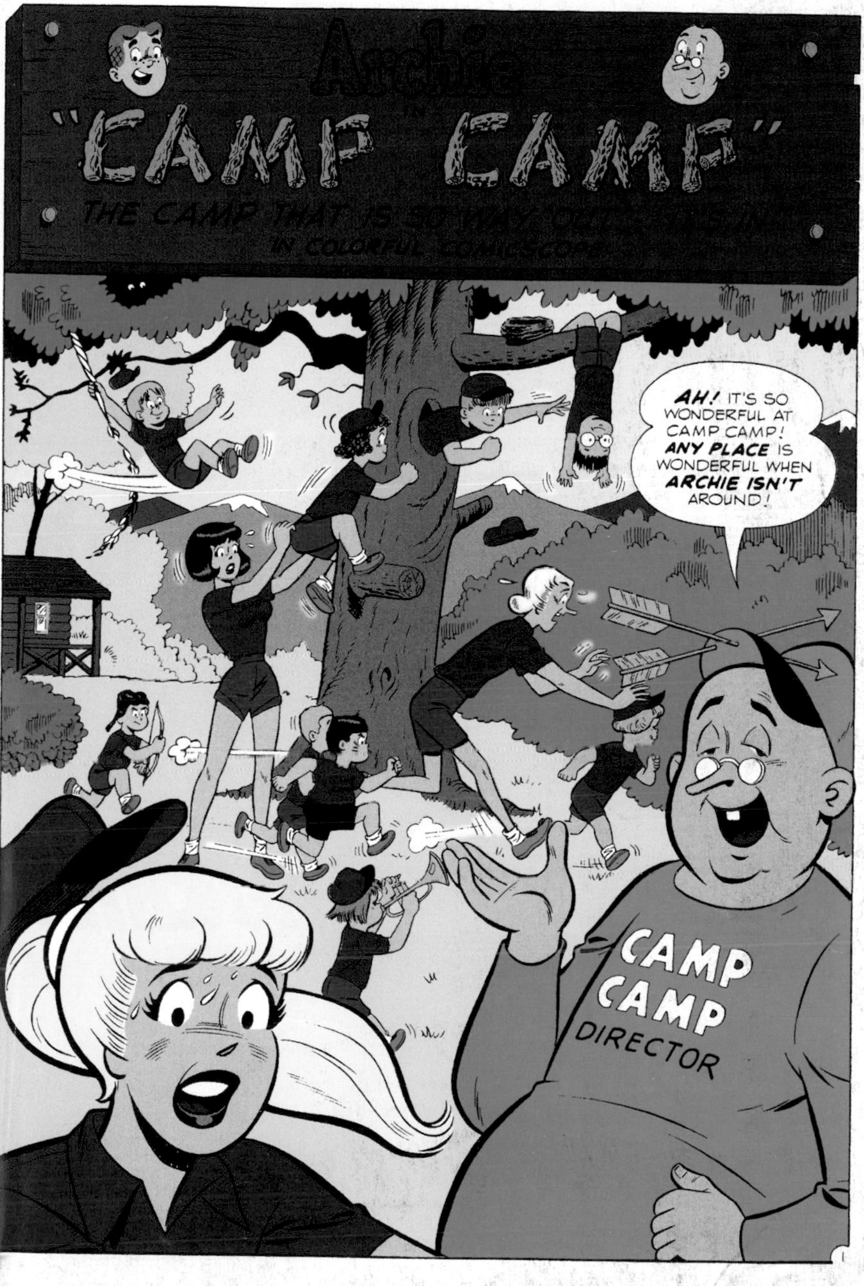
Archie
IN
"CAMP CAMP"
THE CAMP THAT IS SO WAY
IN COLORFUL
AH! IT'S SO WONDERFUL AT CAMP CAMP! ANY PLACE IS WONDERFUL WHEN ARCHIE ISN'T AROUND!
CAMP CAMP DIRECTOR

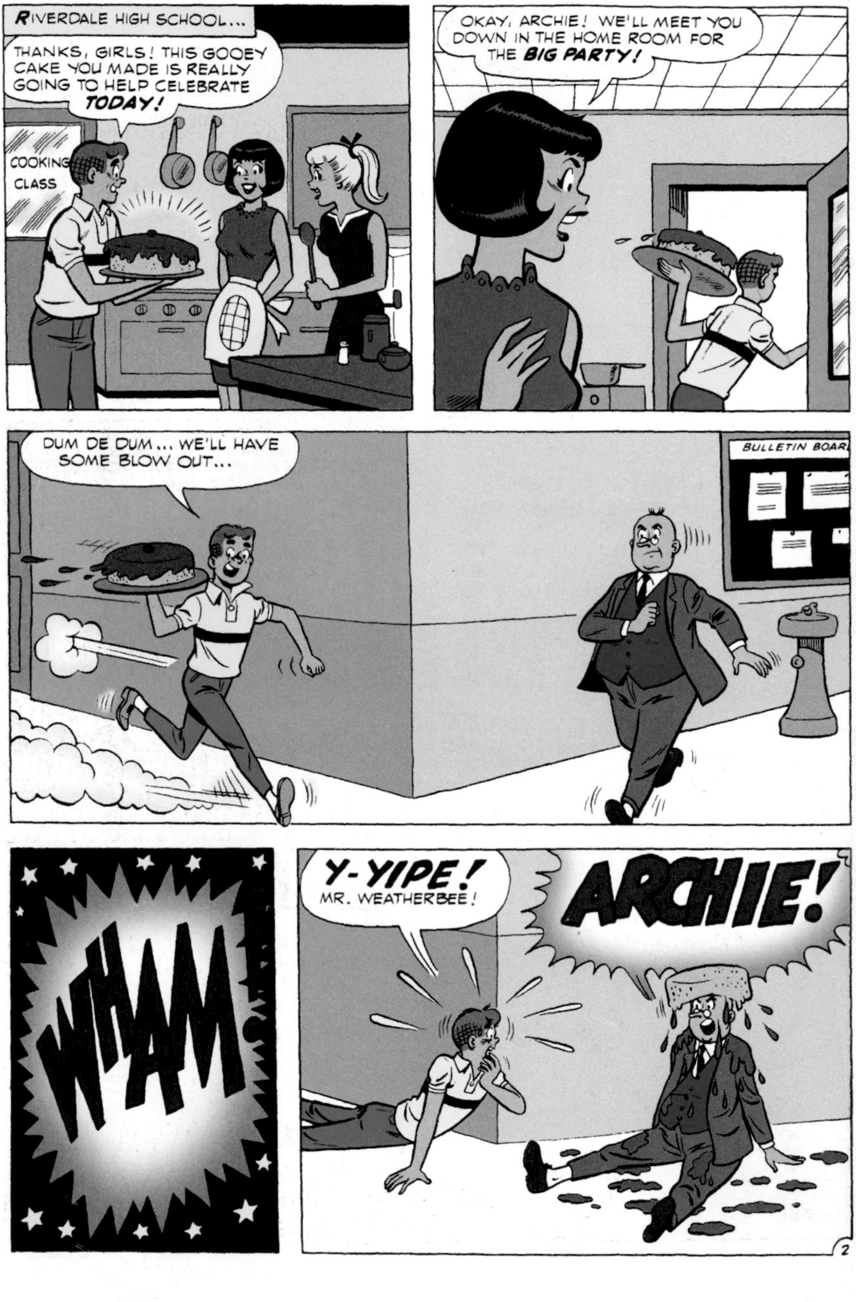
RIVERDALE HIGH SCHOOL...
THANKS, GIRLS! THIS GOOEY CAKE YOU MADE IS REALLY GOING TO HELP CELEBRATE TODAY!
COOKING CLASS
OKAY, ARCHIE! WE'LL MEET YOU DOWN IN THE HOME ROOM FOR THE BIG PARTY!
DUM DE DUM... WE'LL HAVE SOME BLOW OUT...
BULLETIN BOAR
WHAM
Y-YIPE! MR. WEATHERBEE!
ARCHIE!

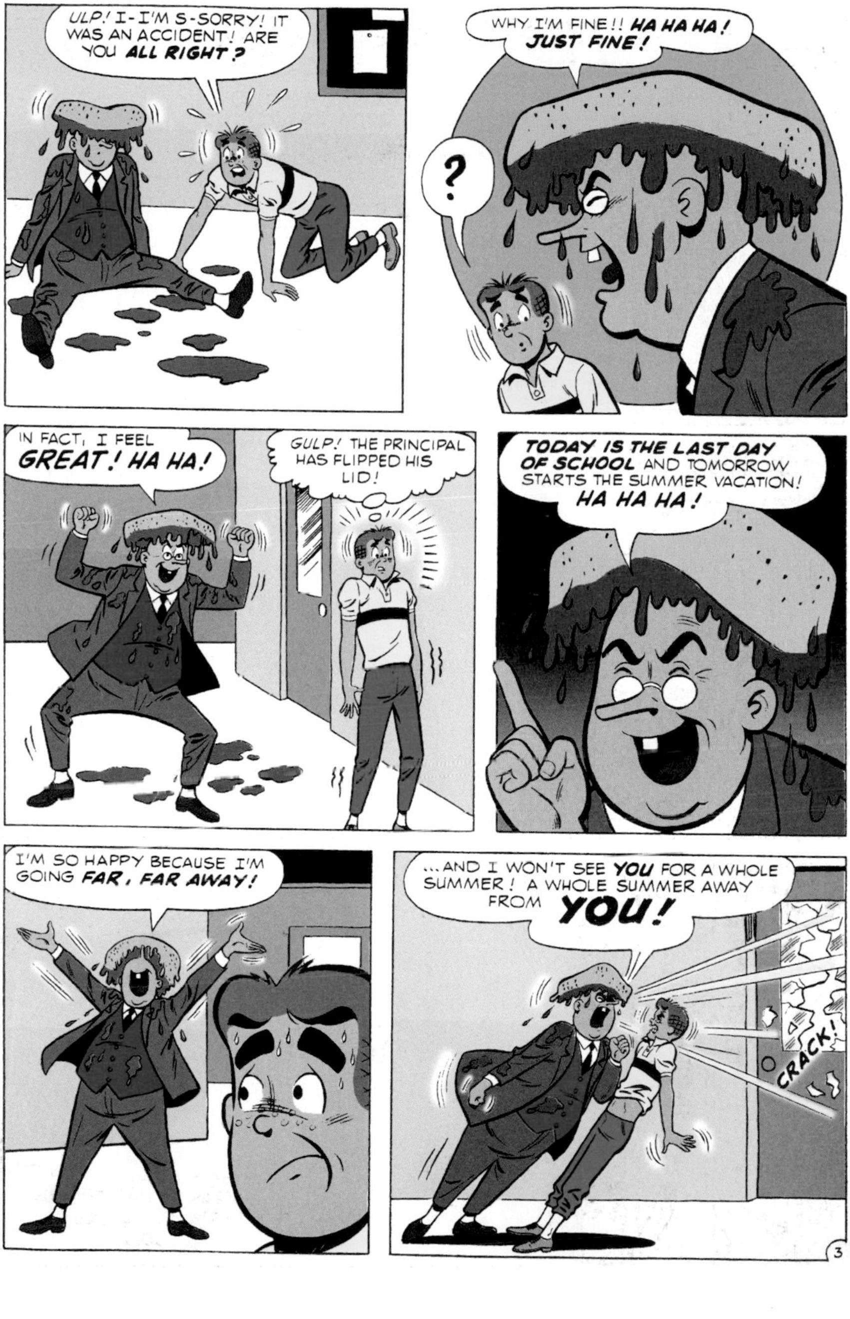
ULP! I-I'M S-SORRY! IT WAS AN ACCIDENT! ARE YOU ALL RIGHT?
WHY I'M FINE!! HA HA HA! JUST FINE!
?
IN FACT, I FEEL GREAT! HA HA!
GULP! THE PRINCIPAL HAS FLIPPED HIS LID!
TODAY IS THE LAST DAY OF SCHOOL AND TOMORROW STARTS THE SUMMER VACATION! HA HA HA!
I'M SO HAPPY BECAUSE I'M GOING FAR, FAR AWAY!
...AND I WON'T SEE YOU FOR A WHOLE SUMMER! A WHOLE SUMMER AWAY FROM YOU!
CRACK!

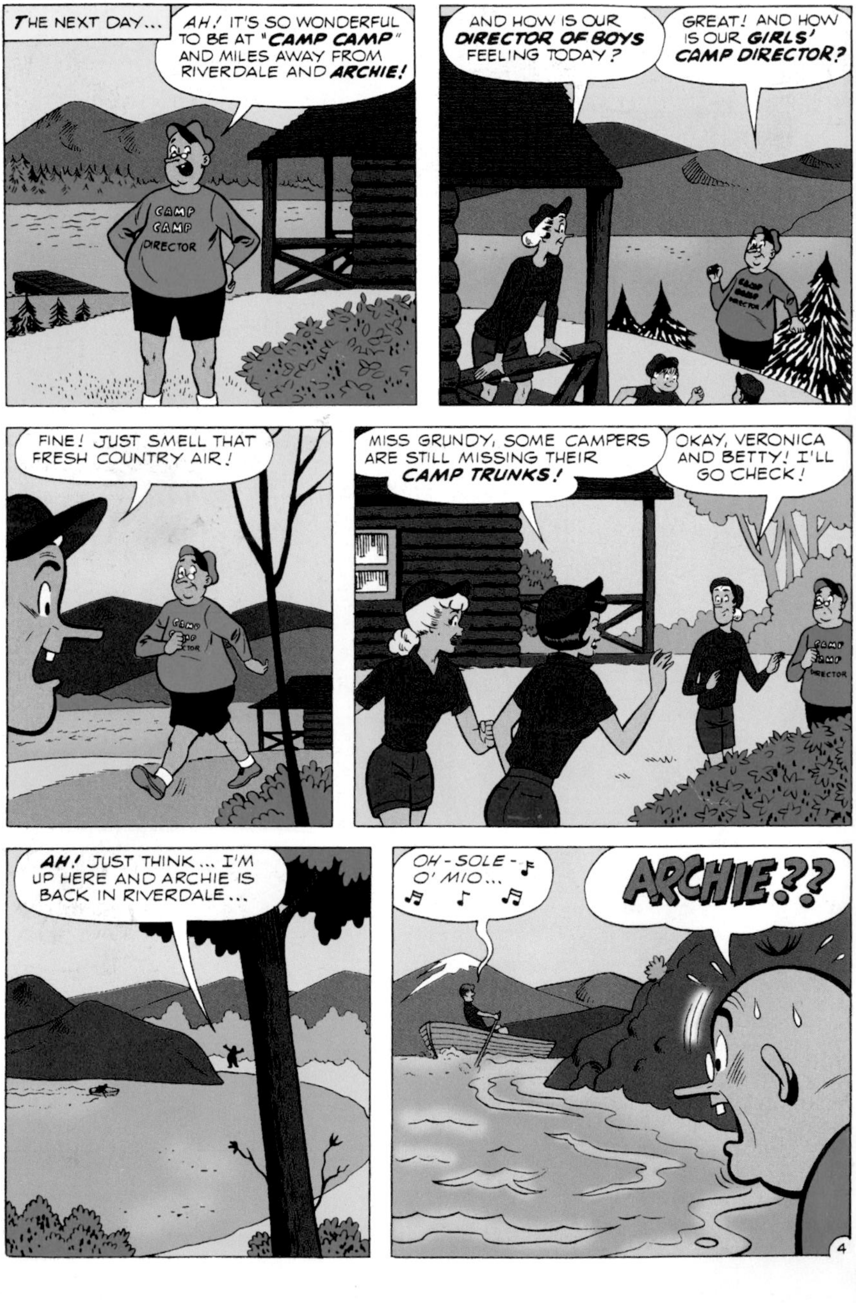
THE NEXT DAY...
AH! IT'S SO WONDERFUL TO BE AT "CAMP CAMP" AND MILES AWAY FROM RIVERDALE AND ARCHIE!
CAMP CAMP DIRECTOR
AND HOW IS OUR DIRECTOR OF BOYS FEELING TODAY?
GREAT! AND HOW IS OUR GIRLS' CAMP DIRECTOR?
FINE! JUST SMELL THAT FRESH COUNTRY AIR!
MISS GRUNDY, SOME CAMPERS ARE STILL MISSING THEIR CAMP TRUNKS!
OKAY, VERONICA AND BETTY! I'LL GO CHECK!
CAMP CAMP DIRECTOR
AH! JUST THINK... I'M UP HERE AND ARCHIE IS BACK IN RIVERDALE...
OH - SOLE - O' MIO...
ARCHIE??

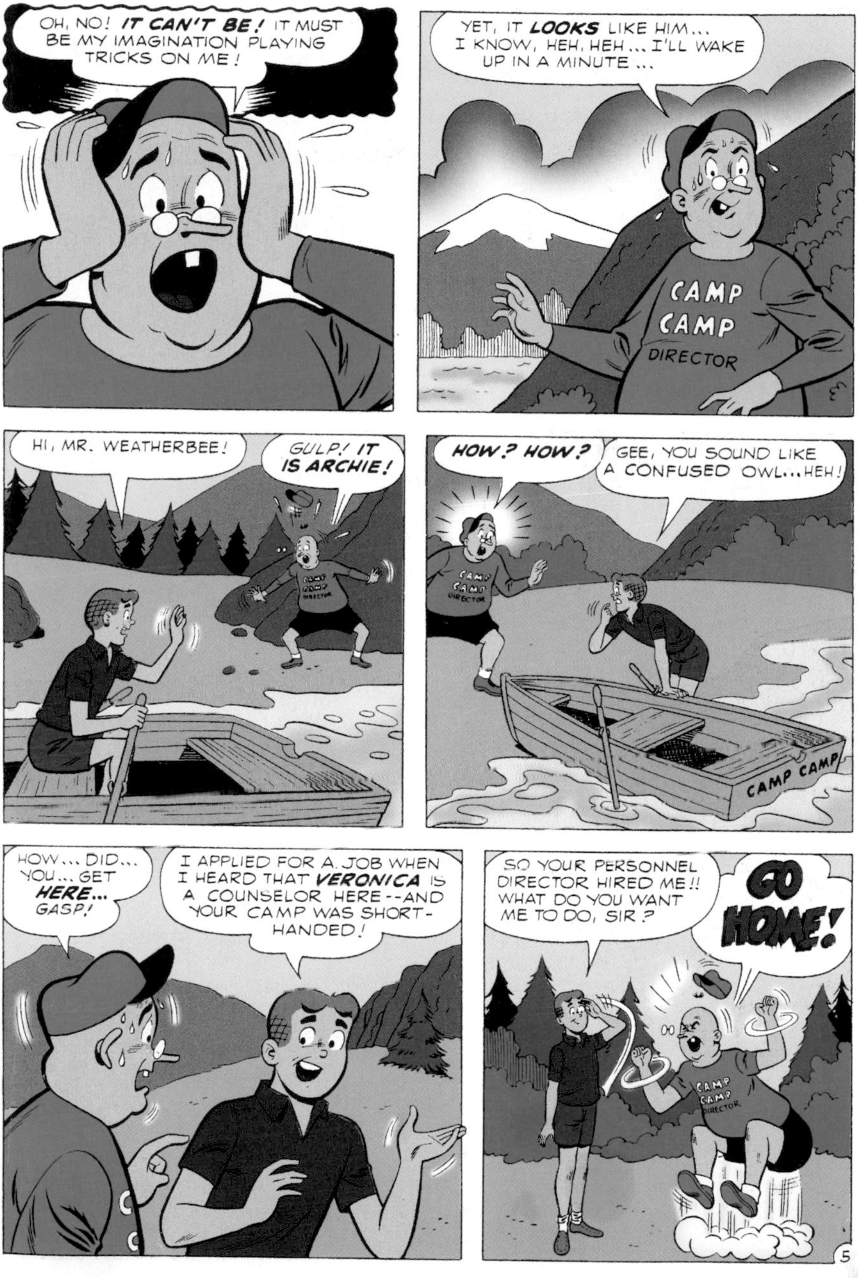
OH, NO! IT CAN'T BE! IT MUST BE MY IMAGINATION PLAYING TRICKS ON ME!
YET, IT LOOKS LIKE HIM... I KNOW, HEH, HEH... I'LL WAKE UP IN A MINUTE...
CAMP CAMP DIRECTOR
HI, MR. WEATHERBEE!
GULP! IT IS ARCHIE!
HOW? HOW?
GEE, YOU SOUND LIKE A CONFUSED OWL...HEH!
CAMP CAMP
HOW... DID... YOU... GET HERE... GASP!
I APPLIED FOR A JOB WHEN I HEARD THAT VERONICA IS A COUNSELOR HERE--AND YOUR CAMP WAS SHORT-HANDED!
SO YOUR PERSONNEL DIRECTOR HIRED ME!! WHAT DO YOU WANT ME TO DO, SIR?
GO HOME!
CAMP CAMP DIRECTOR

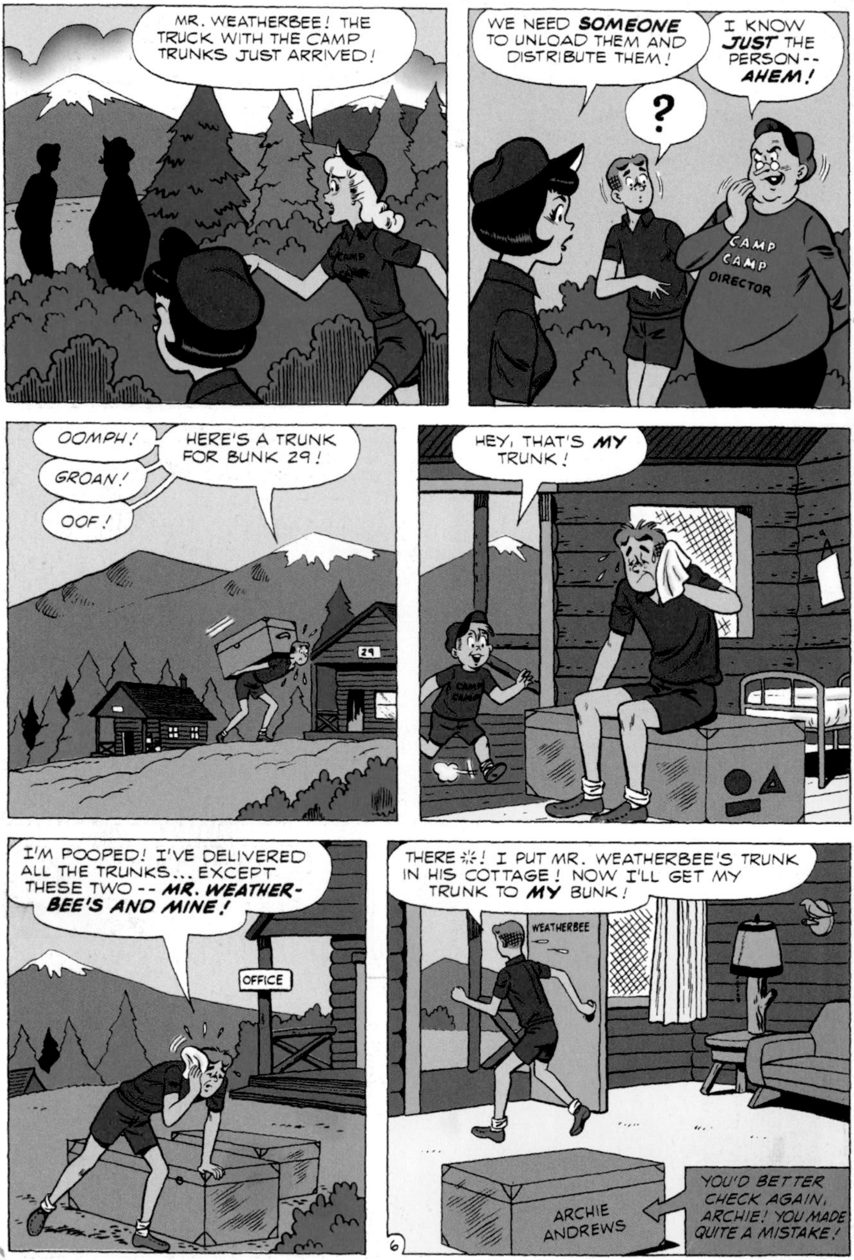
MR. WEATHERBEE! THE TRUCK WITH THE CAMP TRUNKS JUST ARRIVED!
WE NEED **SOMEONE** TO UNLOAD THEM AND DISTRIBUTE THEM!
?
I KNOW **JUST** THE PERSON -- **AHEM!**
CAMP CAMP DIRECTOR
OOMPH!
GROAN!
OOF!
HERE'S A TRUNK FOR BUNK 29!
29
HEY, THAT'S **MY** TRUNK!
I'M POOPED! I'VE DELIVERED ALL THE TRUNKS... EXCEPT THESE TWO -- **MR. WEATHER-BEE'S AND MINE!**
OFFICE
THERE *!*! I PUT MR. WEATHERBEE'S TRUNK IN HIS COTTAGE! NOW I'LL GET MY TRUNK TO **MY** BUNK!
WEATHERBEE
ARCHIE ANDREWS
YOU'D BETTER CHECK AGAIN, ARCHIE! YOU MADE QUITE A MISTAKE!

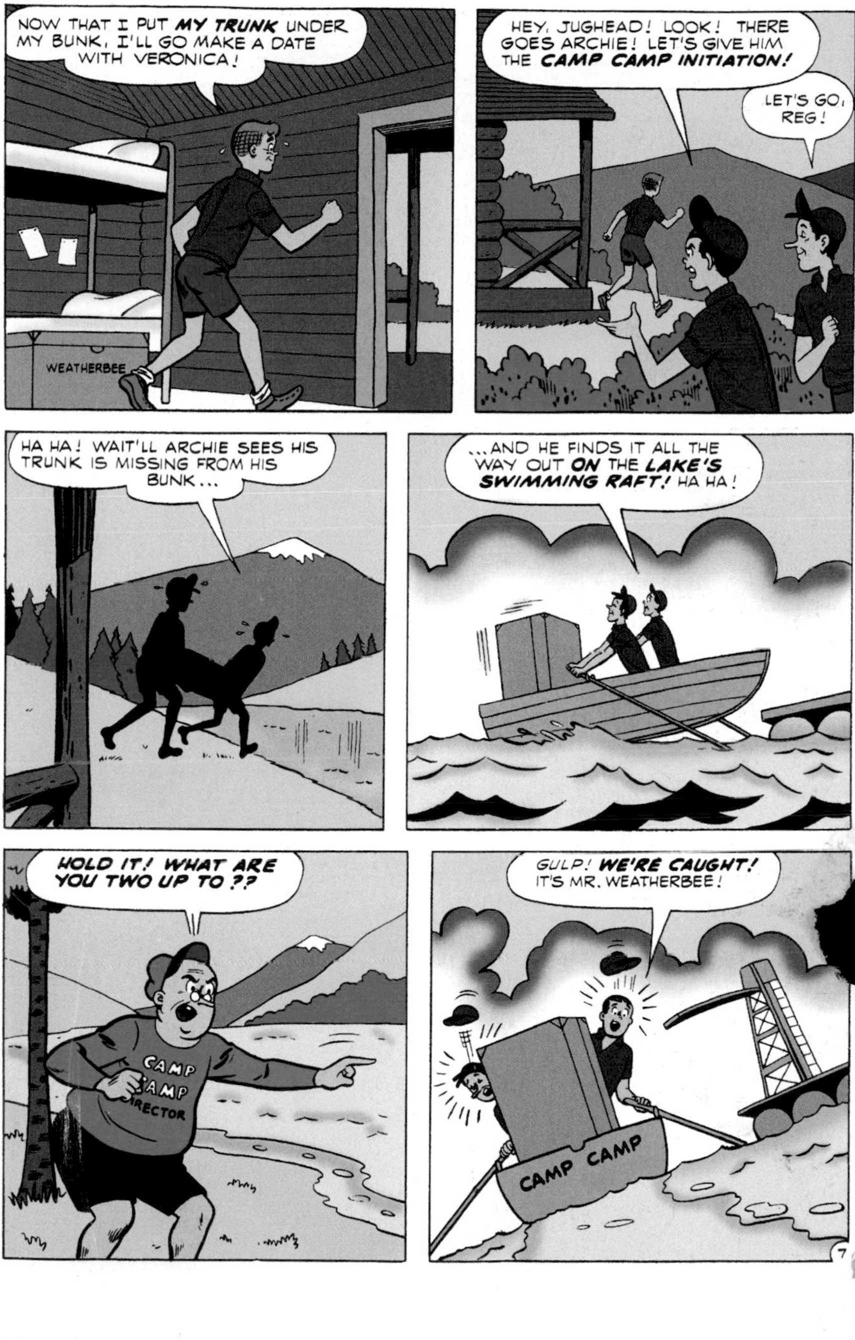
NOW THAT I PUT MY TRUNK UNDER MY BUNK, I'LL GO MAKE A DATE WITH VERONICA!
WEATHERBEE
HEY, JUGHEAD! LOOK! THERE GOES ARCHIE! LET'S GIVE HIM THE CAMP CAMP INITIATION!
LET'S GO, REG!
HA HA! WAIT'LL ARCHIE SEES HIS TRUNK IS MISSING FROM HIS BUNK...
...AND HE FINDS IT ALL THE WAY OUT ON THE LAKE'S SWIMMING RAFT! HA HA!
HOLD IT! WHAT ARE YOU TWO UP TO??
CAMP CAMP DIRECTOR
GULP! WE'RE CAUGHT! IT'S MR. WEATHERBEE!
CAMP CAMP

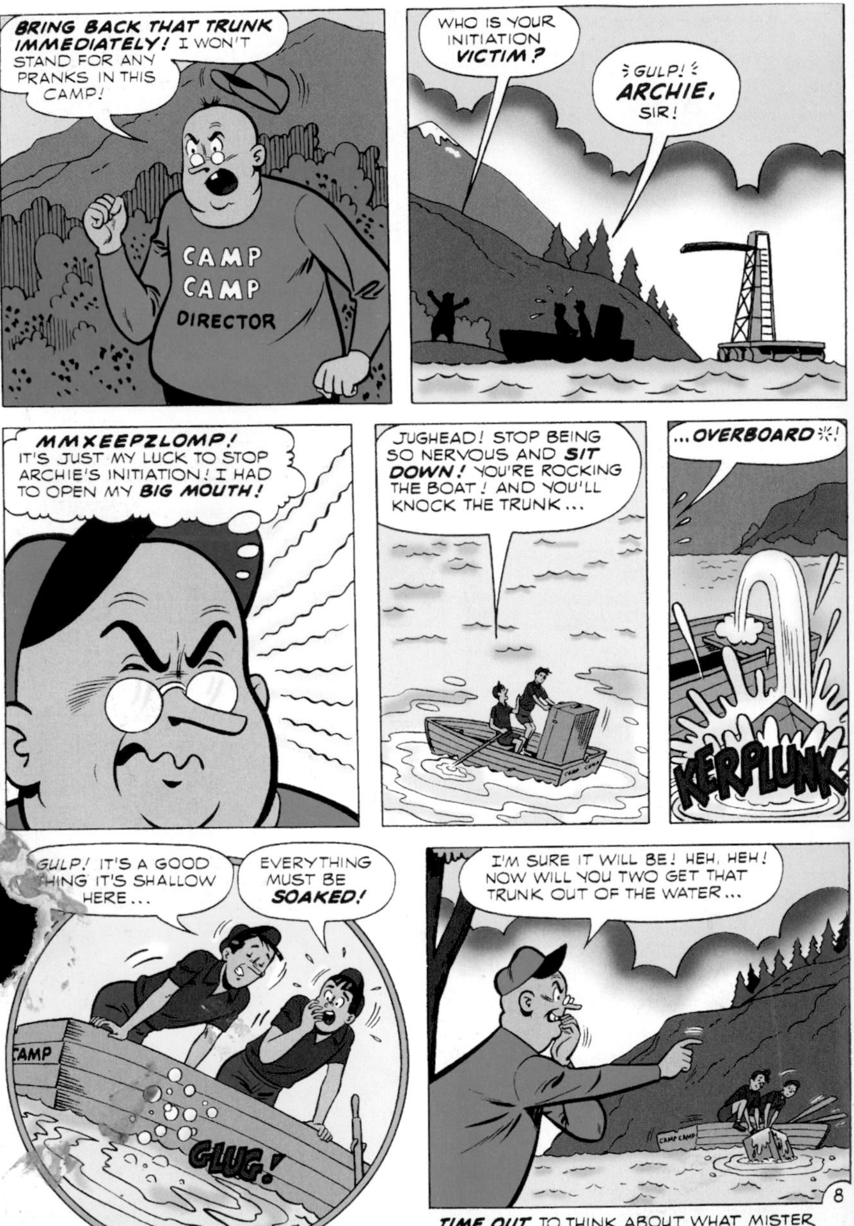

BRING BACK THAT TRUNK IMMEDIATELY! I WON'T STAND FOR ANY PRANKS IN THIS CAMP!
CAMP CAMP DIRECTOR
WHO IS YOUR INITIATION VICTIM?
GULP! ARCHIE, SIR!
MMXEEPZLOMP! IT'S JUST MY LUCK TO STOP ARCHIE'S INITIATION! I HAD TO OPEN MY BIG MOUTH!
JUGHEAD! STOP BEING SO NERVOUS AND SIT DOWN! YOU'RE ROCKING THE BOAT! AND YOU'LL KNOCK THE TRUNK...
...OVERBOARD!
KERPLUNK
GULP! IT'S A GOOD THING IT'S SHALLOW HERE...
EVERYTHING MUST BE SOAKED!
CAMP
GLUG!
I'M SURE IT WILL BE! HEH, HEH! NOW WILL YOU TWO GET THAT TRUNK OUT OF THE WATER...
CAMP CAMP

TIME OUT TO THINK ABOUT WHAT MISTER WEATHERBEE IS GOING TO DO WHEN HE FINDS IT'S HIS TRUNK!

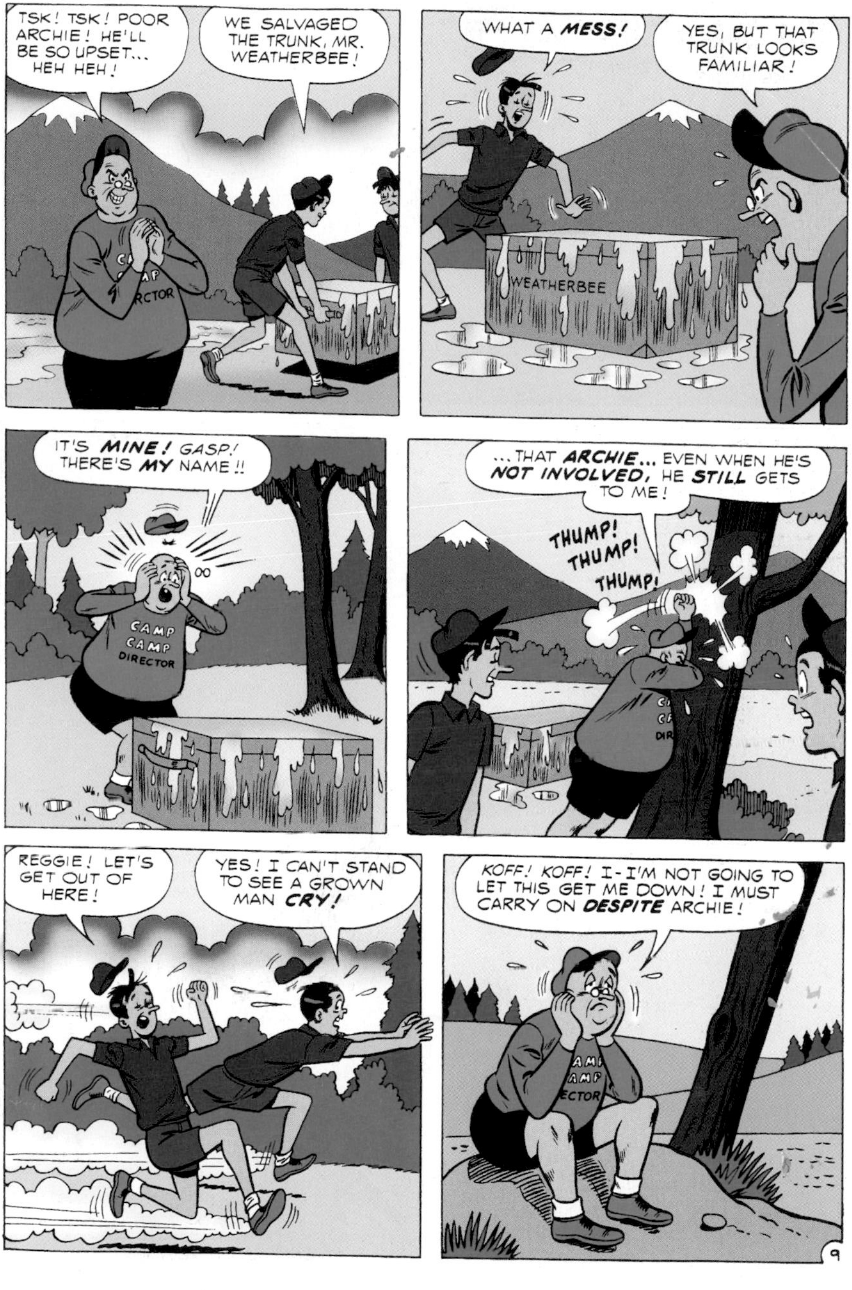
TSK! TSK! POOR ARCHIE! HE'LL BE SO UPSET... HEH HEH!
WE SALVAGED THE TRUNK, MR. WEATHERBEE!
CAMP CAMP DIRECTOR
WHAT A MESS!
YES, BUT THAT TRUNK LOOKS FAMILIAR!
WEATHERBEE
IT'S MINE! GASP! THERE'S MY NAME!!
CAMP CAMP DIRECTOR
...THAT ARCHIE... EVEN WHEN HE'S NOT INVOLVED, HE STILL GETS TO ME!
THUMP! THUMP! THUMP!
REGGIE! LET'S GET OUT OF HERE!
YES! I CAN'T STAND TO SEE A GROWN MAN CRY!
KOFF! KOFF! I-I'M NOT GOING TO LET THIS GET ME DOWN! I MUST CARRY ON DESPITE ARCHIE!

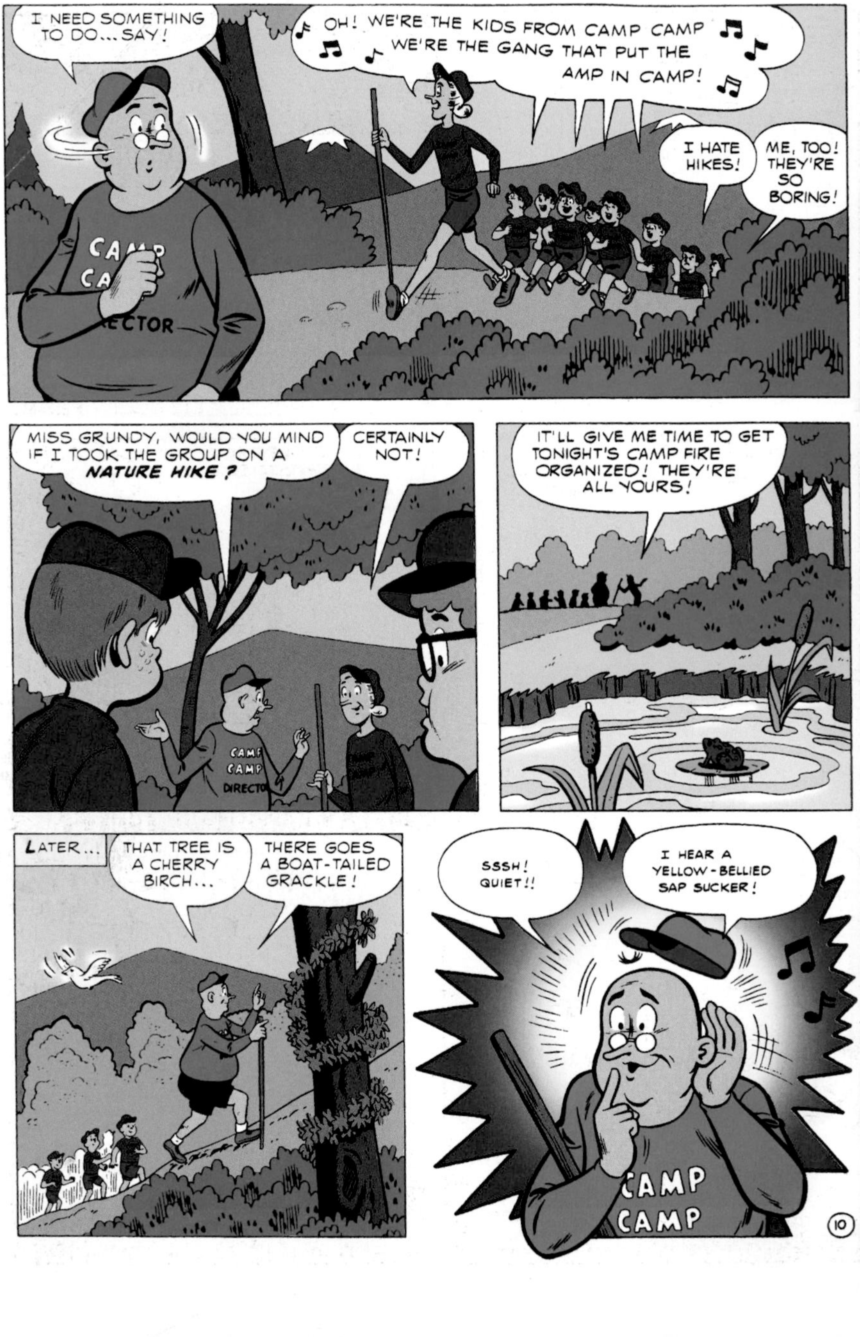
I NEED SOMETHING TO DO... SAY!
OH! WE'RE THE KIDS FROM CAMP CAMP WE'RE THE GANG THAT PUT THE AMP IN CAMP!
I HATE HIKES!
ME, TOO! THEY'RE SO BORING!
CAMP CA... ...ECTOR
MISS GRUNDY, WOULD YOU MIND IF I TOOK THE GROUP ON A ***NATURE HIKE?***
CERTAINLY NOT!
CAMP CAMP DIRECTOR
IT'LL GIVE ME TIME TO GET TONIGHT'S CAMP FIRE ORGANIZED! THEY'RE ALL YOURS!
LATER...
THAT TREE IS A CHERRY BIRCH...
THERE GOES A BOAT-TAILED GRACKLE!
SSSH! QUIET!!
I HEAR A YELLOW-BELLIED SAP SUCKER!
CAMP CAMP

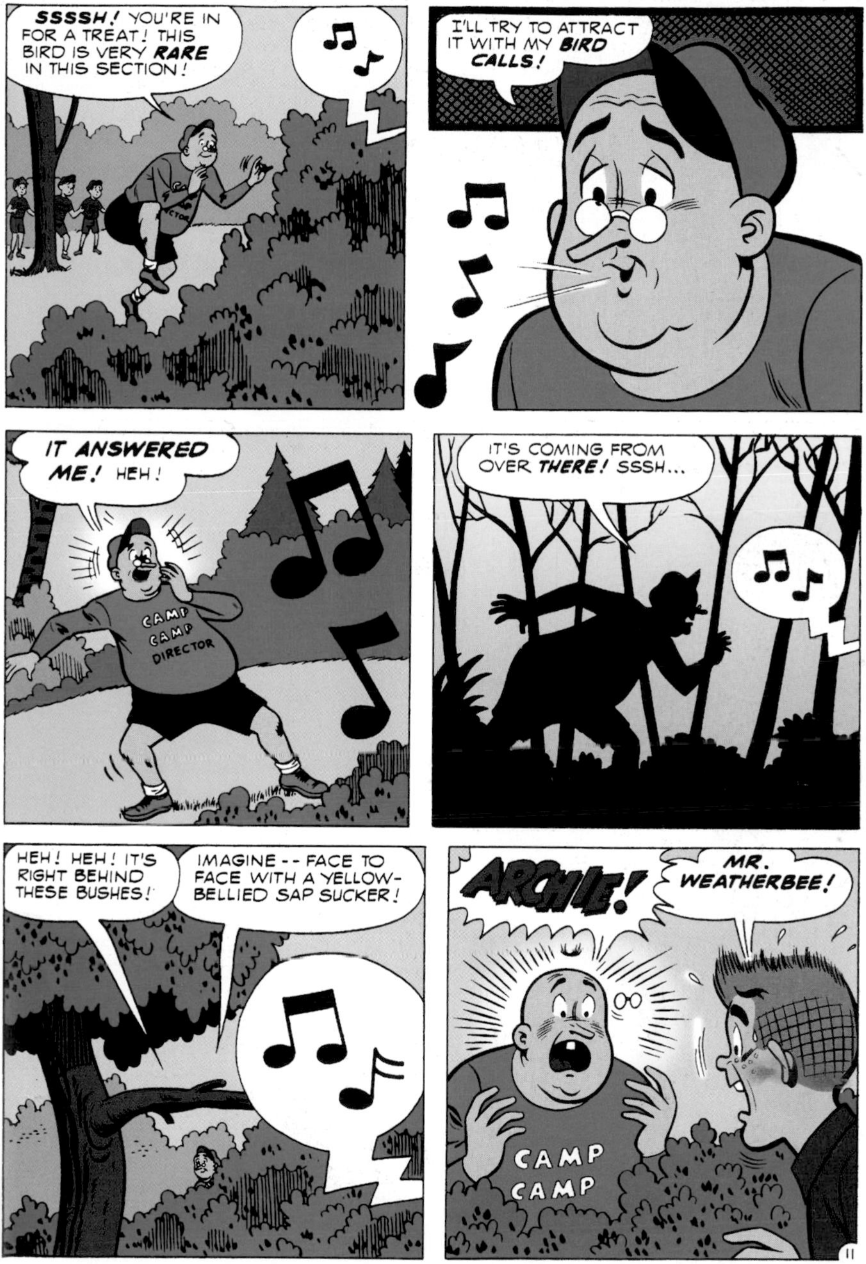

SSSSH! YOU'RE IN FOR A TREAT! THIS BIRD IS VERY RARE IN THIS SECTION!
I'LL TRY TO ATTRACT IT WITH MY BIRD CALLS!
IT ANSWERED ME! HEH!
CAMP CAMP CAMP DIRECTOR
IT'S COMING FROM OVER THERE! SSSH...
HEH! HEH! IT'S RIGHT BEHIND THESE BUSHES!
IMAGINE -- FACE TO FACE WITH A YELLOW-BELLIED SAP SUCKER!
ARCHIE!
MR. WEATHERBEE!
CAMP CAMP

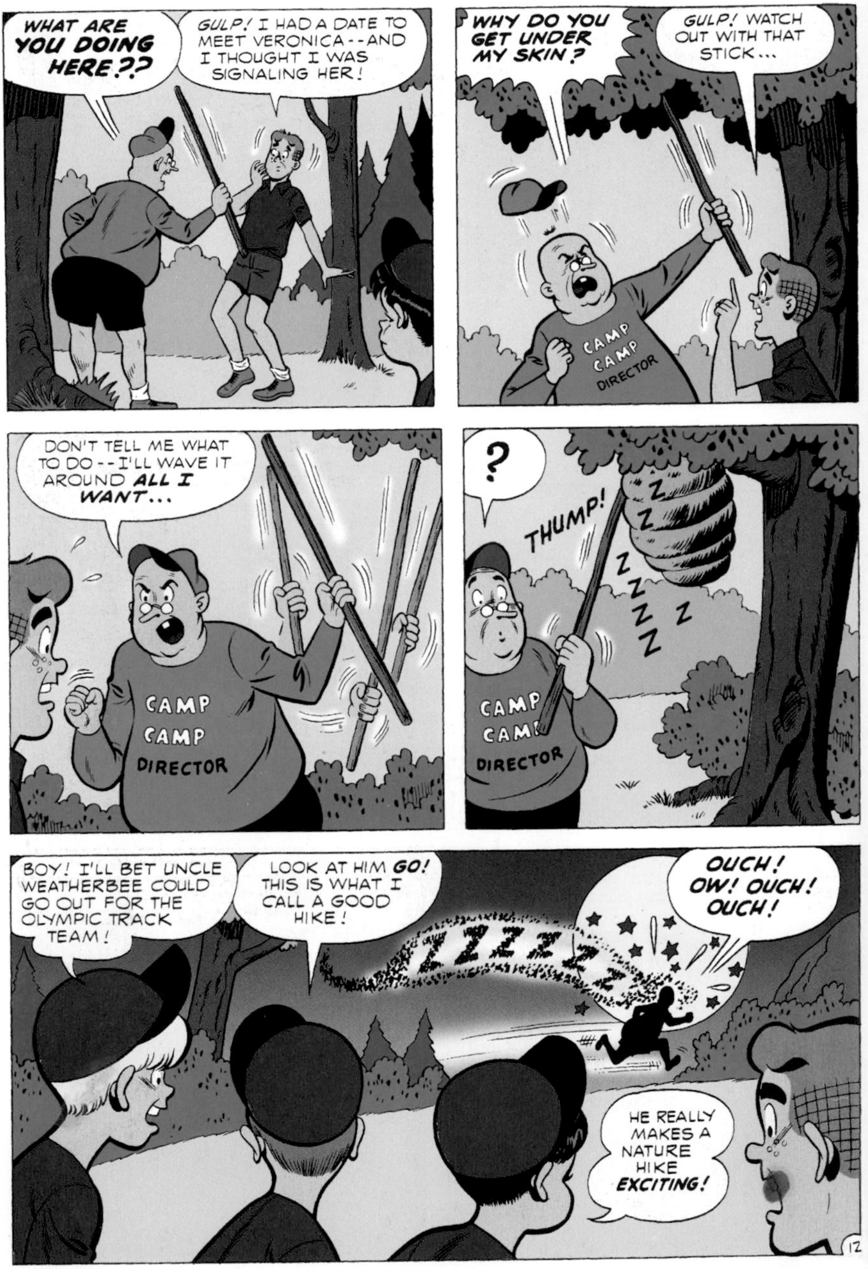
WHAT ARE YOU DOING HERE??
GULP! I HAD A DATE TO MEET VERONICA--AND I THOUGHT I WAS SIGNALING HER!
WHY DO YOU GET UNDER MY SKIN?
GULP! WATCH OUT WITH THAT STICK...
CAMP CAMP DIRECTOR
DON'T TELL ME WHAT TO DO--I'LL WAVE IT AROUND ALL I WANT...
CAMP CAMP DIRECTOR
?
THUMP!
CAMP CAMP DIRECTOR
BOY! I'LL BET UNCLE WEATHERBEE COULD GO OUT FOR THE OLYMPIC TRACK TEAM!
LOOK AT HIM GO! THIS IS WHAT I CALL A GOOD HIKE!
OUCH! OW! OUCH! OUCH!
HE REALLY MAKES A NATURE HIKE EXCITING!

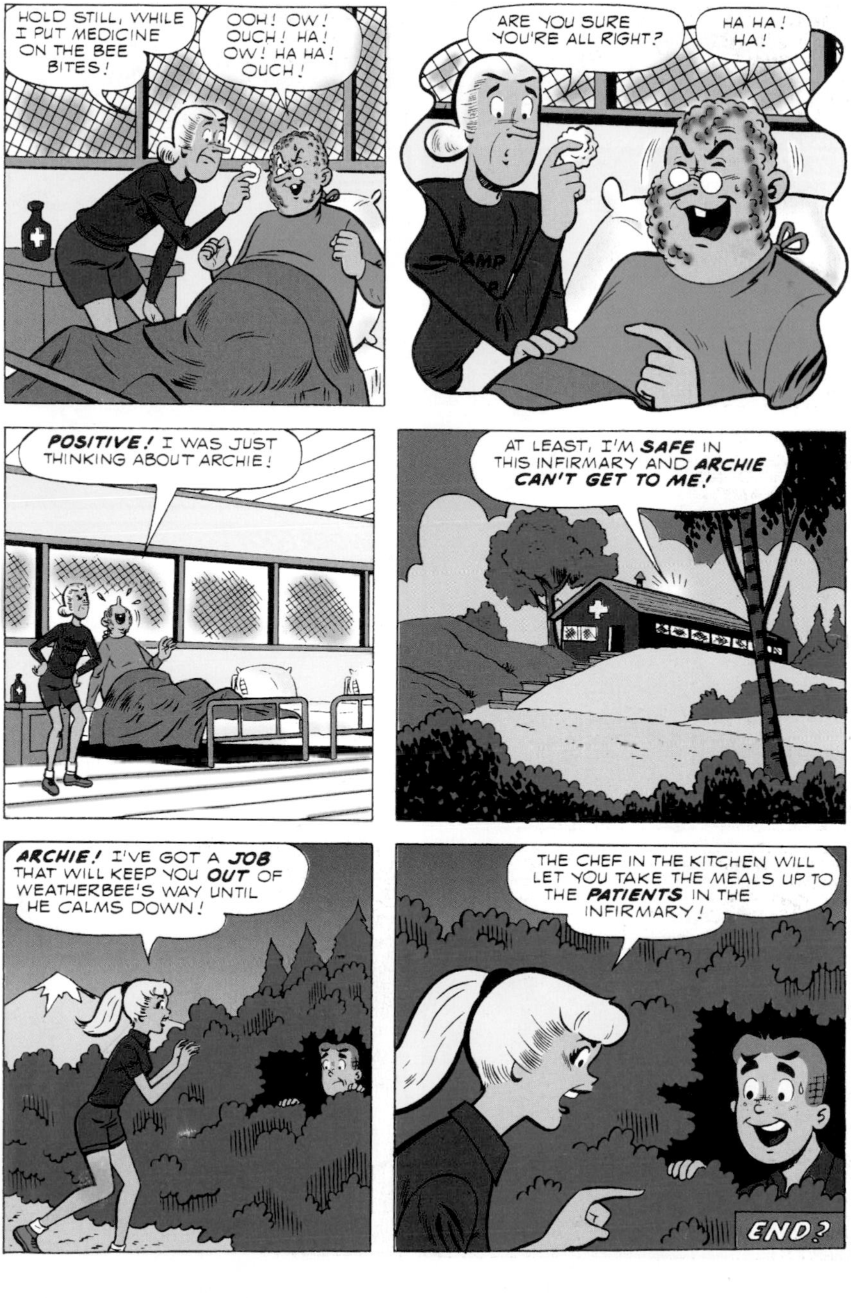
HOLD STILL, WHILE I PUT MEDICINE ON THE BEE BITES!
OOH! OW! OUCH! HA! OW! HA HA! OUCH!
ARE YOU SURE YOU'RE ALL RIGHT?
HA HA! HA!
POSITIVE! I WAS JUST THINKING ABOUT ARCHIE!
AT LEAST, I'M SAFE IN THIS INFIRMARY AND ARCHIE CAN'T GET TO ME!
ARCHIE! I'VE GOT A JOB THAT WILL KEEP YOU OUT OF WEATHERBEE'S WAY UNTIL HE CALMS DOWN!
THE CHEF IN THE KITCHEN WILL LET YOU TAKE THE MEALS UP TO THE PATIENTS IN THE INFIRMARY!
END?

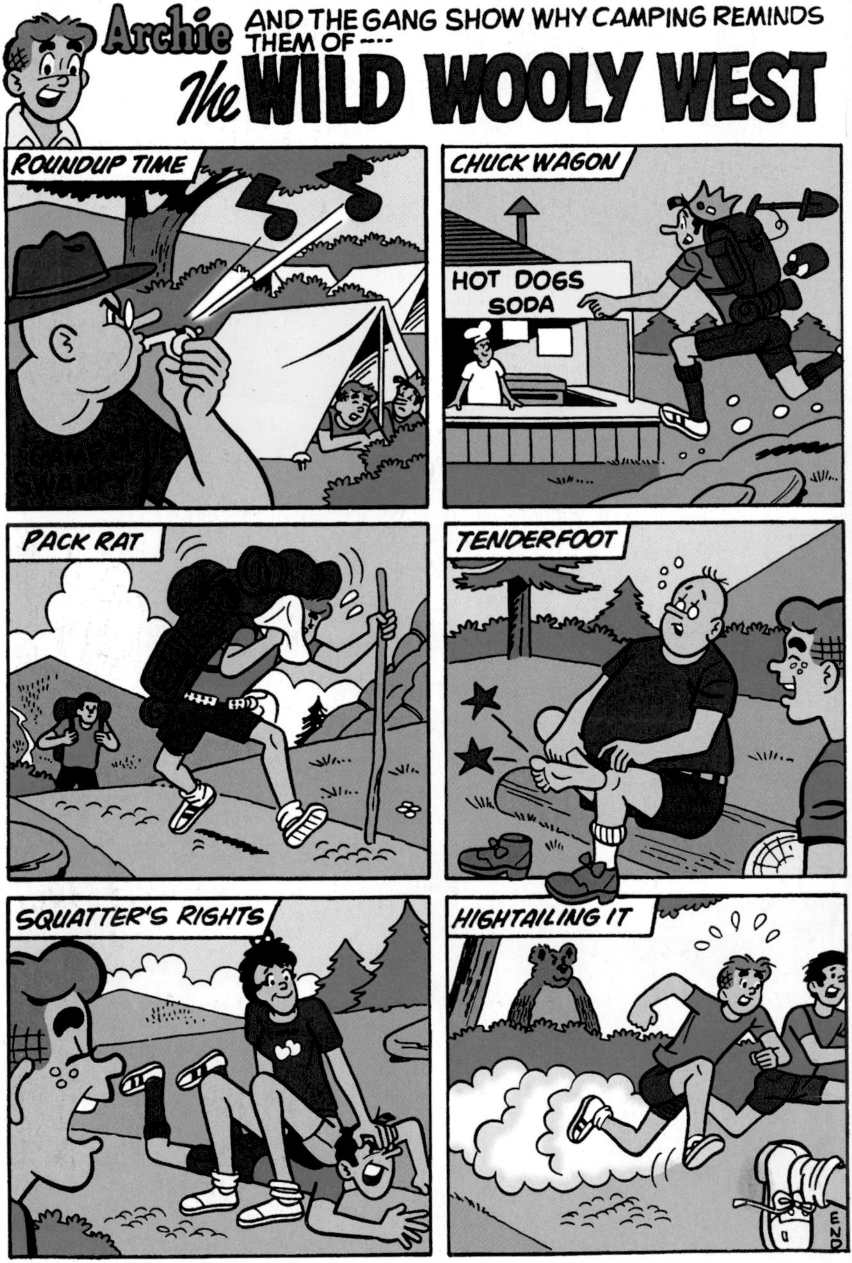
Archie
AND THE GANG SHOW WHY CAMPING REMINDS THEM OF ---
The WILD WOOLY WEST
ROUNDUP TIME
CHUCK WAGON
HOT DOGS
SODA
PACK RAT
TENDERFOOT
SQUATTER'S RIGHTS
HIGHTAILING IT
END

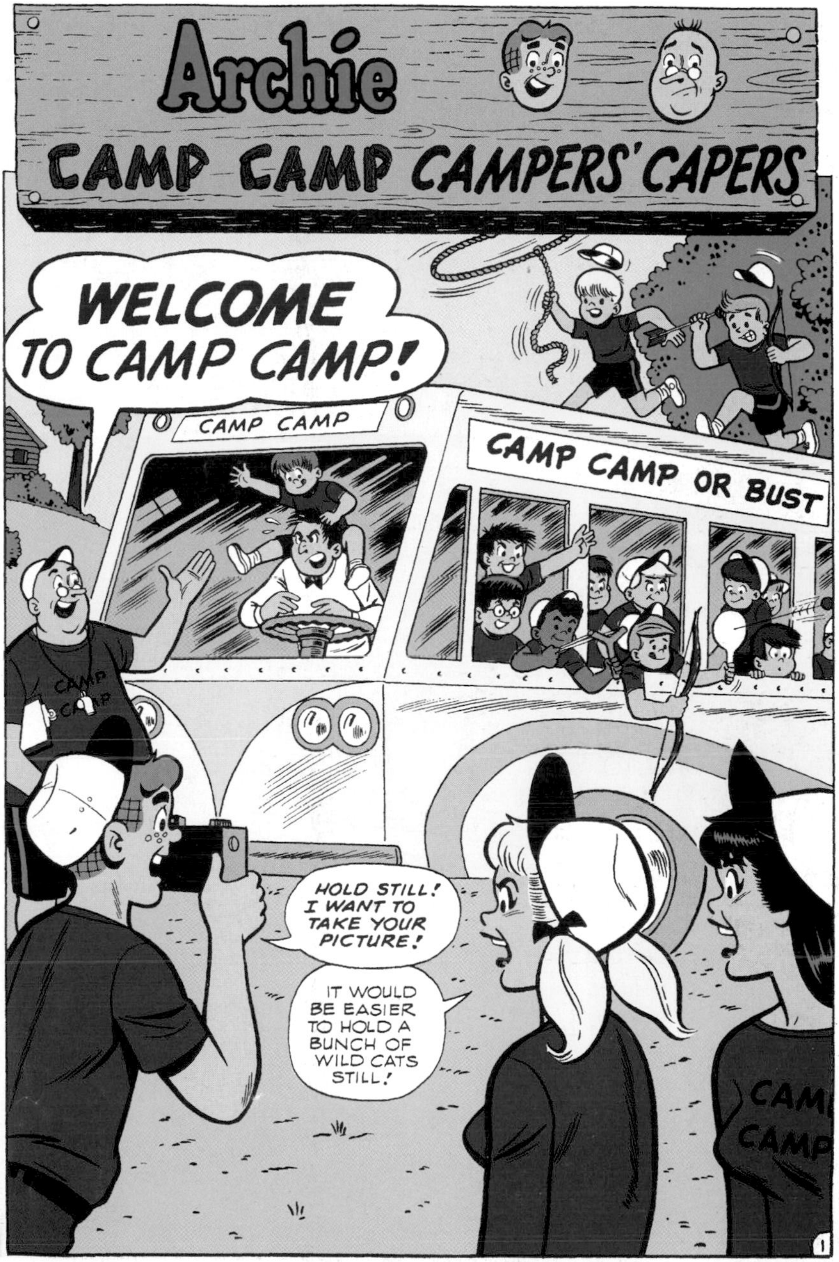
Archie
CAMP CAMP CAMPERS' CAPERS
WELCOME TO CAMP CAMP!
CAMP CAMP
CAMP CAMP OR BUST
HOLD STILL! I WANT TO TAKE YOUR PICTURE!
IT WOULD BE EASIER TO HOLD A BUNCH OF WILD CATS STILL!

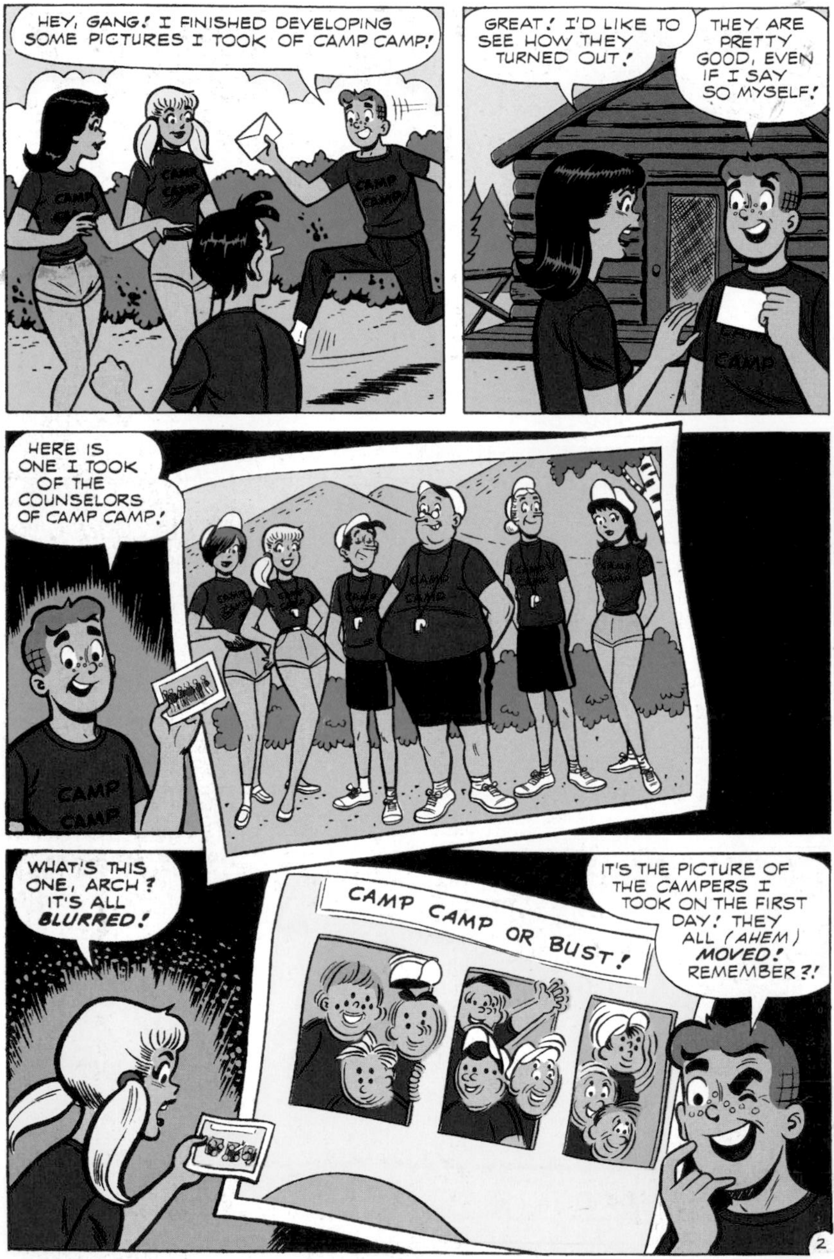

HEY, GANG! I FINISHED DEVELOPING SOME PICTURES I TOOK OF CAMP CAMP!
CAMP CAMP
GREAT! I'D LIKE TO SEE HOW THEY TURNED OUT!
THEY ARE PRETTY GOOD, EVEN IF I SAY SO MYSELF!
HERE IS ONE I TOOK OF THE COUNSELORS OF CAMP CAMP!
WHAT'S THIS ONE, ARCH? IT'S ALL **BLURRED!**
CAMP CAMP OR BUST!
IT'S THE PICTURE OF THE CAMPERS I TOOK ON THE FIRST DAY! THEY ALL *(AHEM)* **MOVED!** REMEMBER?!

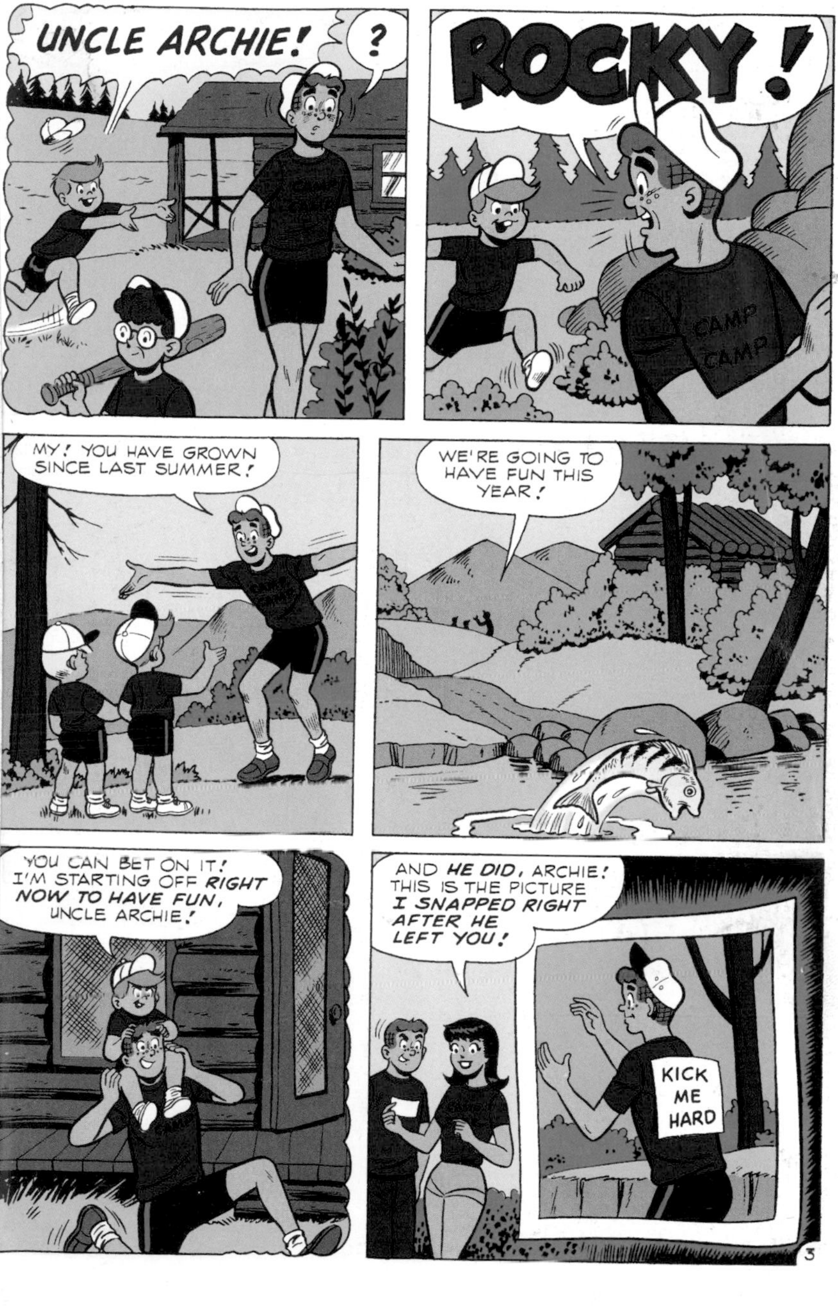
UNCLE ARCHIE!
?
ROCKY!
CAMP CAMP
MY! YOU HAVE GROWN SINCE LAST SUMMER!
WE'RE GOING TO HAVE FUN THIS YEAR!
YOU CAN BET ON IT! I'M STARTING OFF RIGHT NOW TO HAVE FUN, UNCLE ARCHIE!
AND HE DID, ARCHIE! THIS IS THE PICTURE I SNAPPED RIGHT AFTER HE LEFT YOU!
KICK ME HARD

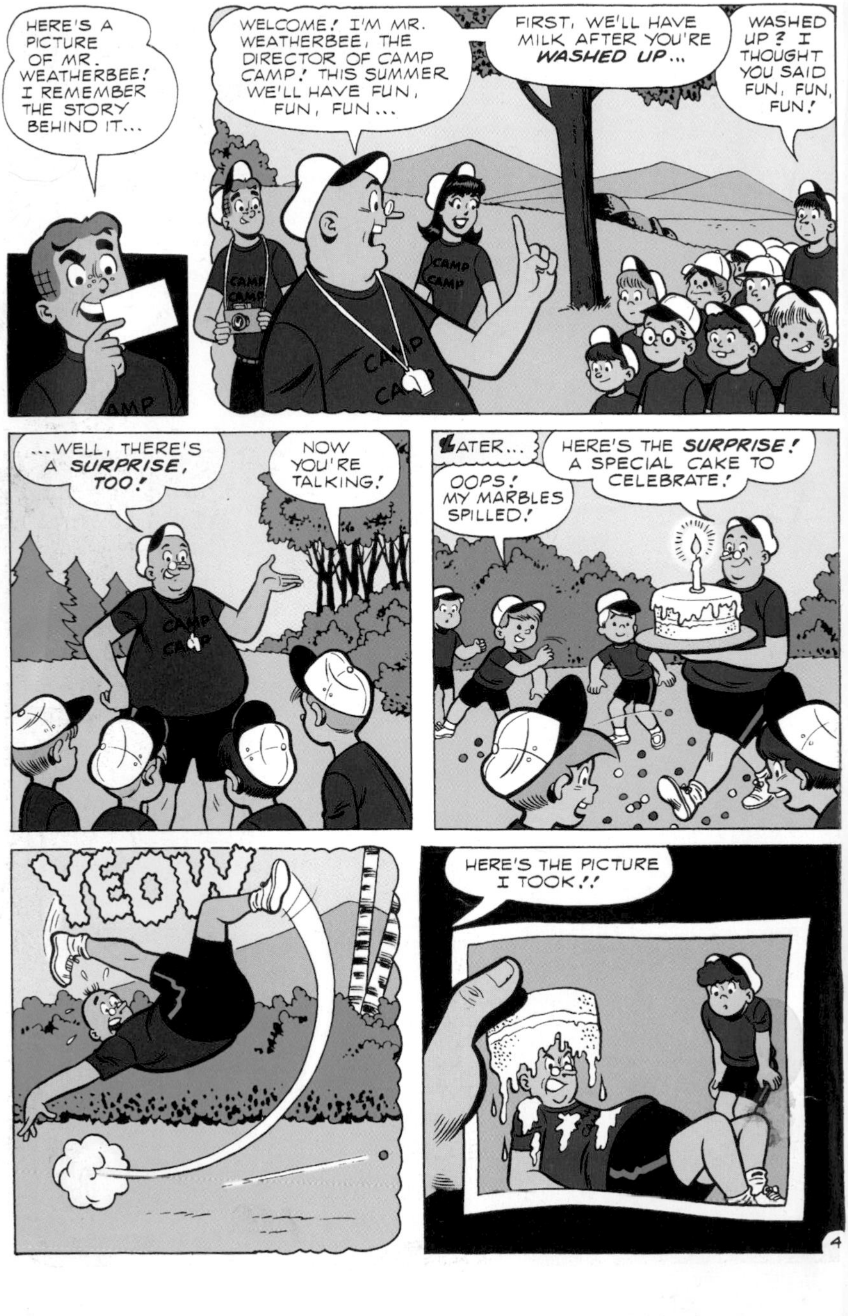
HERE'S A PICTURE OF MR. WEATHERBEE! I REMEMBER THE STORY BEHIND IT...
WELCOME! I'M MR. WEATHERBEE, THE DIRECTOR OF CAMP CAMP! THIS SUMMER WE'LL HAVE FUN, FUN, FUN...
FIRST, WE'LL HAVE MILK AFTER YOU'RE WASHED UP...
WASHED UP? I THOUGHT YOU SAID FUN, FUN, FUN!
CAMP CAMP
...WELL, THERE'S A SURPRISE, TOO!
NOW YOU'RE TALKING!
LATER...
HERE'S THE SURPRISE! A SPECIAL CAKE TO CELEBRATE!
OOPS! MY MARBLES SPILLED!
YEOW
HERE'S THE PICTURE I TOOK!!

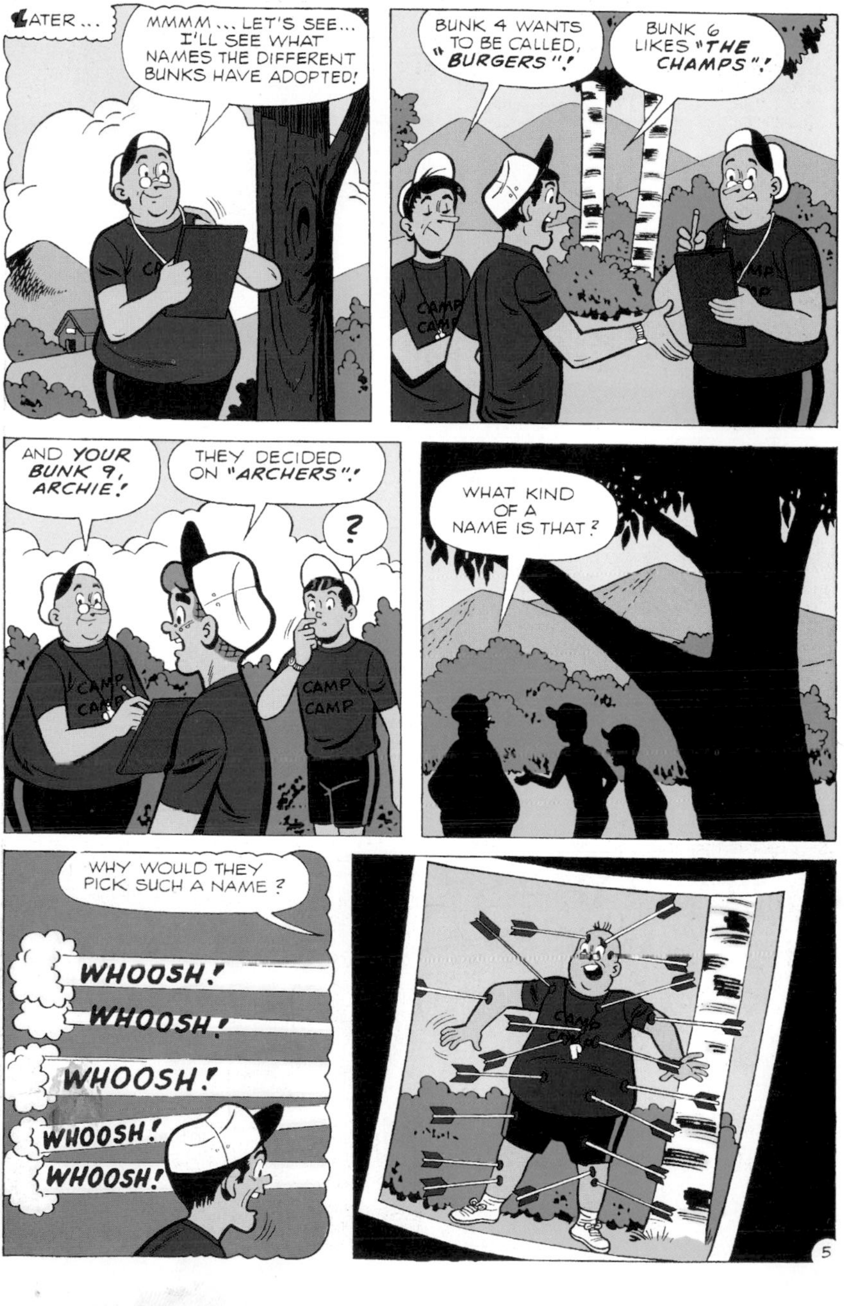
LATER ...
MMMM ... LET'S SEE... I'LL SEE WHAT NAMES THE DIFFERENT BUNKS HAVE ADOPTED!
BUNK 4 WANTS TO BE CALLED, "BURGERS"!
BUNK 6 LIKES "THE CHAMPS"!
AND YOUR BUNK 9, ARCHIE!
THEY DECIDED ON "ARCHERS"!
?
WHAT KIND OF A NAME IS THAT?
WHY WOULD THEY PICK SUCH A NAME?
WHOOSH!
WHOOSH!
WHOOSH!
WHOOSH!
WHOOSH!

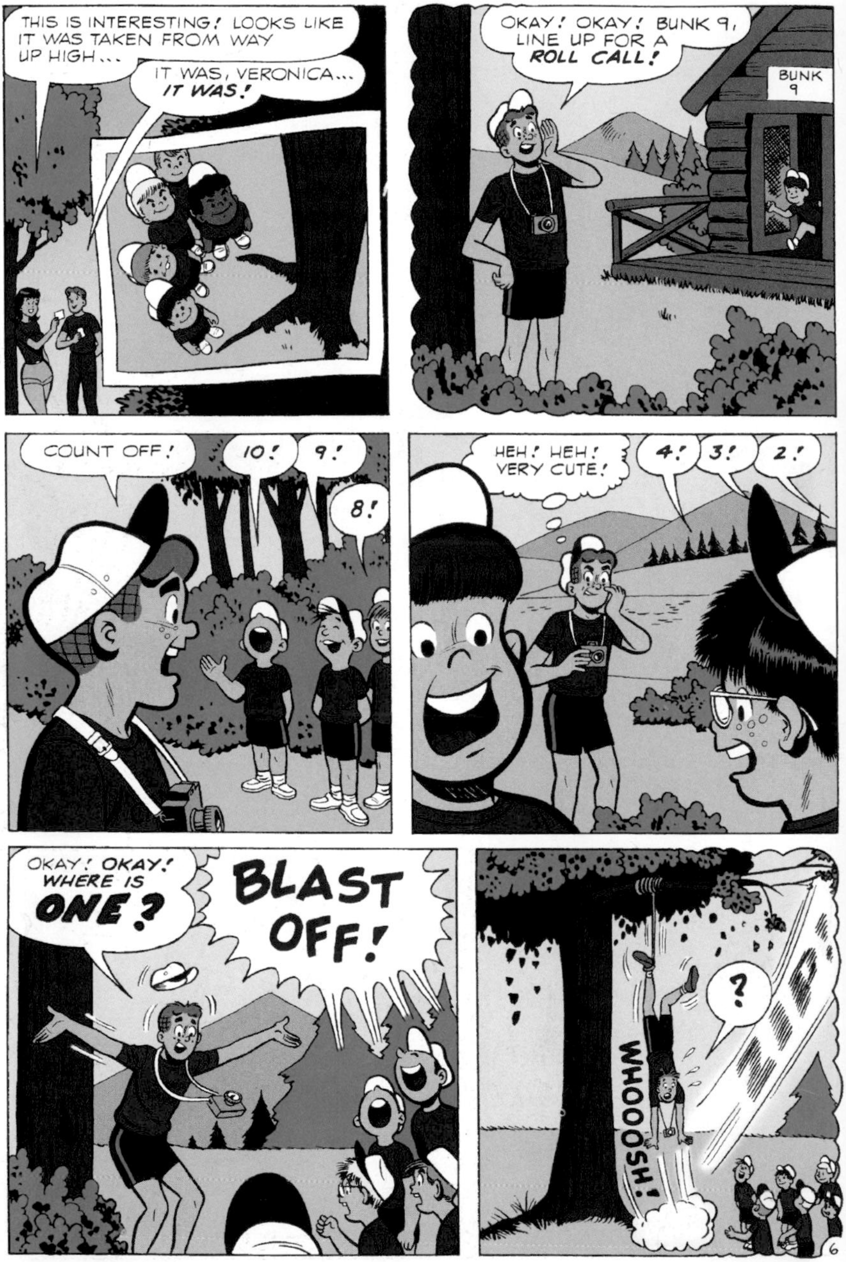
THIS IS INTERESTING! LOOKS LIKE IT WAS TAKEN FROM WAY UP HIGH...
IT WAS, VERONICA... IT WAS!
OKAY! OKAY! BUNK 9, LINE UP FOR A ROLL CALL!
BUNK 9
COUNT OFF!
10!
9!
8!
HEH! HEH! VERY CUTE!
4!
3!
2!
OKAY! OKAY! WHERE IS ONE?
BLAST OFF!
?
WHOOOOSH!

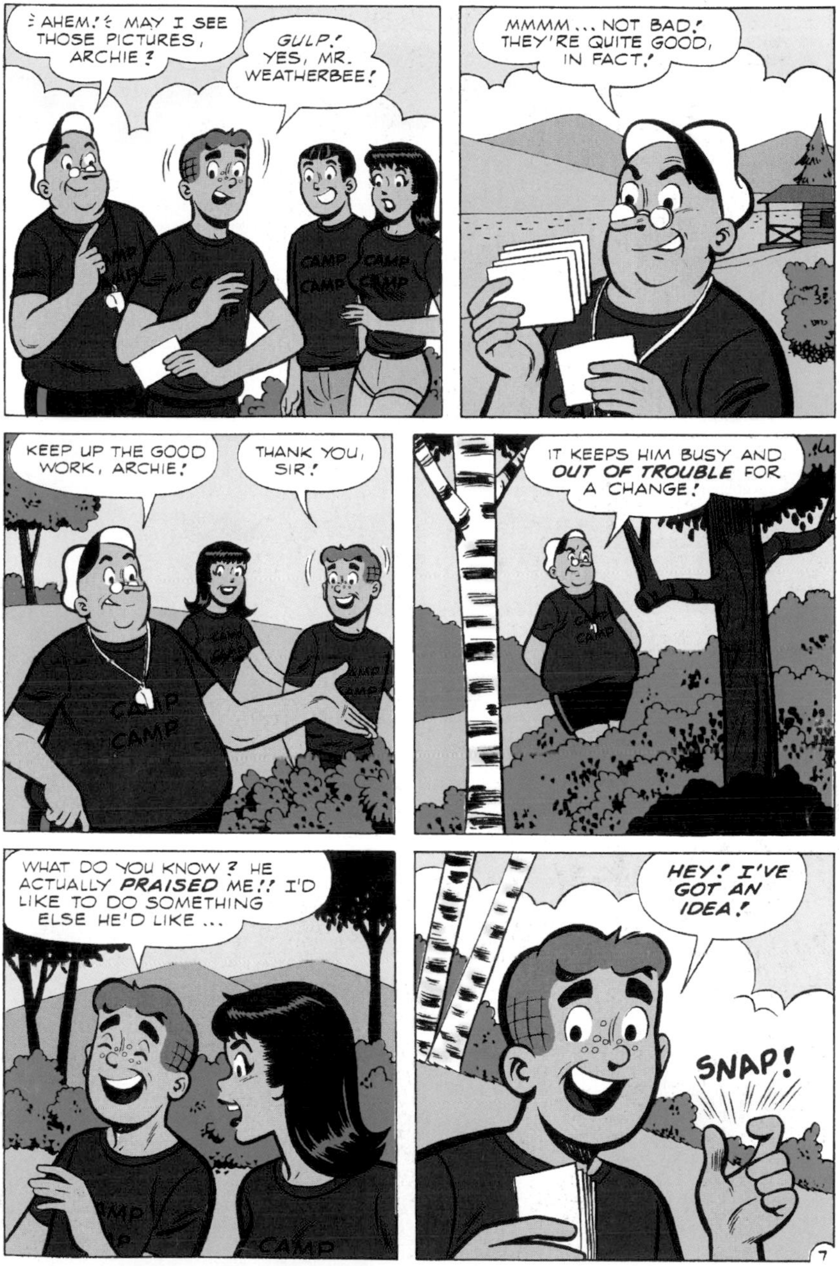

AHEM! MAY I SEE THOSE PICTURES, ARCHIE?
GULP! YES, MR. WEATHERBEE!
MMMM... NOT BAD! THEY'RE QUITE GOOD, IN FACT!
KEEP UP THE GOOD WORK, ARCHIE!
THANK YOU, SIR!
IT KEEPS HIM BUSY AND OUT OF TROUBLE FOR A CHANGE!
WHAT DO YOU KNOW? HE ACTUALLY PRAISED ME!! I'D LIKE TO DO SOMETHING ELSE HE'D LIKE...
HEY! I'VE GOT AN IDEA!
SNAP!

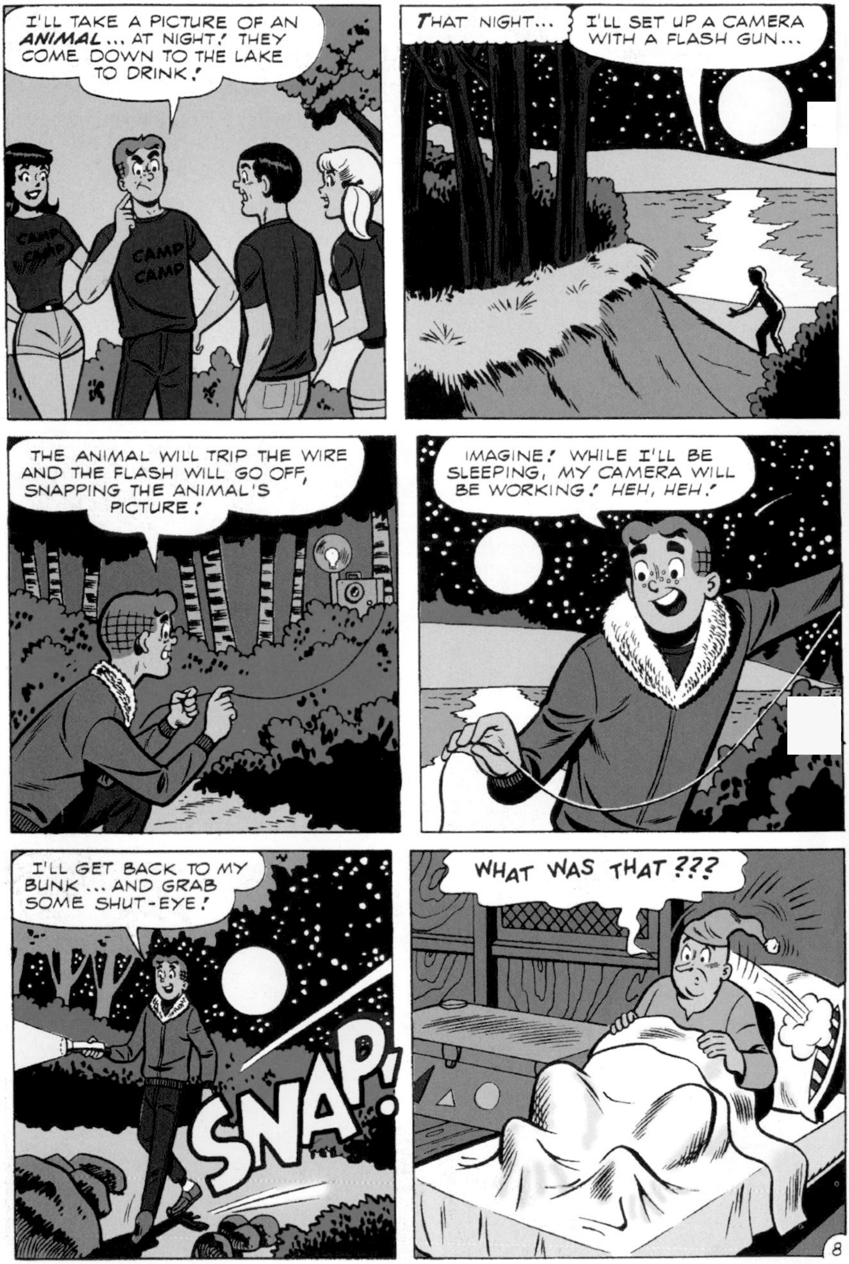
I'LL TAKE A PICTURE OF AN ANIMAL ... AT NIGHT! THEY COME DOWN TO THE LAKE TO DRINK!
CAMP CAMP
CAMP CAMP
THAT NIGHT...
I'LL SET UP A CAMERA WITH A FLASH GUN...
THE ANIMAL WILL TRIP THE WIRE AND THE FLASH WILL GO OFF, SNAPPING THE ANIMAL'S PICTURE!
IMAGINE! WHILE I'LL BE SLEEPING, MY CAMERA WILL BE WORKING! HEH, HEH!
I'LL GET BACK TO MY BUNK ... AND GRAB SOME SHUT-EYE!
SNAP!
WHAT WAS THAT ???

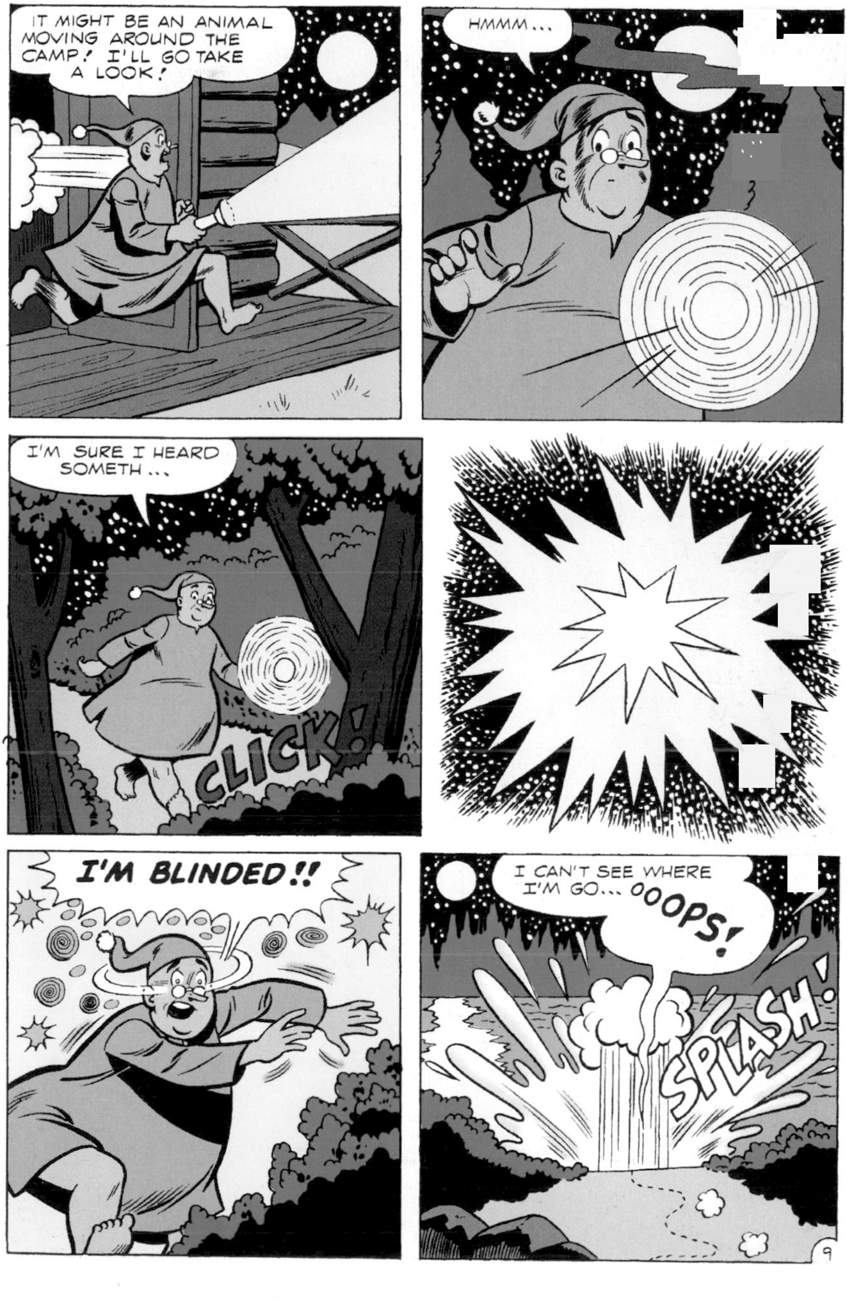

IT MIGHT BE AN ANIMAL MOVING AROUND THE CAMP! I'LL GO TAKE A LOOK!
HMMM...
I'M SURE I HEARD SOMETH...
CLICK!
I'M BLINDED!!
I CAN'T SEE WHERE I'M GO... OOOPS!
SPLASH!

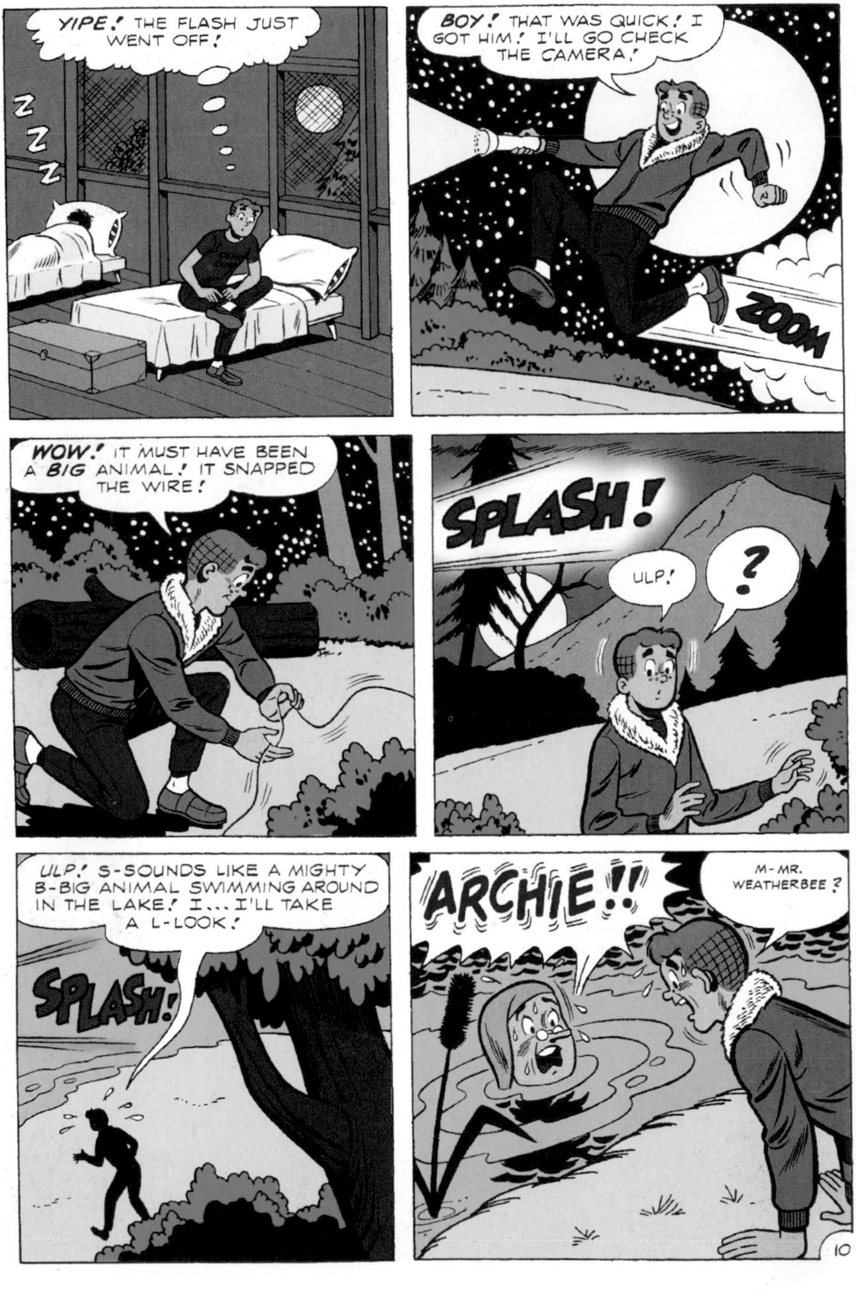
YIPE! THE FLASH JUST WENT OFF!
Z Z Z
BOY! THAT WAS QUICK! I GOT HIM! I'LL GO CHECK THE CAMERA!
ZOOM
WOW! IT MUST HAVE BEEN A BIG ANIMAL! IT SNAPPED THE WIRE!
SPLASH!
ULP!
?
ULP! S-SOUNDS LIKE A MIGHTY B-BIG ANIMAL SWIMMING AROUND IN THE LAKE! I... I'LL TAKE A L-LOOK!
SPLASH!
ARCHIE!!
M-MR. WEATHERBEE?

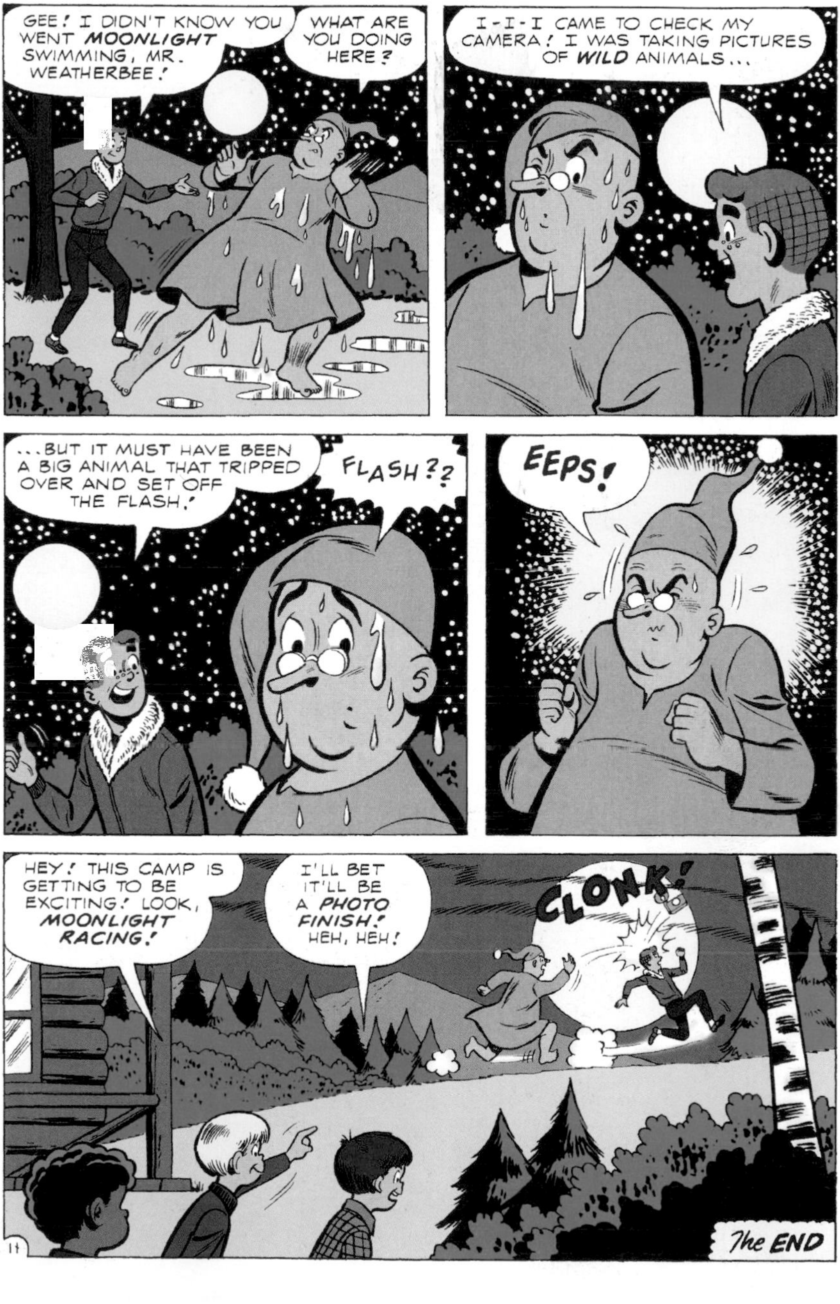
GEE! I DIDN'T KNOW YOU WENT MOONLIGHT SWIMMING, MR. WEATHERBEE!
WHAT ARE YOU DOING HERE?
I-I-I CAME TO CHECK MY CAMERA! I WAS TAKING PICTURES OF WILD ANIMALS...
...BUT IT MUST HAVE BEEN A BIG ANIMAL THAT TRIPPED OVER AND SET OFF THE FLASH!
FLASH??
EEPS!
HEY! THIS CAMP IS GETTING TO BE EXCITING! LOOK, MOONLIGHT RACING!
I'LL BET IT'LL BE A PHOTO FINISH! HEH, HEH!
CLONK!
The END

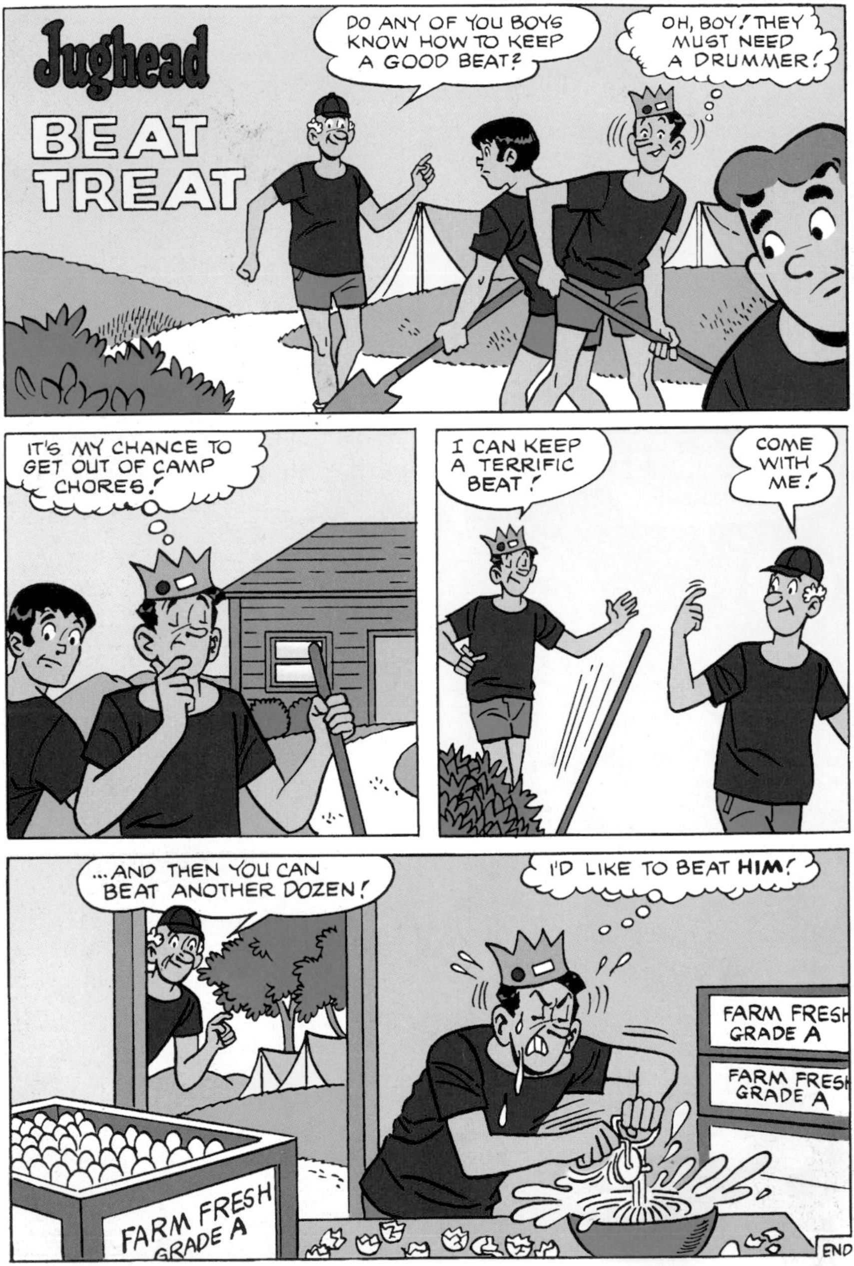
Jughead
BEAT TREAT
DO ANY OF YOU BOYS KNOW HOW TO KEEP A GOOD BEAT?
OH, BOY! THEY MUST NEED A DRUMMER!
IT'S MY CHANCE TO GET OUT OF CAMP CHORES!
I CAN KEEP A TERRIFIC BEAT!
COME WITH ME!
...AND THEN YOU CAN BEAT ANOTHER DOZEN!
I'D LIKE TO BEAT HIM!
FARM FRESH GRADE A
FARM FRESH GRADE A
FARM FRESH GRADE A
END

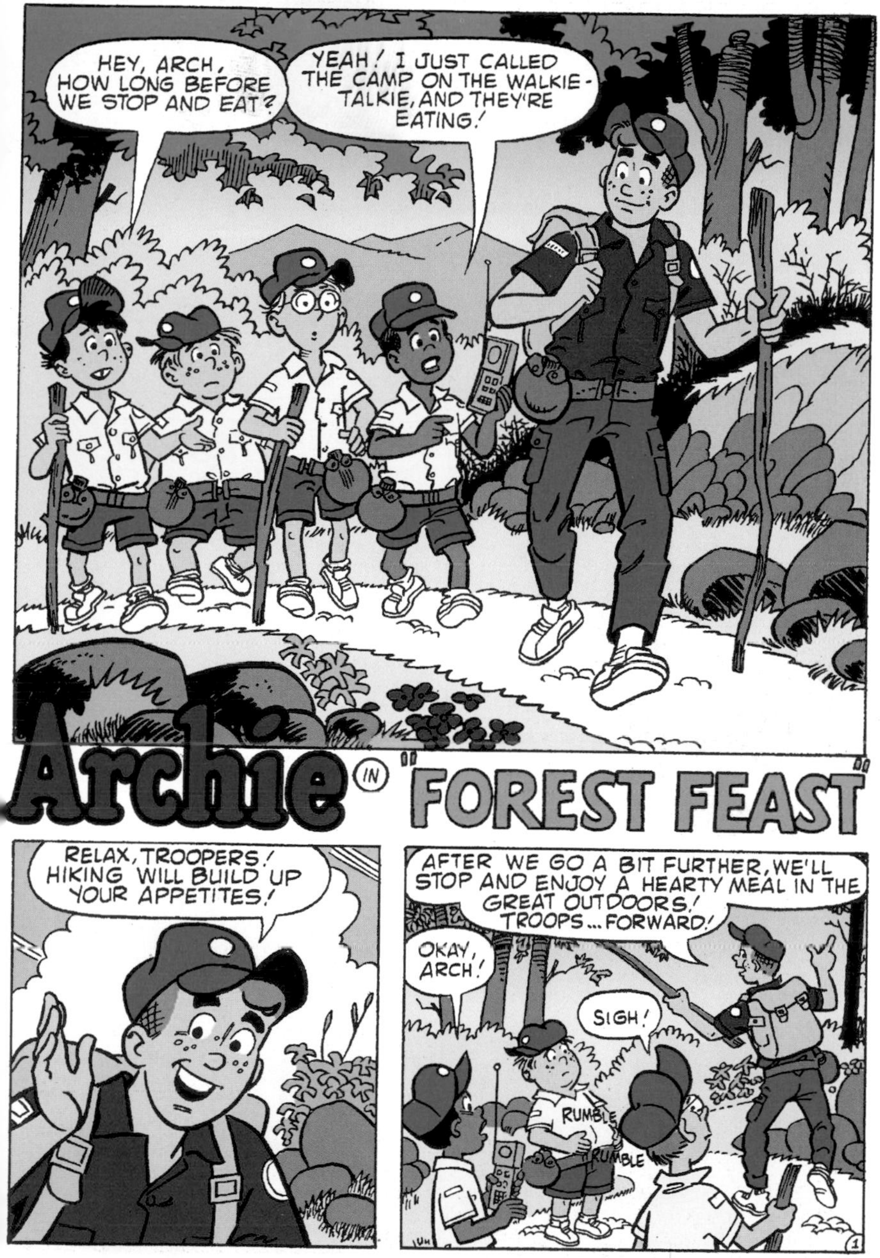
HEY, ARCH, HOW LONG BEFORE WE STOP AND EAT?
YEAH! I JUST CALLED THE CAMP ON THE WALKIE-TALKIE, AND THEY'RE EATING!
Archie (IN) "FOREST FEAST"
RELAX, TROOPERS! HIKING WILL BUILD UP YOUR APPETITES!
AFTER WE GO A BIT FURTHER, WE'LL STOP AND ENJOY A HEARTY MEAL IN THE GREAT OUTDOORS! TROOPS... FORWARD!
OKAY, ARCH!
SIGH!
RUMBLE
RUMBLE
1

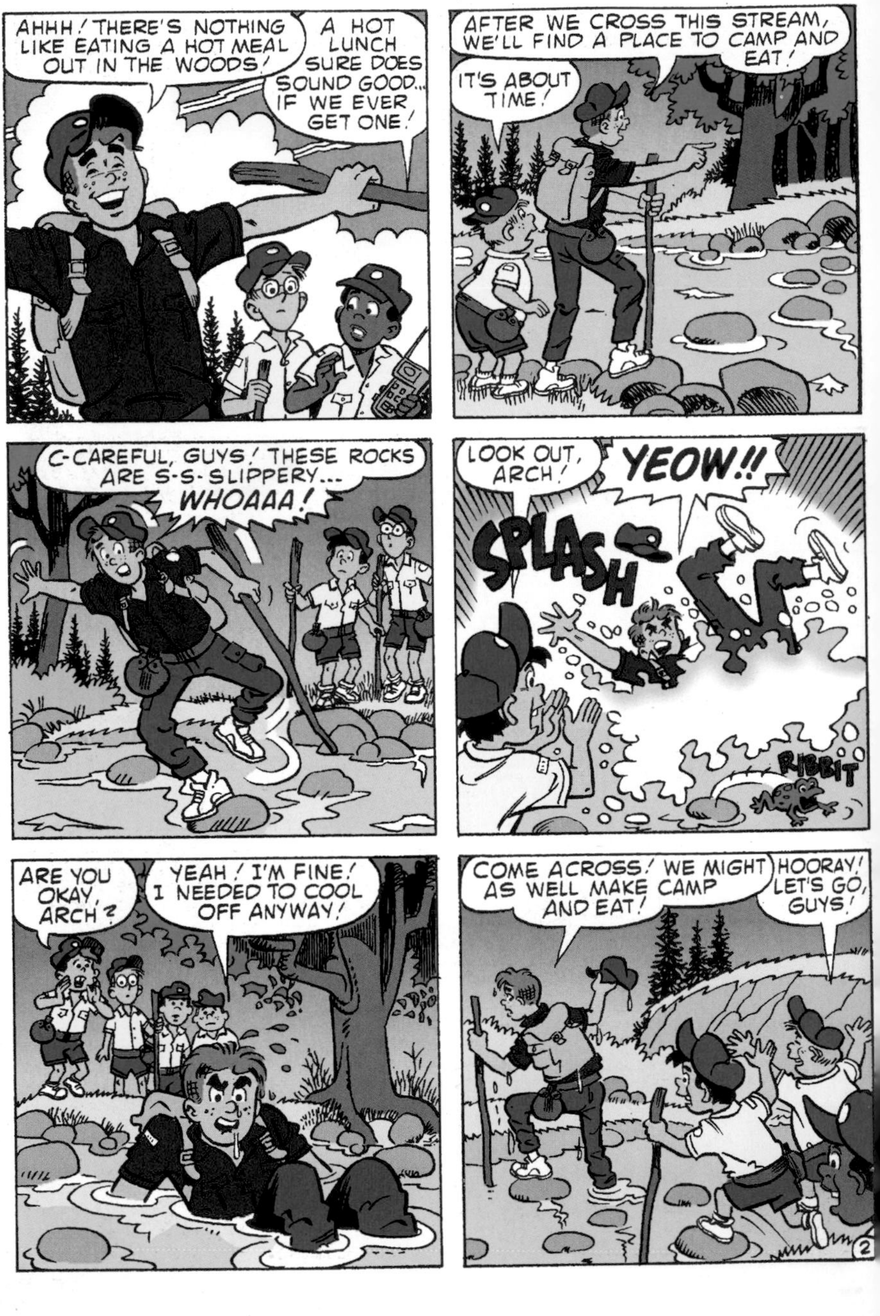
AHHH! THERE'S NOTHING LIKE EATING A HOT MEAL OUT IN THE WOODS!
A HOT LUNCH SURE DOES SOUND GOOD... IF WE EVER GET ONE!
AFTER WE CROSS THIS STREAM, WE'LL FIND A PLACE TO CAMP AND EAT!
IT'S ABOUT TIME!
C-CAREFUL, GUYS! THESE ROCKS ARE S-S-SLIPPERY...
WHOAAA!
LOOK OUT, ARCH!
YEOW!!
SPLASH
RIBBIT
ARE YOU OKAY, ARCH?
YEAH! I'M FINE! I NEEDED TO COOL OFF ANYWAY!
COME ACROSS! WE MIGHT AS WELL MAKE CAMP AND EAT!
HOORAY! LET'S GO, GUYS!

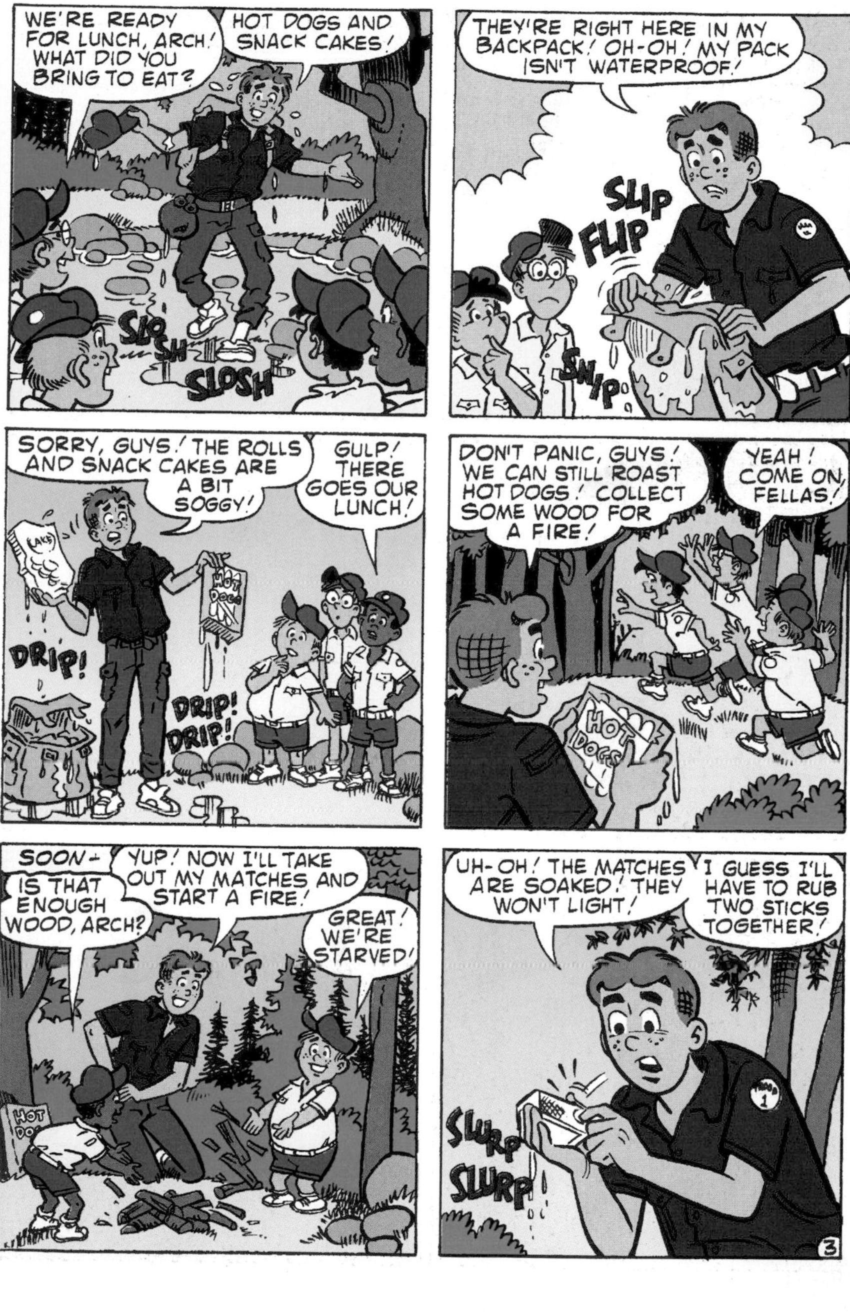
WE'RE READY FOR LUNCH, ARCH! WHAT DID YOU BRING TO EAT?
HOT DOGS AND SNACK CAKES!
SLOSH
SLOSH
THEY'RE RIGHT HERE IN MY BACKPACK! OH-OH! MY PACK ISN'T WATERPROOF!
SLIP
FLIP
SNIP
SORRY, GUYS! THE ROLLS AND SNACK CAKES ARE A BIT SOGGY!
GULP! THERE GOES OUR LUNCH!
CAKE
HOT DOGS
DRIP!
DRIP! DRIP!
DON'T PANIC, GUYS! WE CAN STILL ROAST HOT DOGS! COLLECT SOME WOOD FOR A FIRE!
YEAH! COME ON, FELLAS!
HOT DOGS
SOON—
IS THAT ENOUGH WOOD, ARCH?
YUP! NOW I'LL TAKE OUT MY MATCHES AND START A FIRE!
GREAT! WE'RE STARVED!
UH-OH! THE MATCHES ARE SOAKED! THEY WON'T LIGHT!
I GUESS I'LL HAVE TO RUB TWO STICKS TOGETHER!
SLURP
SLURP

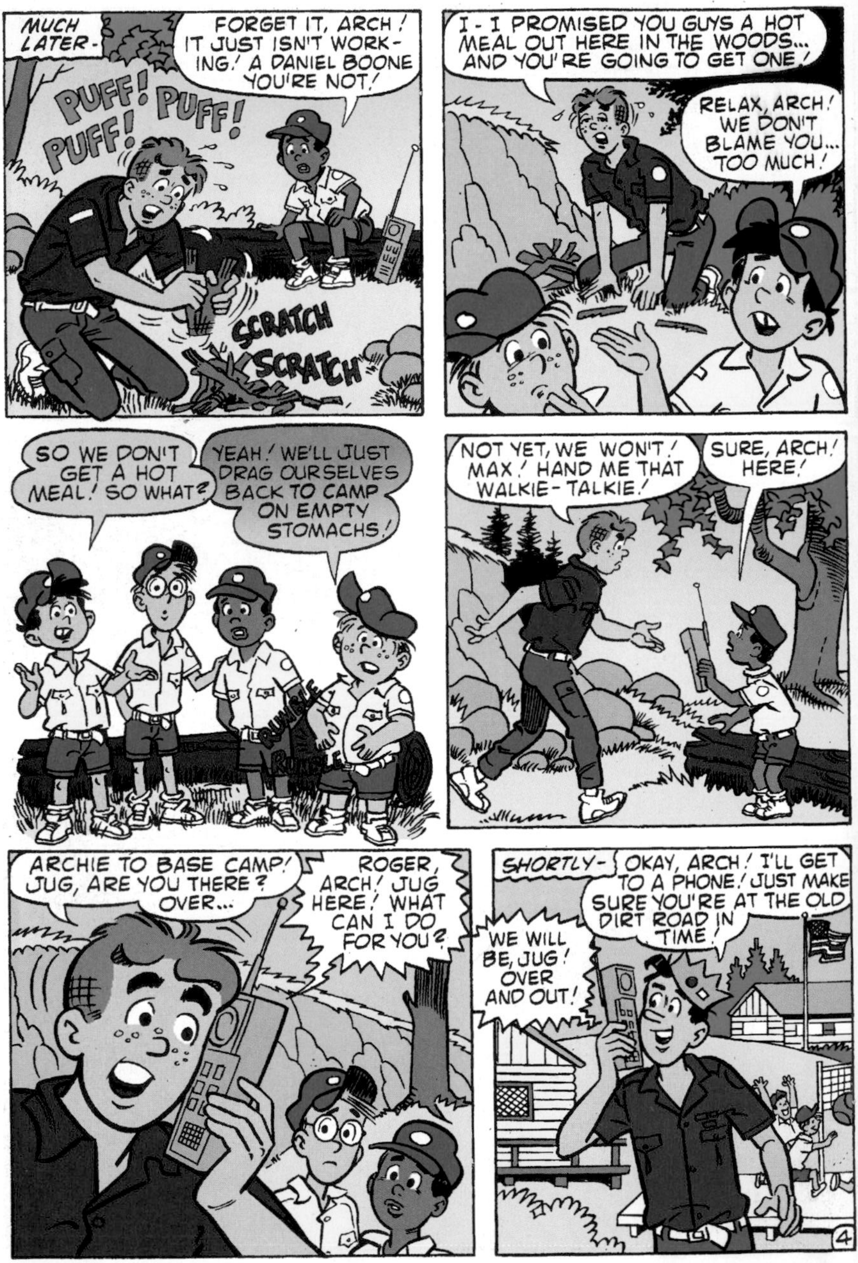
MUCH LATER-
FORGET IT, ARCH! IT JUST ISN'T WORKING! A DANIEL BOONE YOU'RE NOT!
PUFF! PUFF! PUFF!
SCRATCH SCRATCH
I - I PROMISED YOU GUYS A HOT MEAL OUT HERE IN THE WOODS... AND YOU'RE GOING TO GET ONE!
RELAX, ARCH! WE DON'T BLAME YOU... TOO MUCH!
SO WE DON'T GET A HOT MEAL! SO WHAT?
YEAH! WE'LL JUST DRAG OURSELVES BACK TO CAMP ON EMPTY STOMACHS!
RUMBLE
RUMBLE
NOT YET, WE WON'T! MAX! HAND ME THAT WALKIE-TALKIE!
SURE, ARCH! HERE!
ARCHIE TO BASE CAMP! JUG, ARE YOU THERE? OVER...
ROGER, ARCH! JUG HERE! WHAT CAN I DO FOR YOU?
SHORTLY-
OKAY, ARCH! I'LL GET TO A PHONE! JUST MAKE SURE YOU'RE AT THE OLD DIRT ROAD IN TIME!
WE WILL BE, JUG! OVER AND OUT!
4

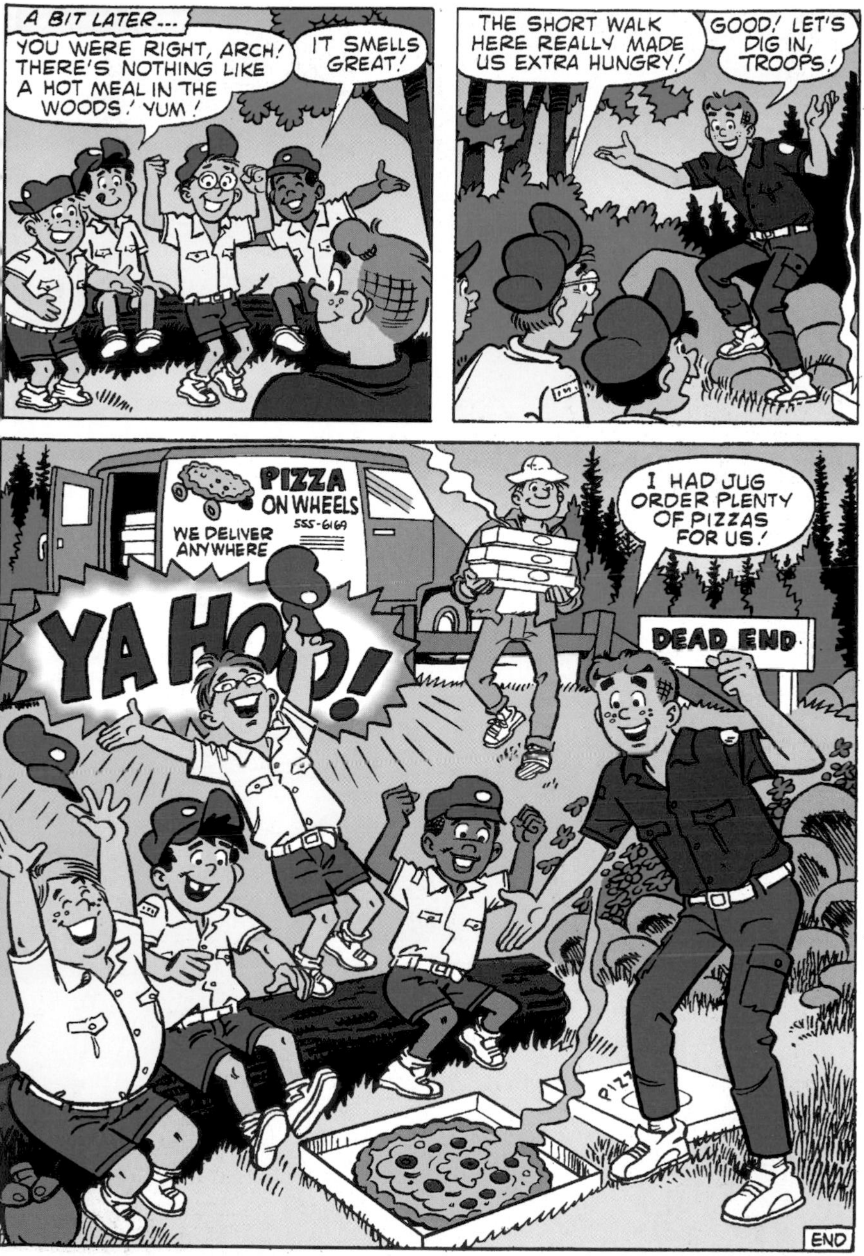
A BIT LATER...
YOU WERE RIGHT, ARCH! THERE'S NOTHING LIKE A HOT MEAL IN THE WOODS! YUM!
IT SMELLS GREAT!
THE SHORT WALK HERE REALLY MADE US EXTRA HUNGRY!
GOOD! LET'S DIG IN, TROOPS!
PIZZA ON WHEELS
555-6169
WE DELIVER ANYWHERE
YAHOO!
I HAD JUG ORDER PLENTY OF PIZZAS FOR US!
DEAD END
END

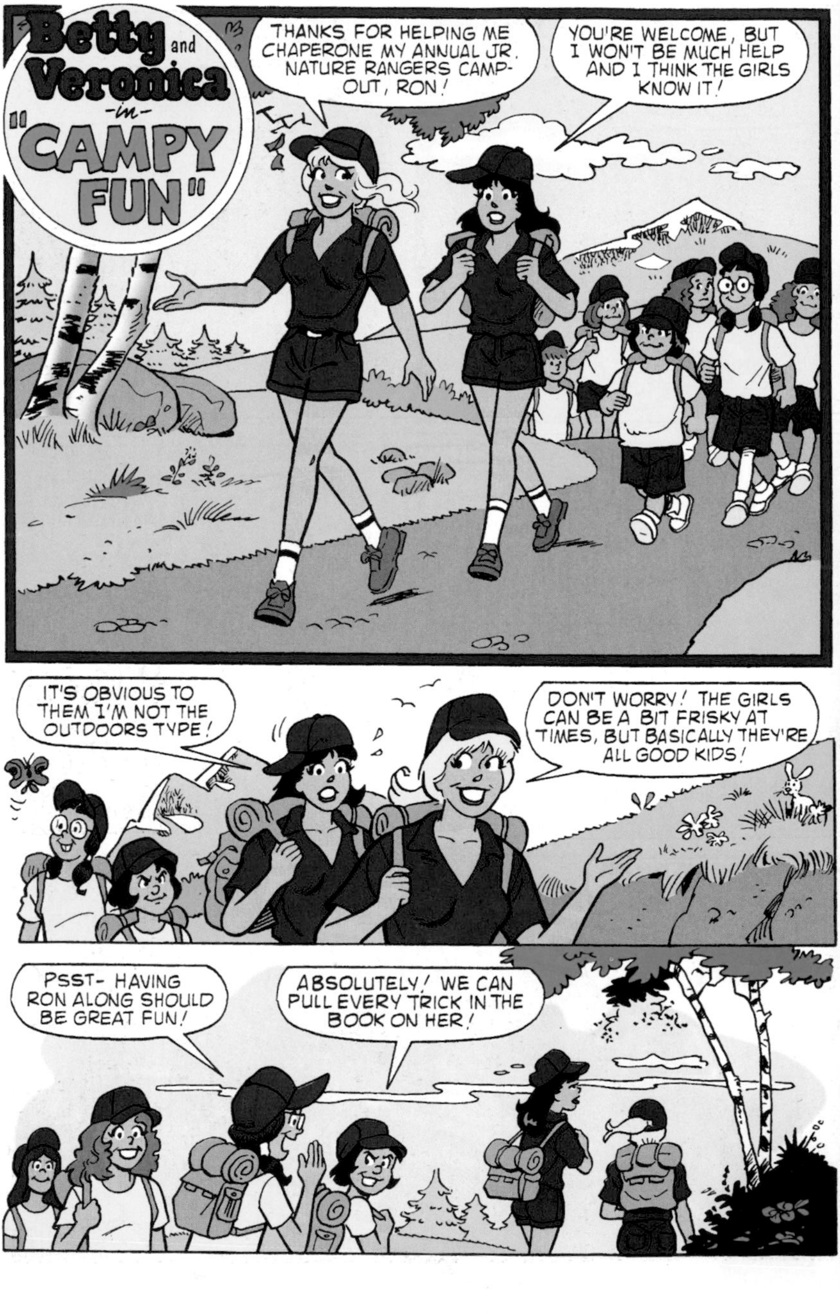
Betty and Veronica -in- "CAMPY FUN"
THANKS FOR HELPING ME CHAPERONE MY ANNUAL JR. NATURE RANGERS CAMP-OUT, RON!
YOU'RE WELCOME, BUT I WON'T BE MUCH HELP AND I THINK THE GIRLS KNOW IT!
IT'S OBVIOUS TO THEM I'M NOT THE OUTDOORS TYPE!
DON'T WORRY! THE GIRLS CAN BE A BIT FRISKY AT TIMES, BUT BASICALLY THEY'RE ALL GOOD KIDS!
PSST- HAVING RON ALONG SHOULD BE GREAT FUN!
ABSOLUTELY! WE CAN PULL EVERY TRICK IN THE BOOK ON HER!

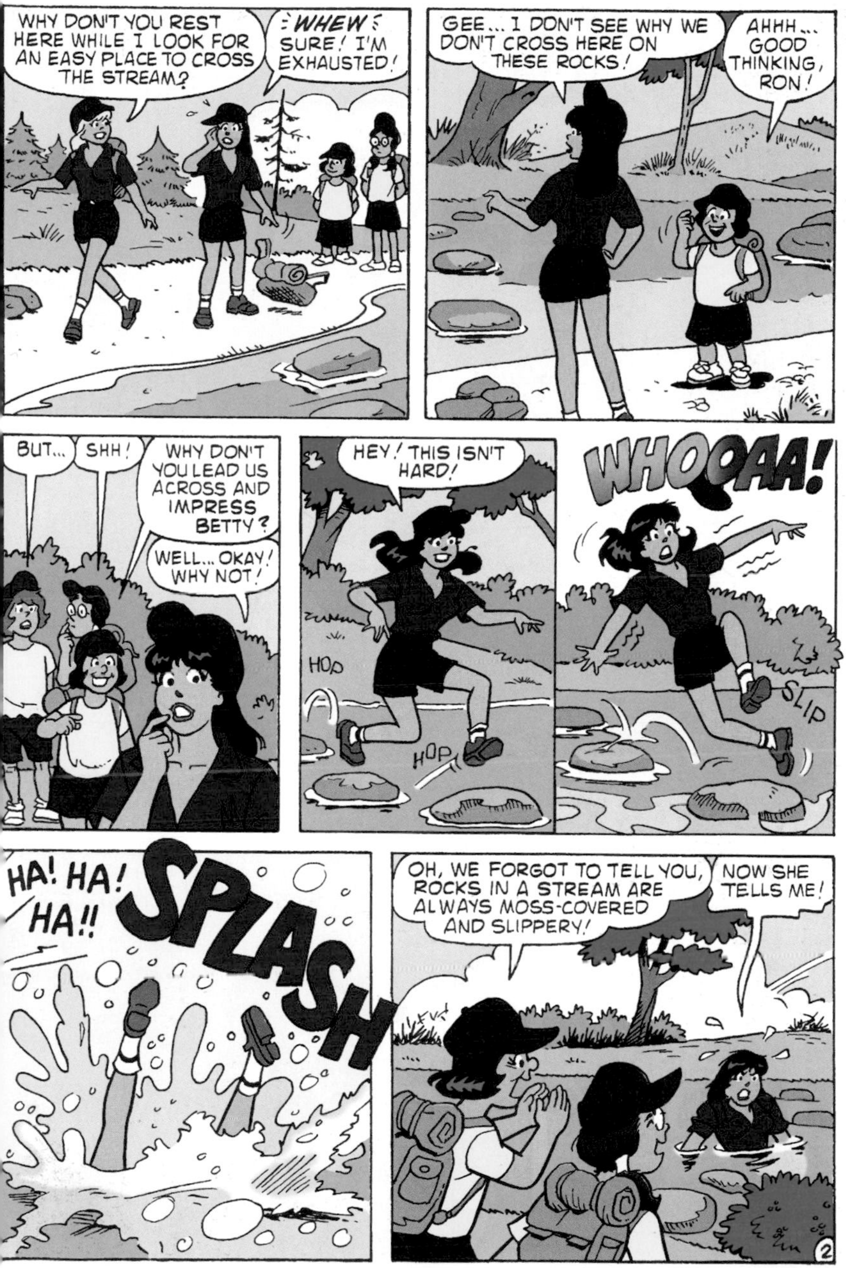

WHY DON'T YOU REST HERE WHILE I LOOK FOR AN EASY PLACE TO CROSS THE STREAM?
WHEW SURE! I'M EXHAUSTED!
GEE... I DON'T SEE WHY WE DON'T CROSS HERE ON THESE ROCKS!
AHHH... GOOD THINKING, RON!
BUT...
SHH!
WHY DON'T YOU LEAD US ACROSS AND IMPRESS BETTY?
WELL... OKAY! WHY NOT!
HEY! THIS ISN'T HARD!
HOP
HOP
WHOOAA!
SLIP
HA! HA! HA!!
SPLASH
OH, WE FORGOT TO TELL YOU, ROCKS IN A STREAM ARE ALWAYS MOSS-COVERED AND SLIPPERY!
NOW SHE TELLS ME!
2

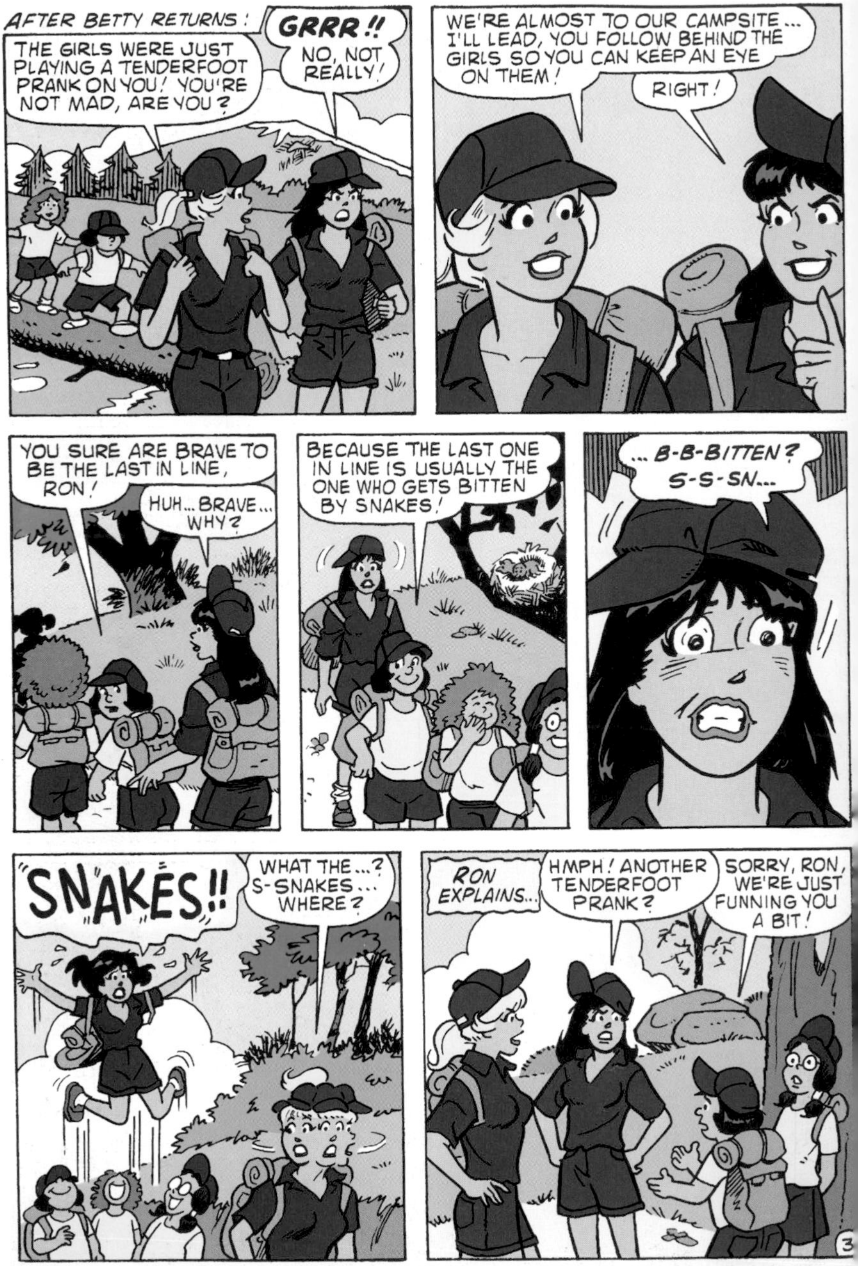
AFTER BETTY RETURNS :
THE GIRLS WERE JUST PLAYING A TENDERFOOT PRANK ON YOU! YOU'RE NOT MAD, ARE YOU ?
GRRR !!
NO, NOT REALLY!
WE'RE ALMOST TO OUR CAMPSITE... I'LL LEAD, YOU FOLLOW BEHIND THE GIRLS SO YOU CAN KEEP AN EYE ON THEM!
RIGHT!
YOU SURE ARE BRAVE TO BE THE LAST IN LINE, RON!
HUH... BRAVE... WHY?
BECAUSE THE LAST ONE IN LINE IS USUALLY THE ONE WHO GETS BITTEN BY SNAKES!
... B-B-BITTEN? S-S-SN...
SNAKES!!
WHAT THE...? S-SNAKES... WHERE?
RON EXPLAINS...
HMPH! ANOTHER TENDERFOOT PRANK?
SORRY, RON, WE'RE JUST FUNNING YOU A BIT!
3

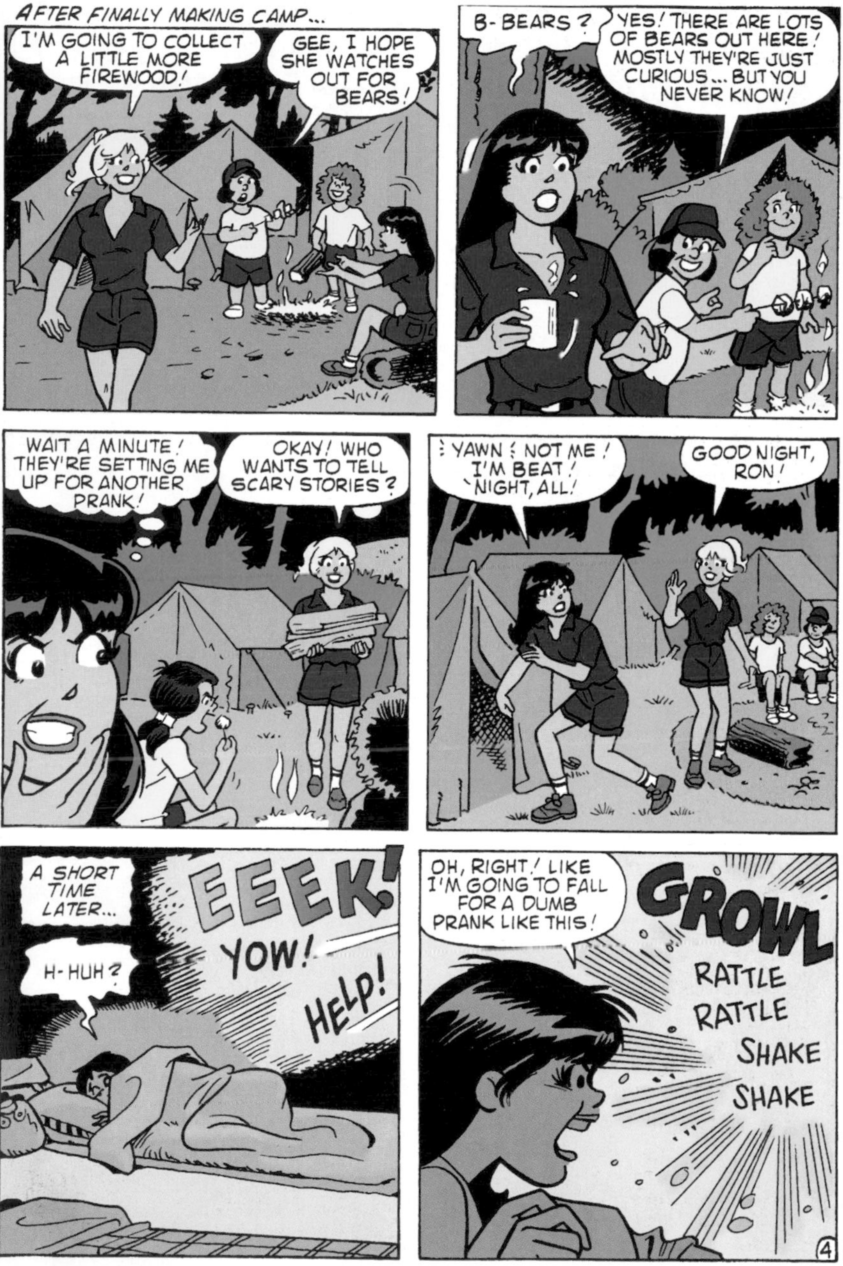
AFTER FINALLY MAKING CAMP...
I'M GOING TO COLLECT A LITTLE MORE FIREWOOD!
GEE, I HOPE SHE WATCHES OUT FOR BEARS!
B-BEARS?
YES! THERE ARE LOTS OF BEARS OUT HERE! MOSTLY THEY'RE JUST CURIOUS... BUT YOU NEVER KNOW!
WAIT A MINUTE! THEY'RE SETTING ME UP FOR ANOTHER PRANK!
OKAY! WHO WANTS TO TELL SCARY STORIES?
:YAWN: NOT ME! I'M BEAT! 'NIGHT, ALL!
GOOD NIGHT, RON!
A SHORT TIME LATER...
EEEK!
YOW!
HELP!
H-HUH?
OH, RIGHT! LIKE I'M GOING TO FALL FOR A DUMB PRANK LIKE THIS!
GROWL
RATTLE
RATTLE
SHAKE
SHAKE
4

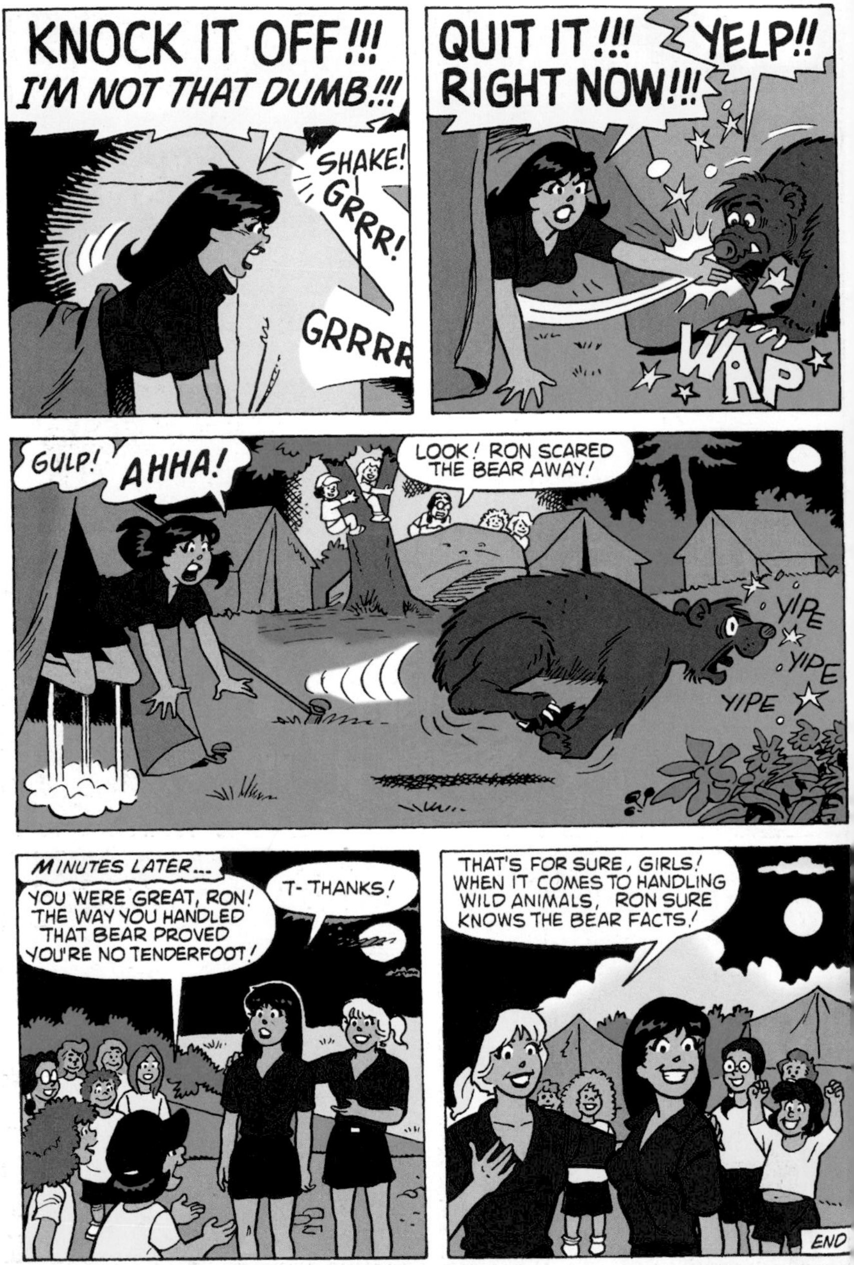
KNOCK IT OFF!!!
I'M NOT THAT DUMB!!!
SHAKE!
G!
GRRRR!
GRRRR
QUIT IT!!!
RIGHT NOW!!!
YELP!!
WAP
GULP!
AHHA!
LOOK! RON SCARED THE BEAR AWAY!
YIPE
YIPE
YIPE
MINUTES LATER...
YOU WERE GREAT, RON! THE WAY YOU HANDLED THAT BEAR PROVED YOU'RE NO TENDERFOOT!
T- THANKS!
THAT'S FOR SURE, GIRLS! WHEN IT COMES TO HANDLING WILD ANIMALS, RON SURE KNOWS THE BEAR FACTS!
END

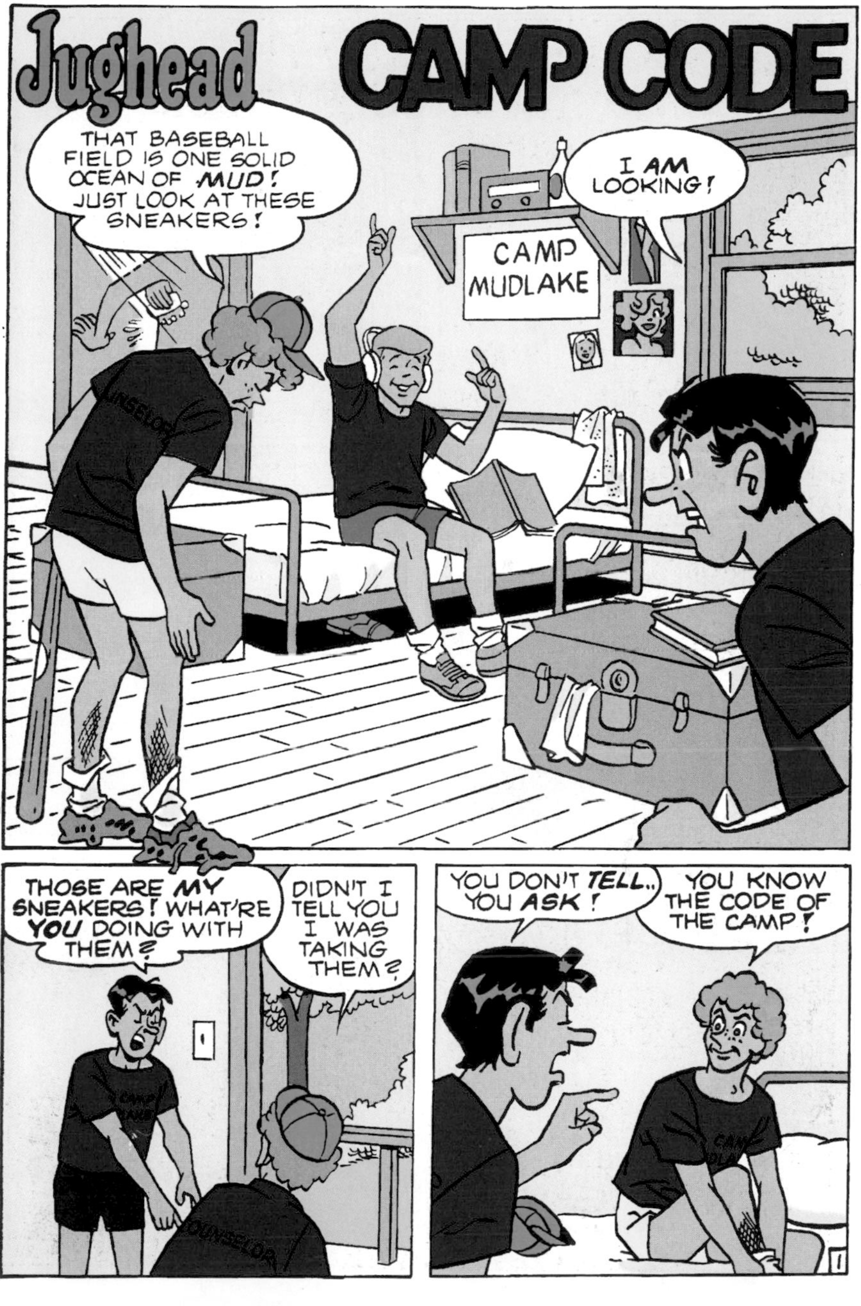
Jughead
CAMP CODE
THAT BASEBALL FIELD IS ONE SOLID OCEAN OF MUD! JUST LOOK AT THESE SNEAKERS!
I AM LOOKING!
CAMP MUDLAKE
THOSE ARE MY SNEAKERS! WHAT'RE YOU DOING WITH THEM?
DIDN'T I TELL YOU I WAS TAKING THEM?
YOU DON'T TELL.. YOU ASK!
YOU KNOW THE CODE OF THE CAMP!
1

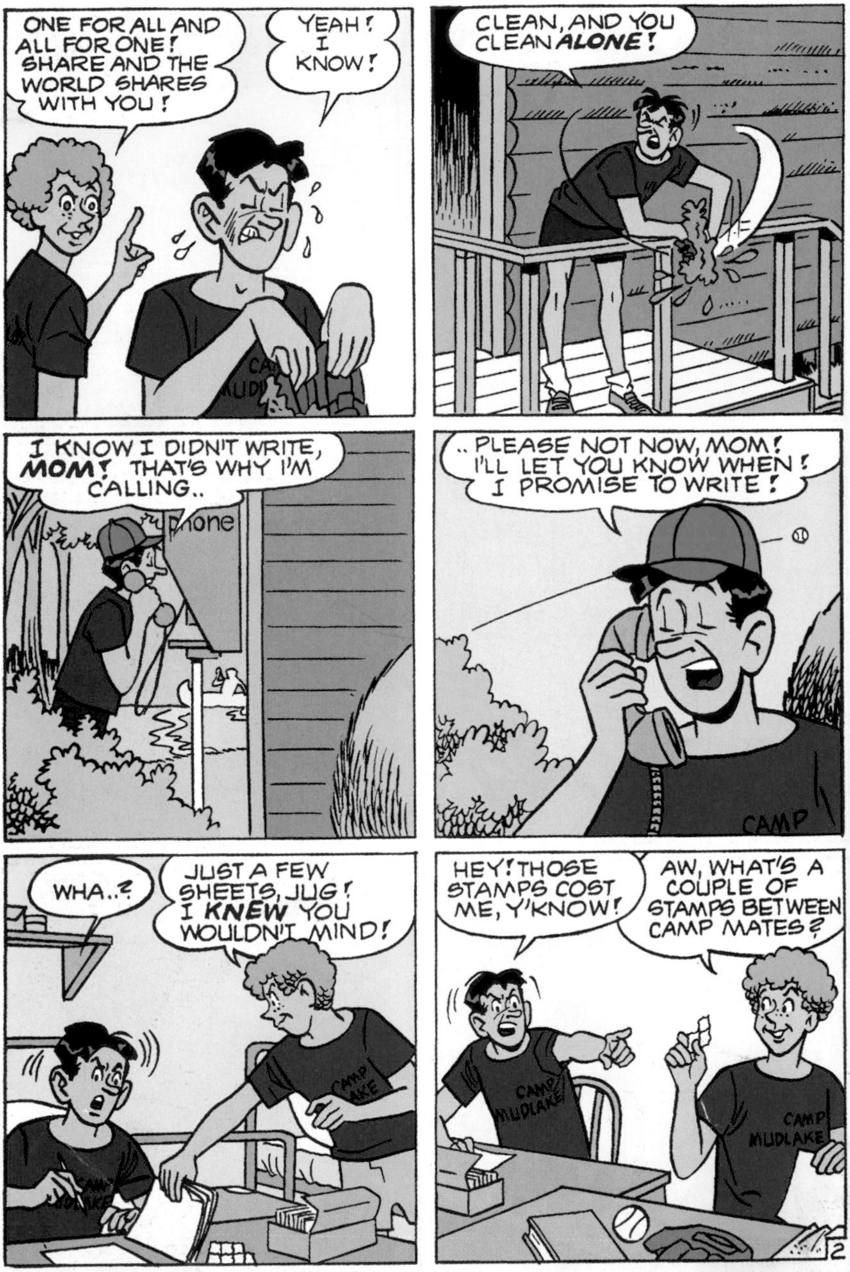
ONE FOR ALL AND ALL FOR ONE! SHARE AND THE WORLD SHARES WITH YOU!
YEAH! I KNOW!
CLEAN, AND YOU CLEAN ALONE!
I KNOW I DIDN'T WRITE, MOM! THAT'S WHY I'M CALLING..
phone
.. PLEASE NOT NOW, MOM! I'LL LET YOU KNOW WHEN! I PROMISE TO WRITE!
CAMP
WHA..?
JUST A FEW SHEETS, JUG! I KNEW YOU WOULDN'T MIND!
HEY! THOSE STAMPS COST ME, Y'KNOW!
AW, WHAT'S A COUPLE OF STAMPS BETWEEN CAMP MATES?
CAMP MUDLAKE
CAMP MUDLAKE

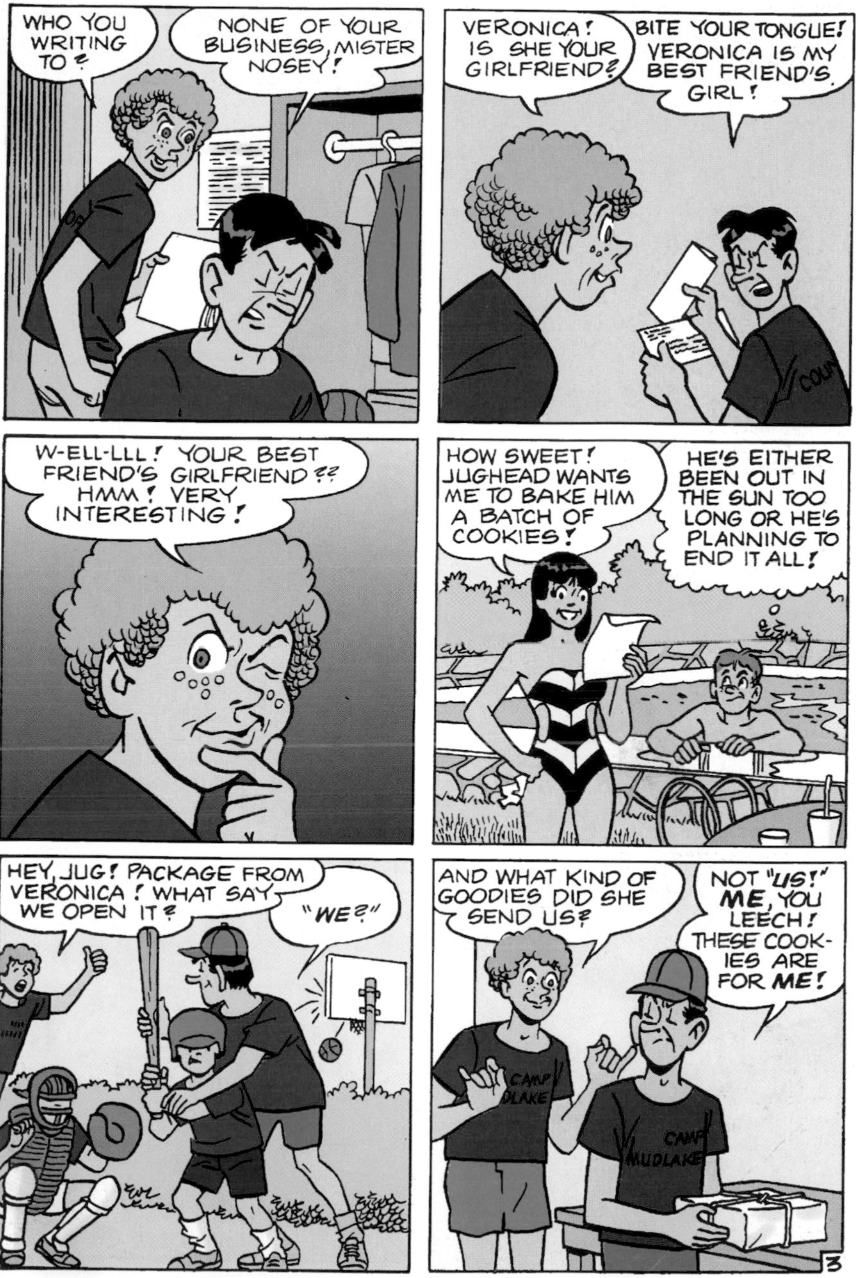
WHO YOU WRITING TO?
NONE OF YOUR BUSINESS, MISTER NOSEY!
VERONICA! IS SHE YOUR GIRLFRIEND?
BITE YOUR TONGUE! VERONICA IS MY BEST FRIEND'S GIRL!
W-ELL-LLL! YOUR BEST FRIEND'S GIRLFRIEND?? HMM! VERY INTERESTING!
HOW SWEET! JUGHEAD WANTS ME TO BAKE HIM A BATCH OF COOKIES!
HE'S EITHER BEEN OUT IN THE SUN TOO LONG OR HE'S PLANNING TO END IT ALL!
HEY, JUG! PACKAGE FROM VERONICA! WHAT SAY WE OPEN IT?
"WE?"
AND WHAT KIND OF GOODIES DID SHE SEND US?
NOT "US!" ME, YOU LEECH! THESE COOKIES ARE FOR ME!
CAMP MUDLAKE

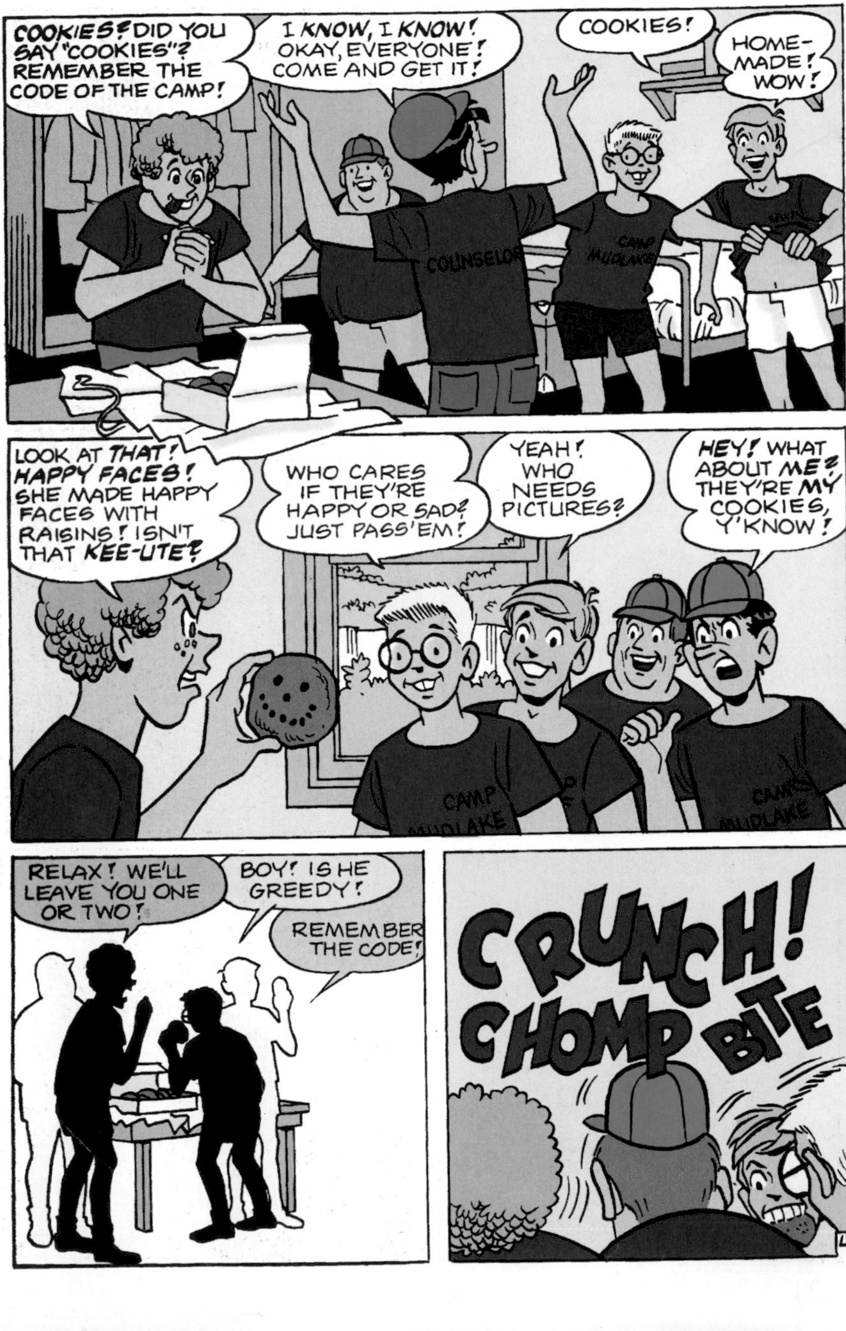
COOKIES? DID YOU SAY "COOKIES"? REMEMBER THE CODE OF THE CAMP!
I KNOW, I KNOW! OKAY, EVERYONE! COME AND GET IT!
COOKIES!
HOME-MADE! WOW!
COUNSELOR
CAMP MUDLAKE
LOOK AT THAT! HAPPY FACES! SHE MADE HAPPY FACES WITH RAISINS! ISN'T THAT KEE-UTE?
WHO CARES IF THEY'RE HAPPY OR SAD? JUST PASS'EM!
YEAH! WHO NEEDS PICTURES?
HEY! WHAT ABOUT ME? THEY'RE MY COOKIES, Y'KNOW!
CAMP MUDLAKE
CAMP MUDLAKE
RELAX! WE'LL LEAVE YOU ONE OR TWO!
BOY! IS HE GREEDY!
REMEMBER THE CODE!
CRUNCH! CHOMP BITE

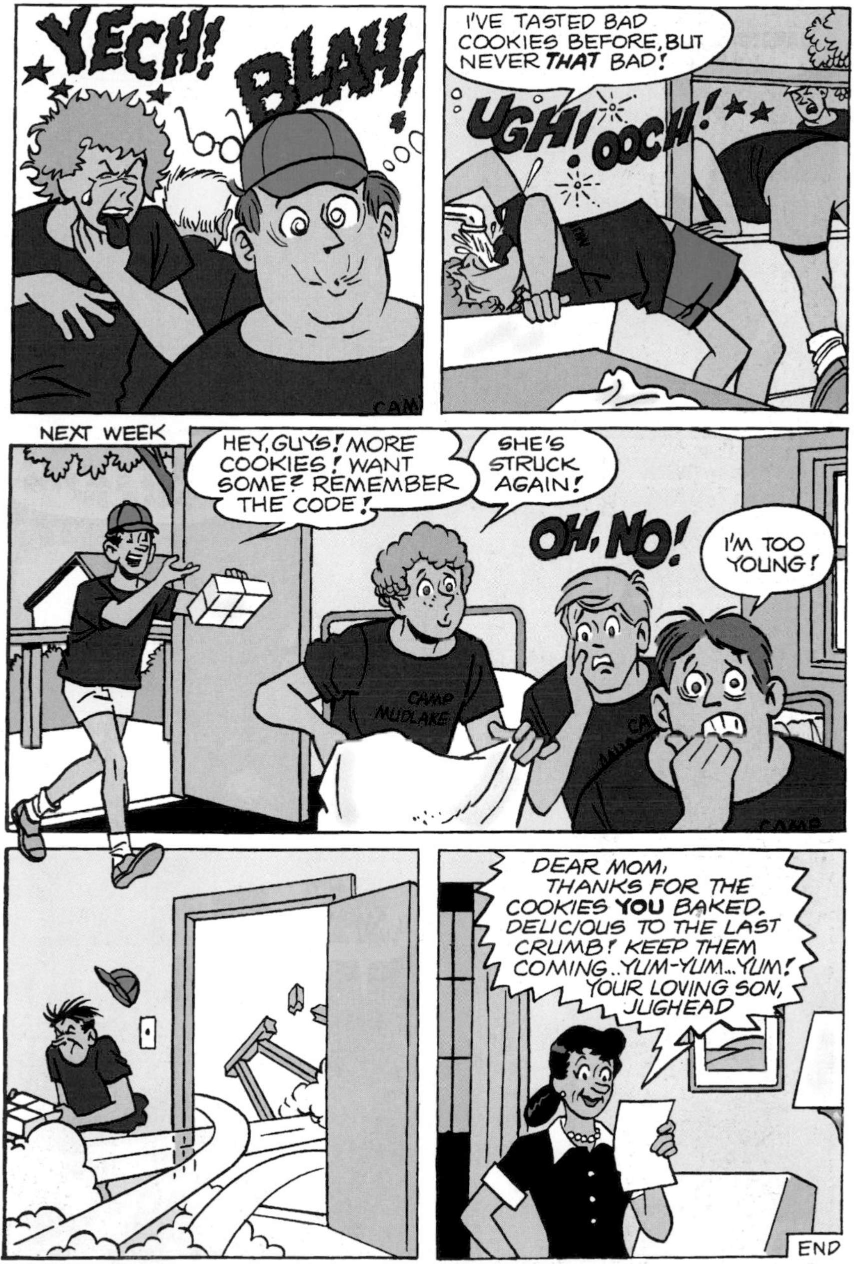
YECH!
BLAH!
I'VE TASTED BAD COOKIES BEFORE, BUT NEVER THAT BAD!
UGH!
OOCH!
NEXT WEEK
HEY, GUYS! MORE COOKIES! WANT SOME? REMEMBER THE CODE!
SHE'S STRUCK AGAIN!
OH, NO!
I'M TOO YOUNG!
CAMP MUDLAKE
DEAR MOM, THANKS FOR THE COOKIES YOU BAKED. DELICIOUS TO THE LAST CRUMB! KEEP THEM COMING..YUM-YUM...YUM! YOUR LOVING SON, JUGHEAD
END

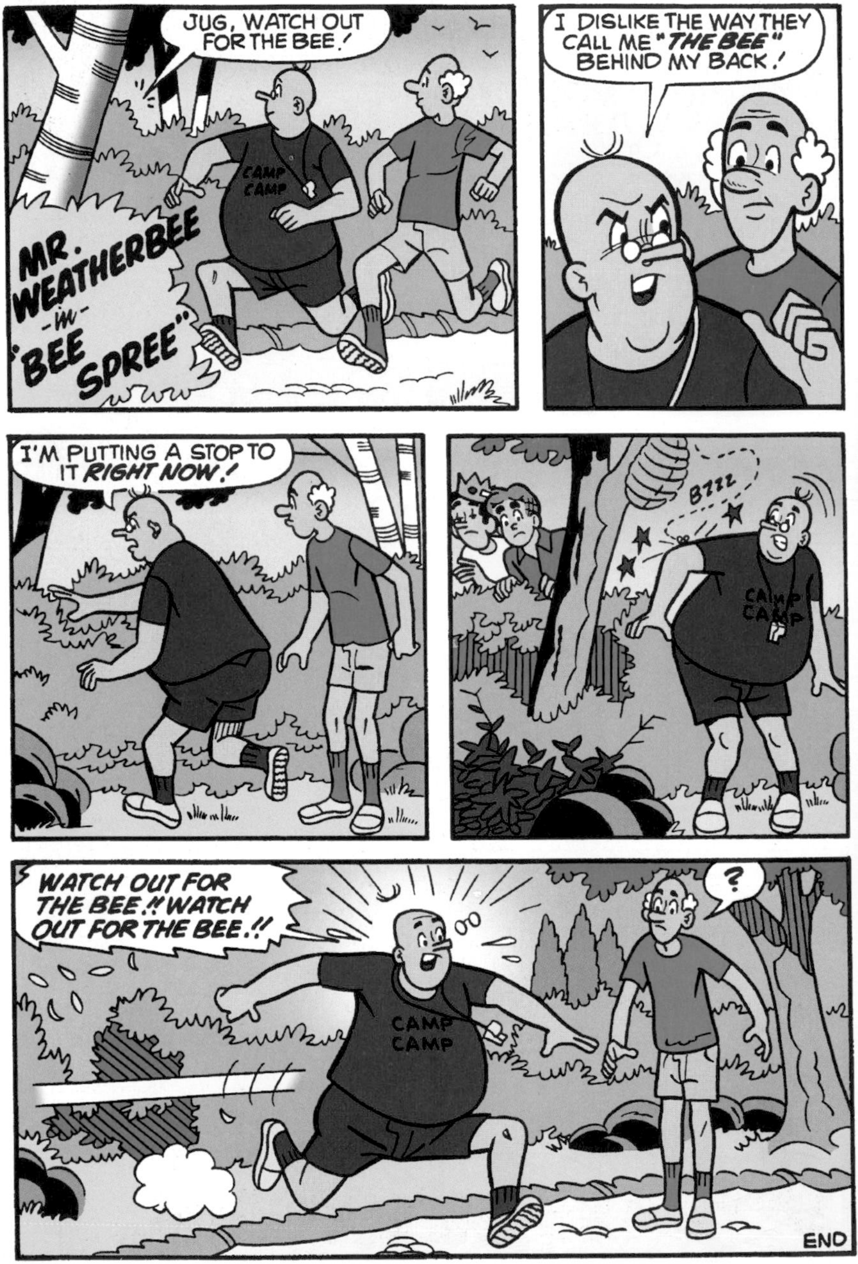

JUG, WATCH OUT FOR THE BEE!
MR. WEATHERBEE -in- "BEE SPREE"
CAMP CAMP
I DISLIKE THE WAY THEY CALL ME "THE BEE" BEHIND MY BACK!
I'M PUTTING A STOP TO IT RIGHT NOW!
BZZZ
CAMP CAMP
WATCH OUT FOR THE BEE!! WATCH OUT FOR THE BEE!!
?
CAMP CAMP
END

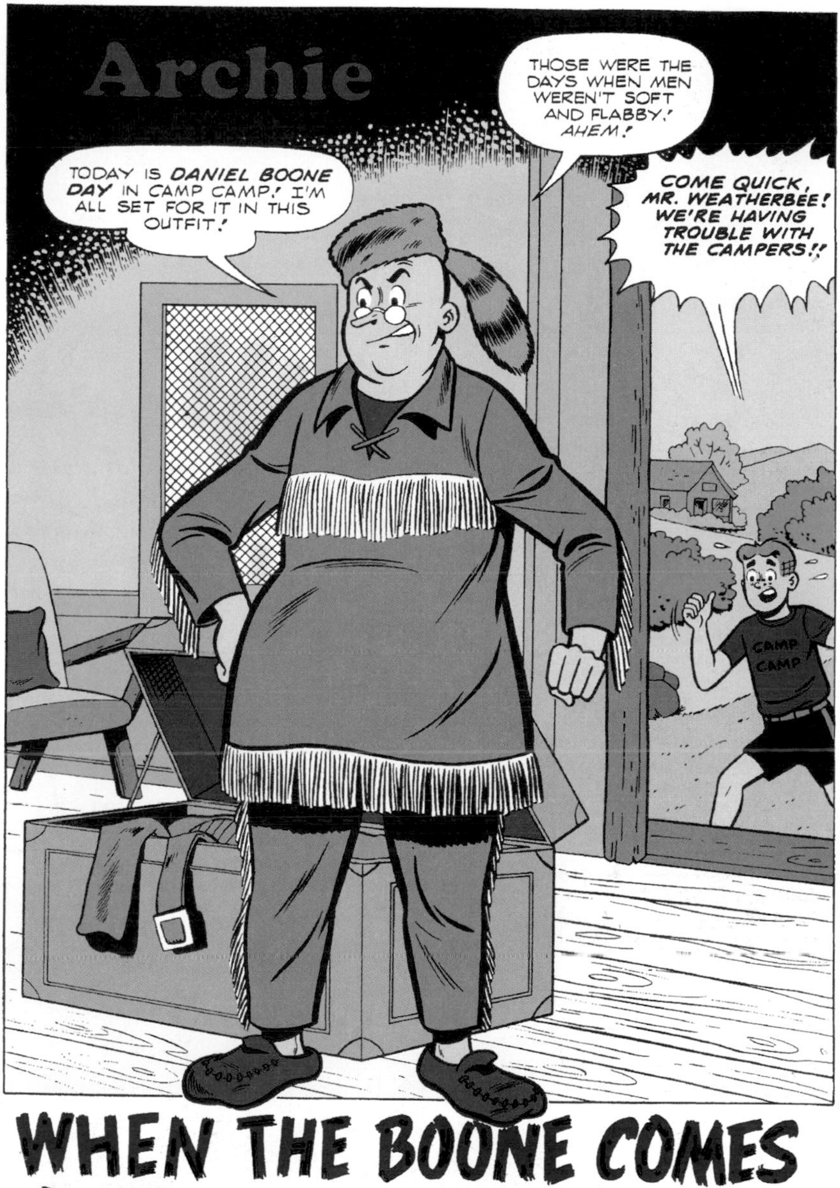
Archie
TODAY IS DANIEL BOONE DAY IN CAMP CAMP! I'M ALL SET FOR IT IN THIS OUTFIT!
THOSE WERE THE DAYS WHEN MEN WEREN'T SOFT AND FLABBY! AHEM!
COME QUICK, MR. WEATHERBEE! WE'RE HAVING TROUBLE WITH THE CAMPERS!!
CAMP CAMP

WHEN THE BOONE COMES OVER THE MOUNTAIN...

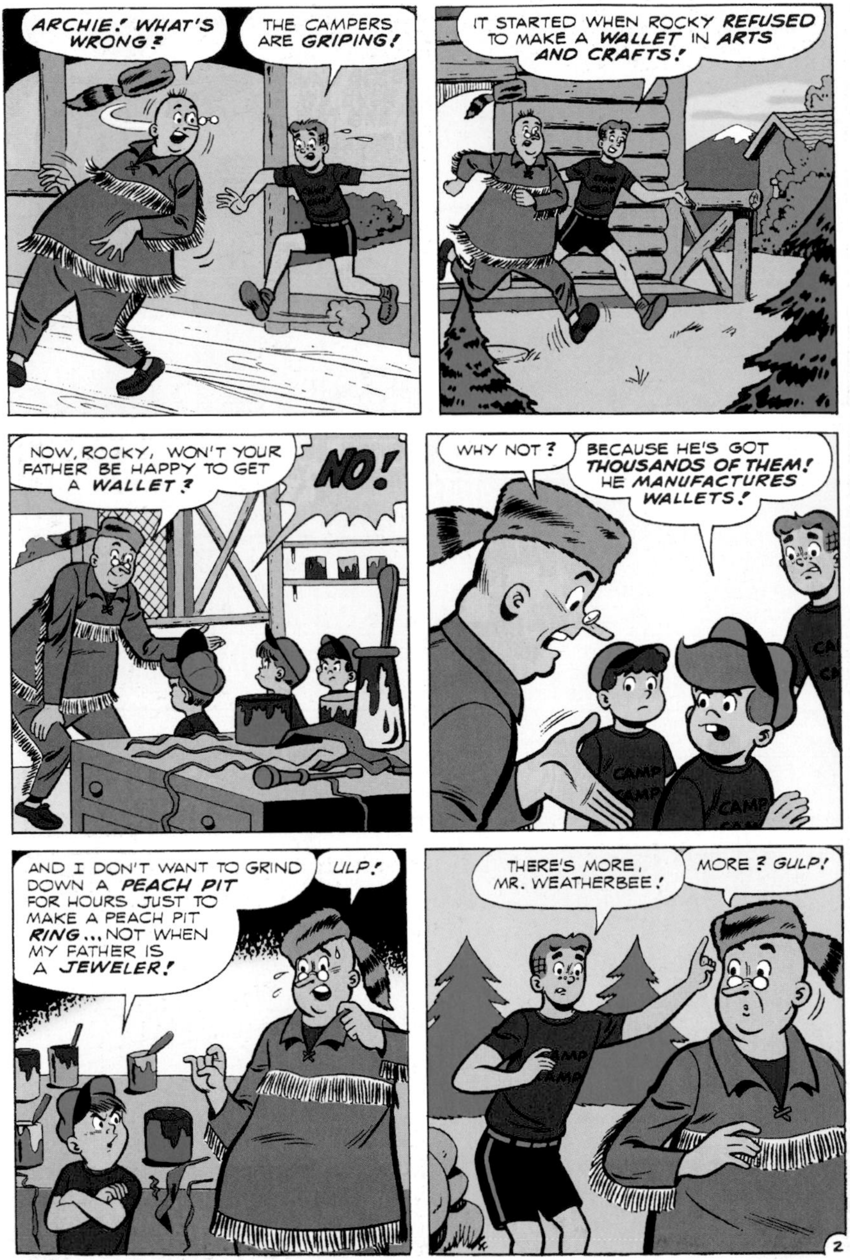

ARCHIE! WHAT'S WRONG?
THE CAMPERS ARE GRIPING!
IT STARTED WHEN ROCKY REFUSED TO MAKE A WALLET IN ARTS AND CRAFTS!
NOW, ROCKY, WON'T YOUR FATHER BE HAPPY TO GET A WALLET?
NO!
WHY NOT?
BECAUSE HE'S GOT THOUSANDS OF THEM! HE MANUFACTURES WALLETS!
AND I DON'T WANT TO GRIND DOWN A PEACH PIT FOR HOURS JUST TO MAKE A PEACH PIT RING... NOT WHEN MY FATHER IS A JEWELER!
ULP!
THERE'S MORE, MR. WEATHERBEE!
MORE? GULP!

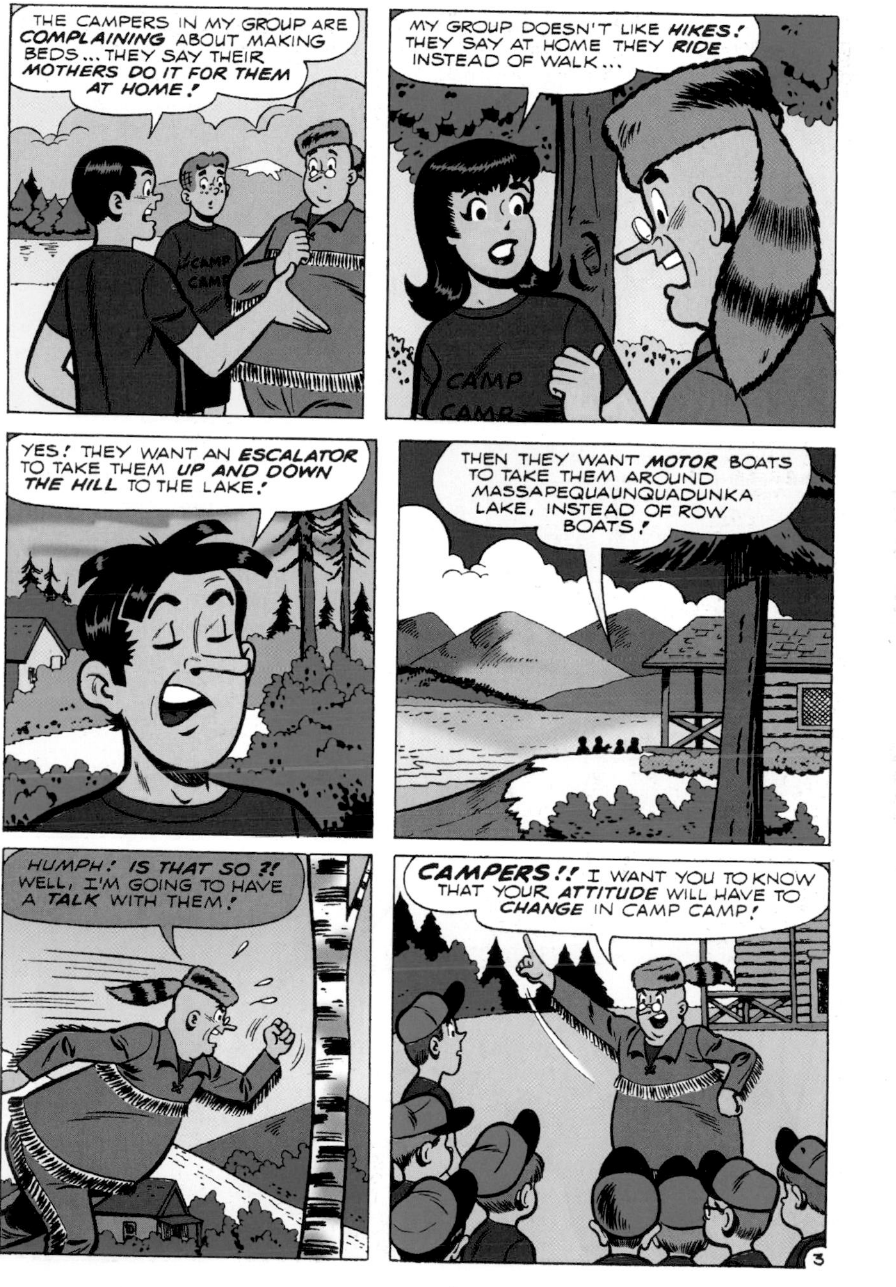
THE CAMPERS IN MY GROUP ARE COMPLAINING ABOUT MAKING BEDS... THEY SAY THEIR MOTHERS DO IT FOR THEM AT HOME!
CAMP CAMP
MY GROUP DOESN'T LIKE HIKES! THEY SAY AT HOME THEY RIDE INSTEAD OF WALK...
CAMP CAMP
YES! THEY WANT AN ESCALATOR TO TAKE THEM UP AND DOWN THE HILL TO THE LAKE!
THEN THEY WANT MOTOR BOATS TO TAKE THEM AROUND MASSAPEQUAUNQUADUNKA LAKE, INSTEAD OF ROW BOATS!
HUMPH! IS THAT SO ?! WELL, I'M GOING TO HAVE A TALK WITH THEM!
CAMPERS!! I WANT YOU TO KNOW THAT YOUR ATTITUDE WILL HAVE TO CHANGE IN CAMP CAMP!

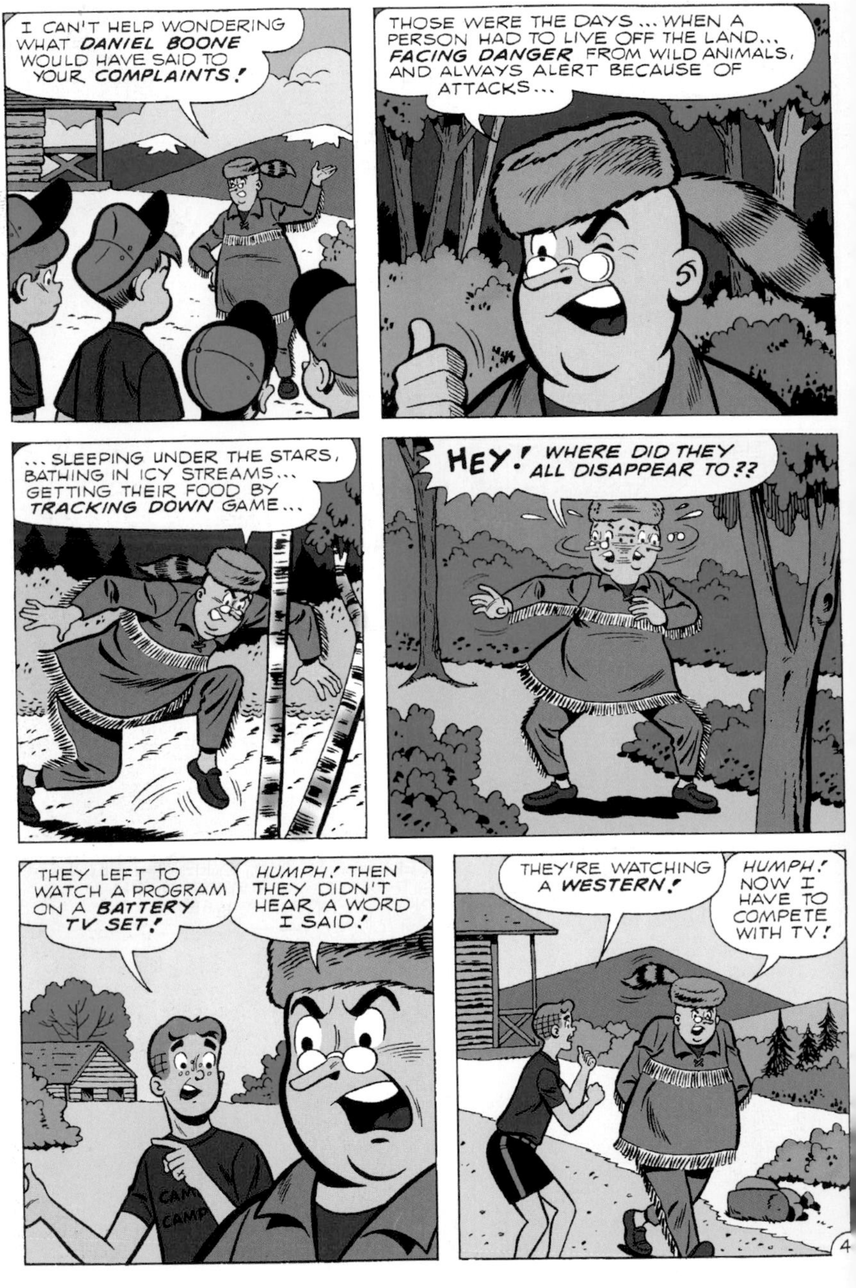
I CAN'T HELP WONDERING WHAT DANIEL BOONE WOULD HAVE SAID TO YOUR COMPLAINTS!
THOSE WERE THE DAYS... WHEN A PERSON HAD TO LIVE OFF THE LAND... FACING DANGER FROM WILD ANIMALS, AND ALWAYS ALERT BECAUSE OF ATTACKS...
...SLEEPING UNDER THE STARS, BATHING IN ICY STREAMS... GETTING THEIR FOOD BY TRACKING DOWN GAME...
HEY! WHERE DID THEY ALL DISAPPEAR TO??
THEY LEFT TO WATCH A PROGRAM ON A BATTERY TV SET!
HUMPH! THEN THEY DIDN'T HEAR A WORD I SAID!
THEY'RE WATCHING A WESTERN!
HUMPH! NOW I HAVE TO COMPETE WITH TV!

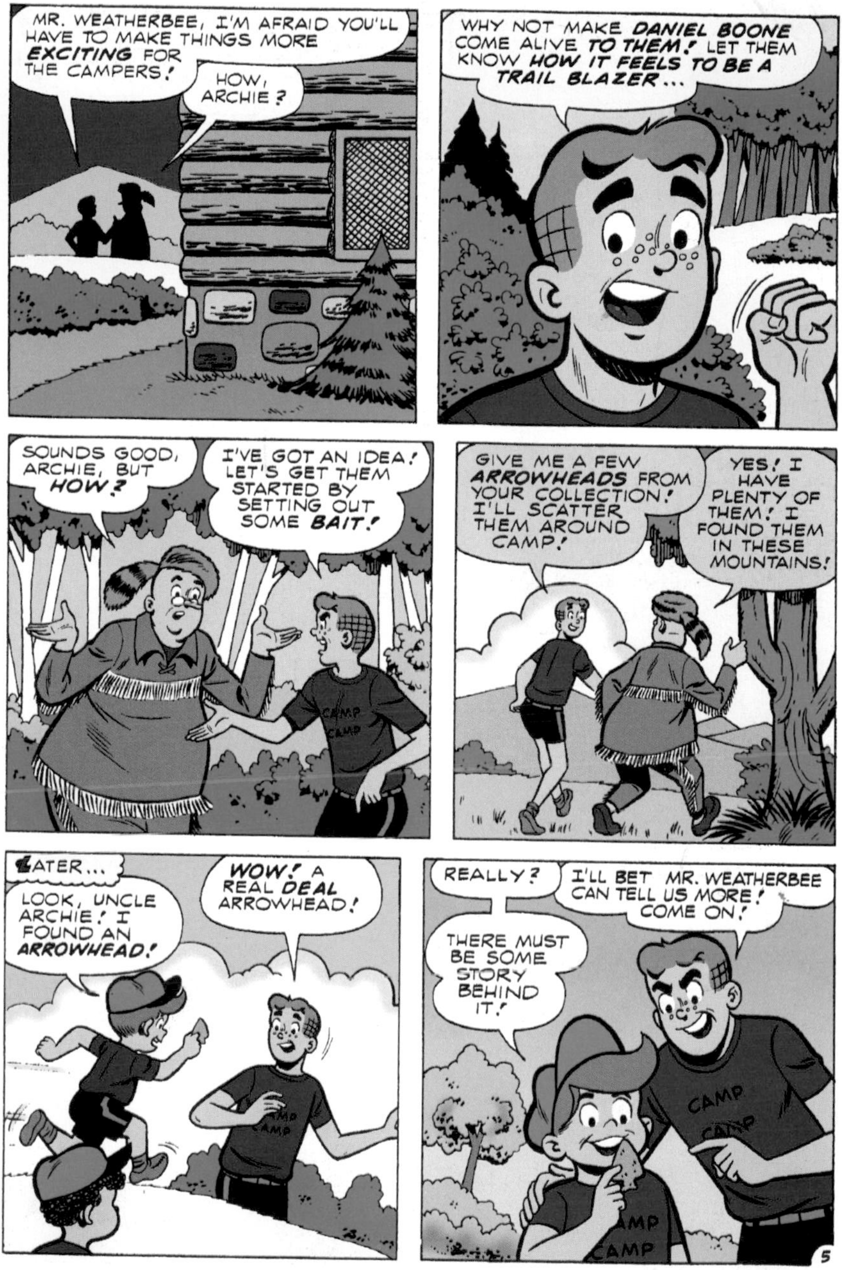
MR. WEATHERBEE, I'M AFRAID YOU'LL HAVE TO MAKE THINGS MORE EXCITING FOR THE CAMPERS!
HOW, ARCHIE?
WHY NOT MAKE DANIEL BOONE COME ALIVE TO THEM! LET THEM KNOW HOW IT FEELS TO BE A TRAIL BLAZER...
SOUNDS GOOD, ARCHIE, BUT HOW?
I'VE GOT AN IDEA! LET'S GET THEM STARTED BY SETTING OUT SOME BAIT!
CAMP CAMP
GIVE ME A FEW ARROWHEADS FROM YOUR COLLECTION! I'LL SCATTER THEM AROUND CAMP!
YES! I HAVE PLENTY OF THEM! I FOUND THEM IN THESE MOUNTAINS!
LATER...
LOOK, UNCLE ARCHIE! I FOUND AN ARROWHEAD!
WOW! A REAL DEAL ARROWHEAD!
REALLY?
THERE MUST BE SOME STORY BEHIND IT!
I'LL BET MR. WEATHERBEE CAN TELL US MORE! COME ON!
CAMP

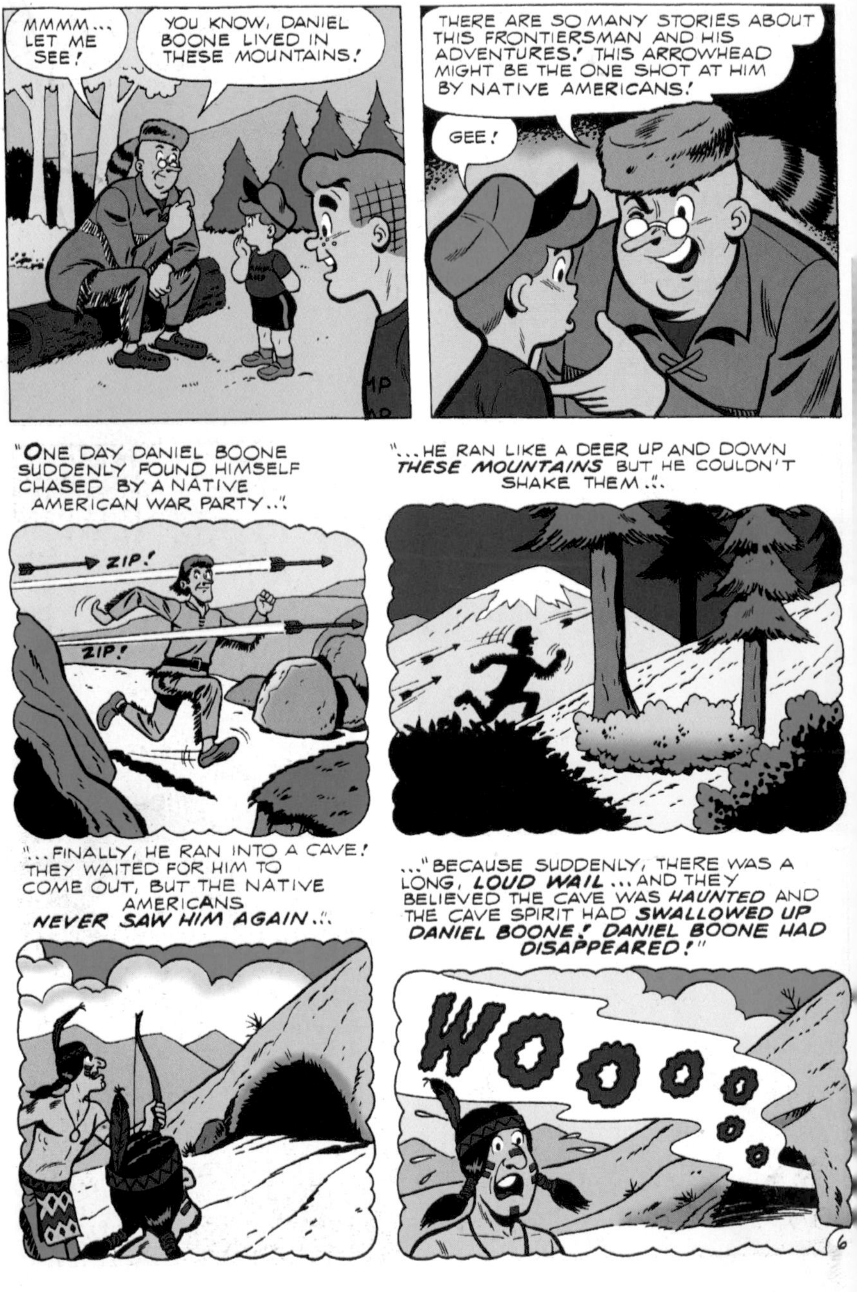
MMMM... LET ME SEE!
YOU KNOW, DANIEL BOONE LIVED IN THESE MOUNTAINS!
THERE ARE SO MANY STORIES ABOUT THIS FRONTIERSMAN AND HIS ADVENTURES! THIS ARROWHEAD MIGHT BE THE ONE SHOT AT HIM BY NATIVE AMERICANS!
GEE!
"ONE DAY DANIEL BOONE SUDDENLY FOUND HIMSELF CHASED BY A NATIVE AMERICAN WAR PARTY...
ZIP!
ZIP!
"...HE RAN LIKE A DEER UP AND DOWN THESE MOUNTAINS BUT HE COULDN'T SHAKE THEM...
"...FINALLY, HE RAN INTO A CAVE! THEY WAITED FOR HIM TO COME OUT, BUT THE NATIVE AMERICANS NEVER SAW HIM AGAIN...
..."BECAUSE SUDDENLY, THERE WAS A LONG, LOUD WAIL ... AND THEY BELIEVED THE CAVE WAS HAUNTED AND THE CAVE SPIRIT HAD SWALLOWED UP DANIEL BOONE! DANIEL BOONE HAD DISAPPEARED!"
WOOOOOO

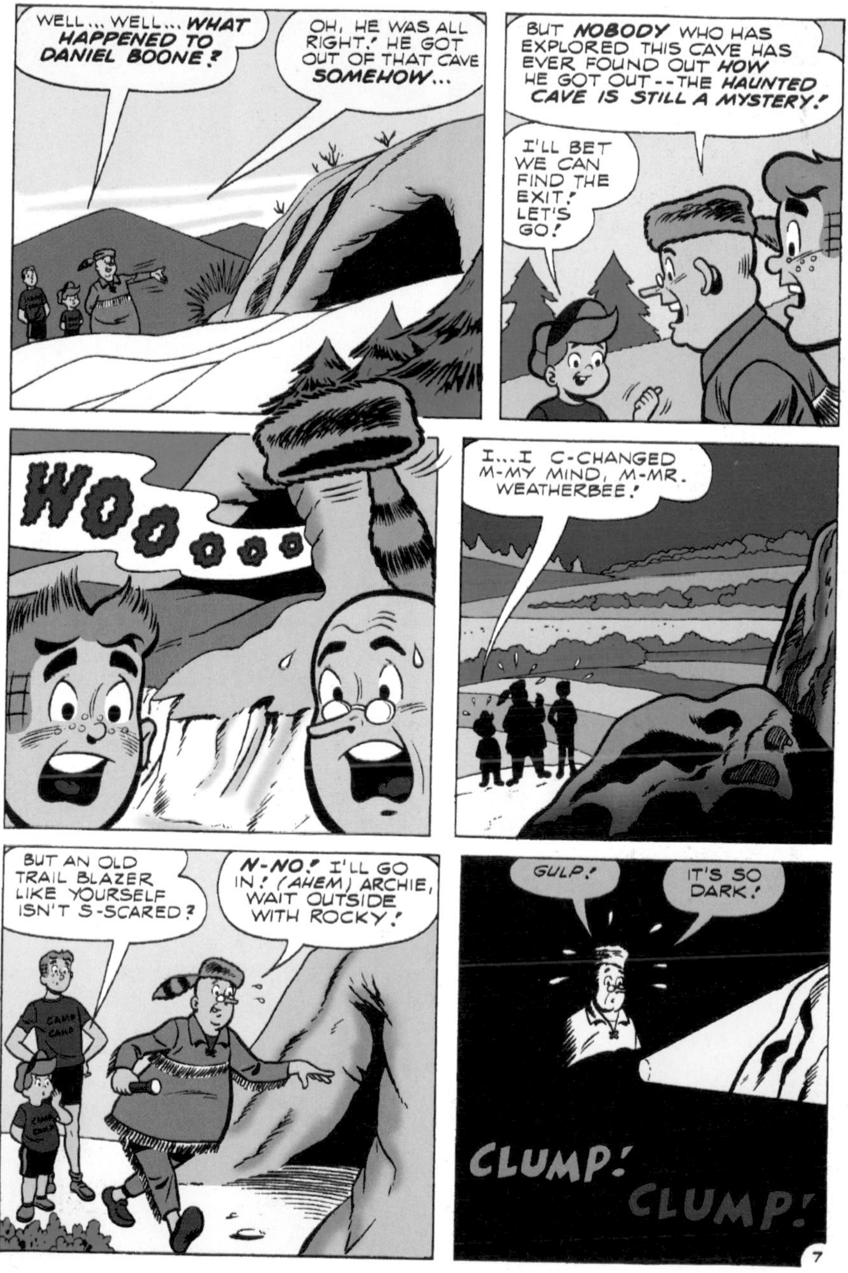
WELL... WELL... WHAT HAPPENED TO DANIEL BOONE?
OH, HE WAS ALL RIGHT! HE GOT OUT OF THAT CAVE SOMEHOW...
BUT NOBODY WHO HAS EXPLORED THIS CAVE HAS EVER FOUND OUT HOW HE GOT OUT -- THE HAUNTED CAVE IS STILL A MYSTERY!
I'LL BET WE CAN FIND THE EXIT! LET'S GO!
WOOOOO
I... I C-CHANGED M-MY MIND, M-MR. WEATHERBEE!
BUT AN OLD TRAIL BLAZER LIKE YOURSELF ISN'T S-SCARED?
N-NO! I'LL GO IN! (AHEM) ARCHIE, WAIT OUTSIDE WITH ROCKY!
GULP!
IT'S SO DARK!
CLUMP!
CLUMP!

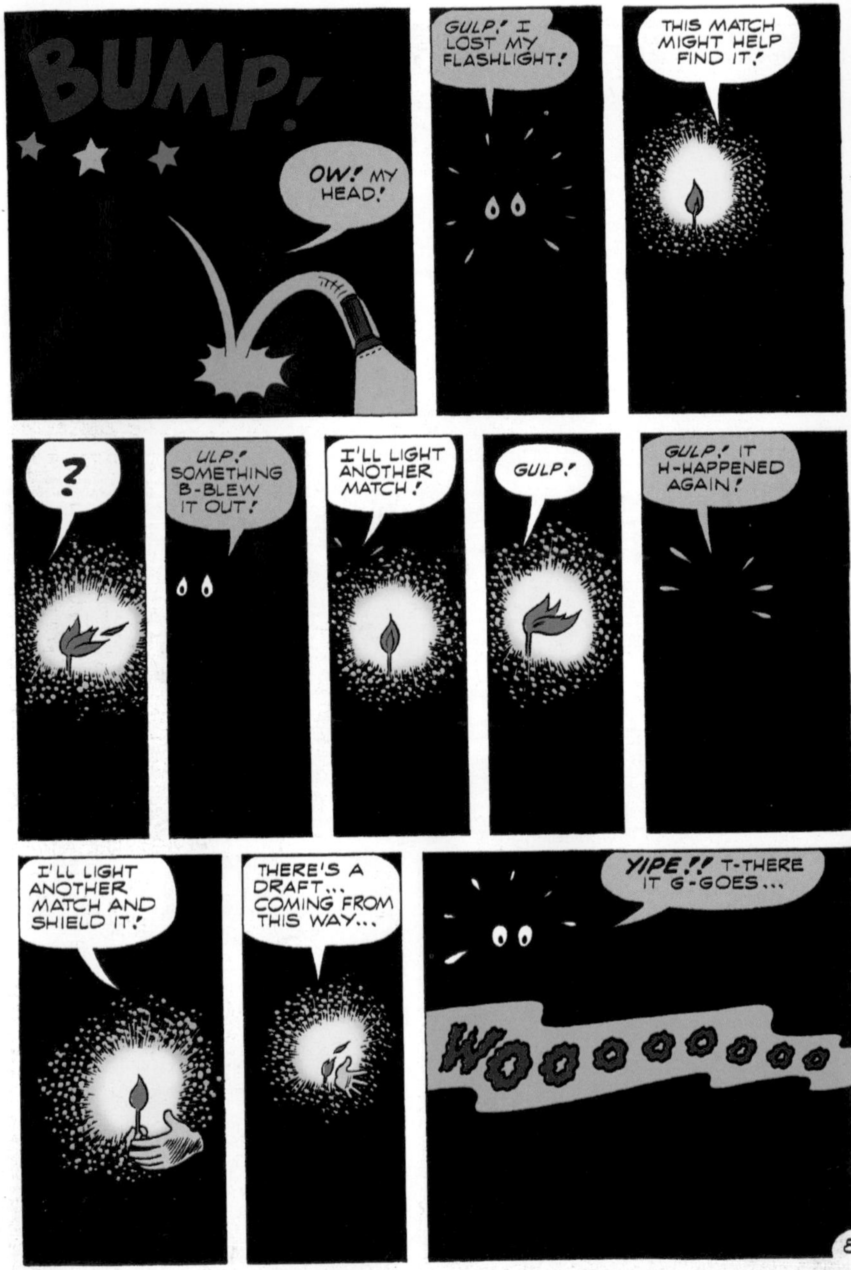
BUMP!
OW! MY HEAD!
GULP! I LOST MY FLASHLIGHT!
THIS MATCH MIGHT HELP FIND IT!
?
ULP! SOMETHING B-BLEW IT OUT!
I'LL LIGHT ANOTHER MATCH!
GULP!
GULP! IT H-HAPPENED AGAIN!
I'LL LIGHT ANOTHER MATCH AND SHIELD IT!
THERE'S A DRAFT... COMING FROM THIS WAY...
YIPE!!! T-THERE IT G-GOES...
WOoooooooo

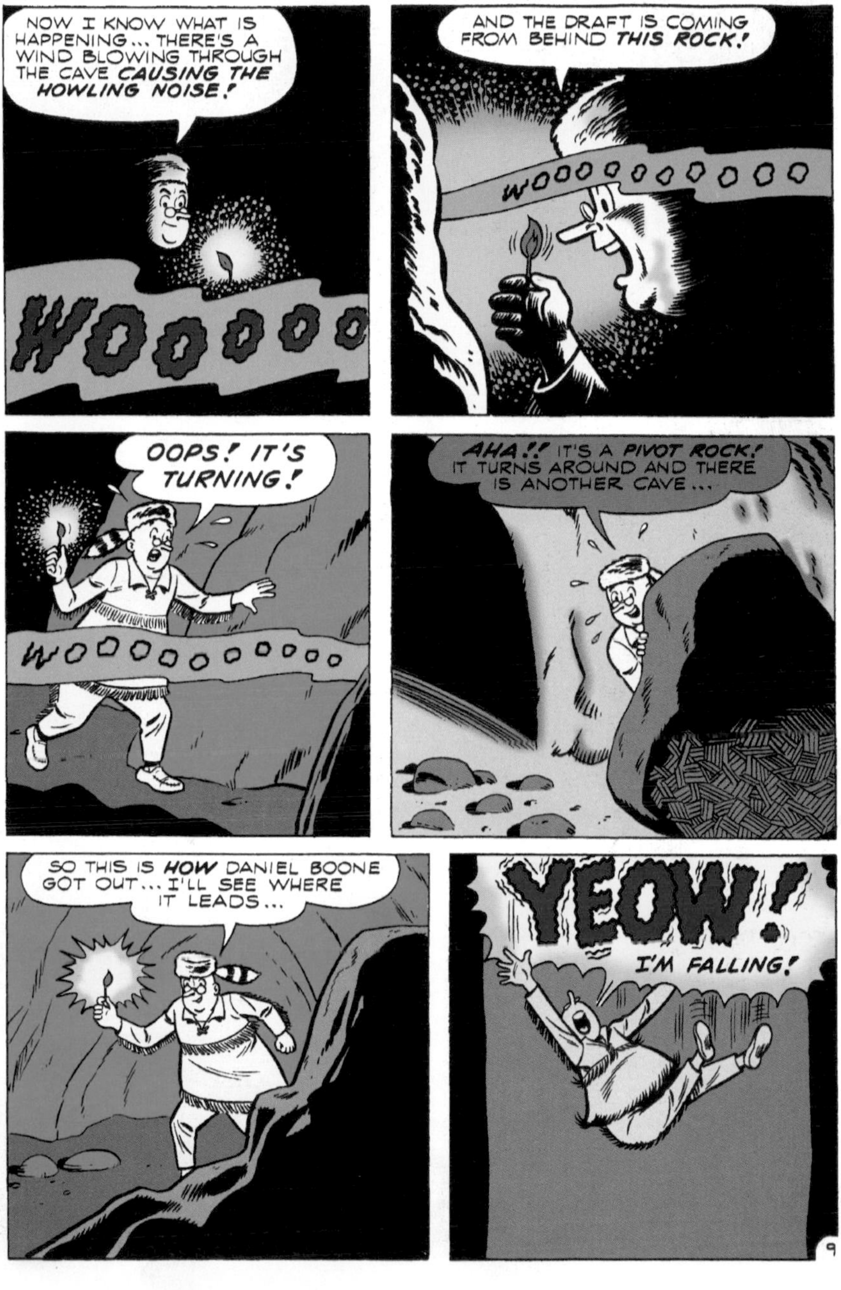
NOW I KNOW WHAT IS HAPPENING... THERE'S A WIND BLOWING THROUGH THE CAVE CAUSING THE HOWLING NOISE!
WOOOOO
AND THE DRAFT IS COMING FROM BEHIND THIS ROCK!
WOOOOOOOOOOOO
OOPS! IT'S TURNING!
WOOOOOOOOOOOO
AHA!! IT'S A PIVOT ROCK! IT TURNS AROUND AND THERE IS ANOTHER CAVE...
SO THIS IS HOW DANIEL BOONE GOT OUT... I'LL SEE WHERE IT LEADS...
YEOW!
I'M FALLING!

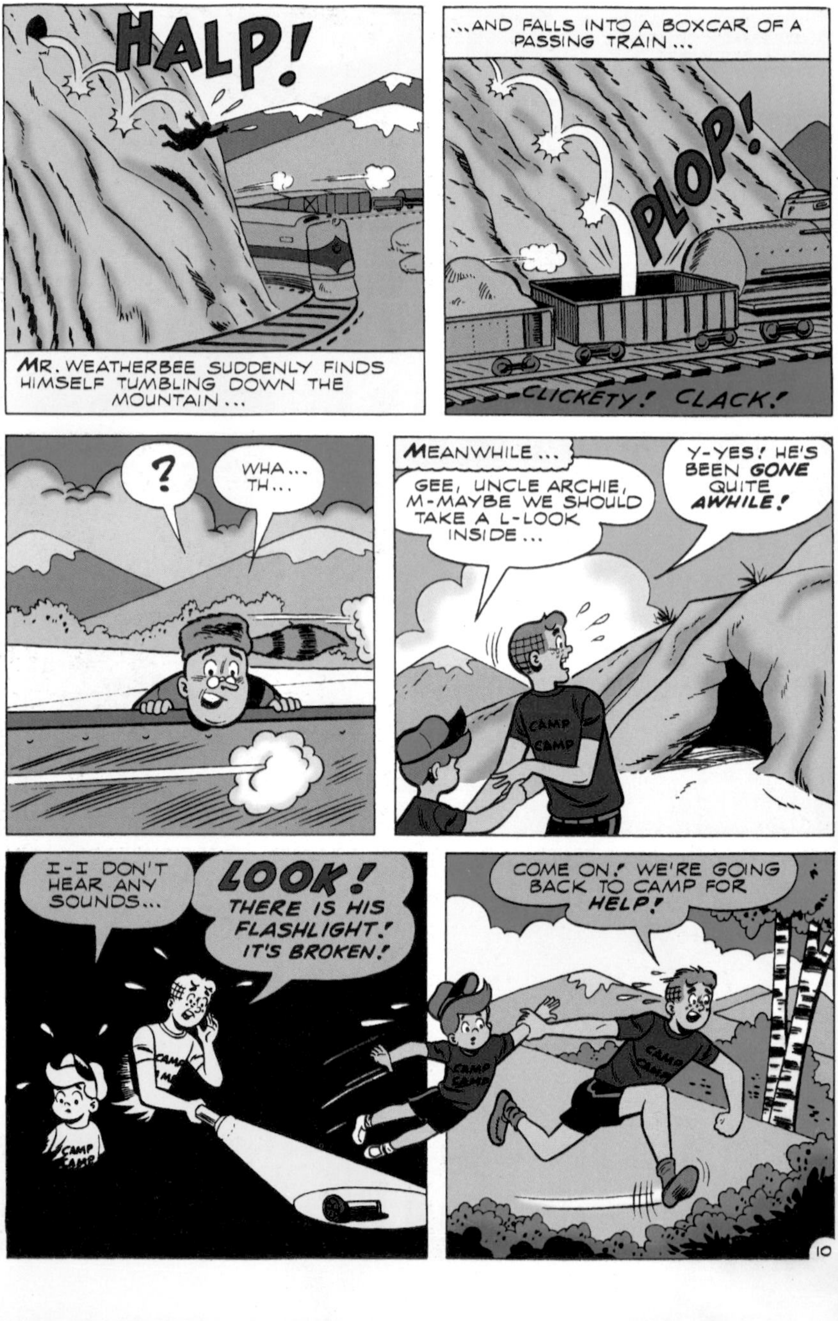
HALP!
MR. WEATHERBEE SUDDENLY FINDS HIMSELF TUMBLING DOWN THE MOUNTAIN...
...AND FALLS INTO A BOXCAR OF A PASSING TRAIN...
PLOP!
CLICKETY! CLACK!
?
WHA... TH...
MEANWHILE...
GEE, UNCLE ARCHIE, M-MAYBE WE SHOULD TAKE A L-LOOK INSIDE...
Y-YES! HE'S BEEN GONE QUITE AWHILE!
I-I DON'T HEAR ANY SOUNDS...
LOOK! THERE IS HIS FLASHLIGHT! IT'S BROKEN!
COME ON! WE'RE GOING BACK TO CAMP FOR HELP!

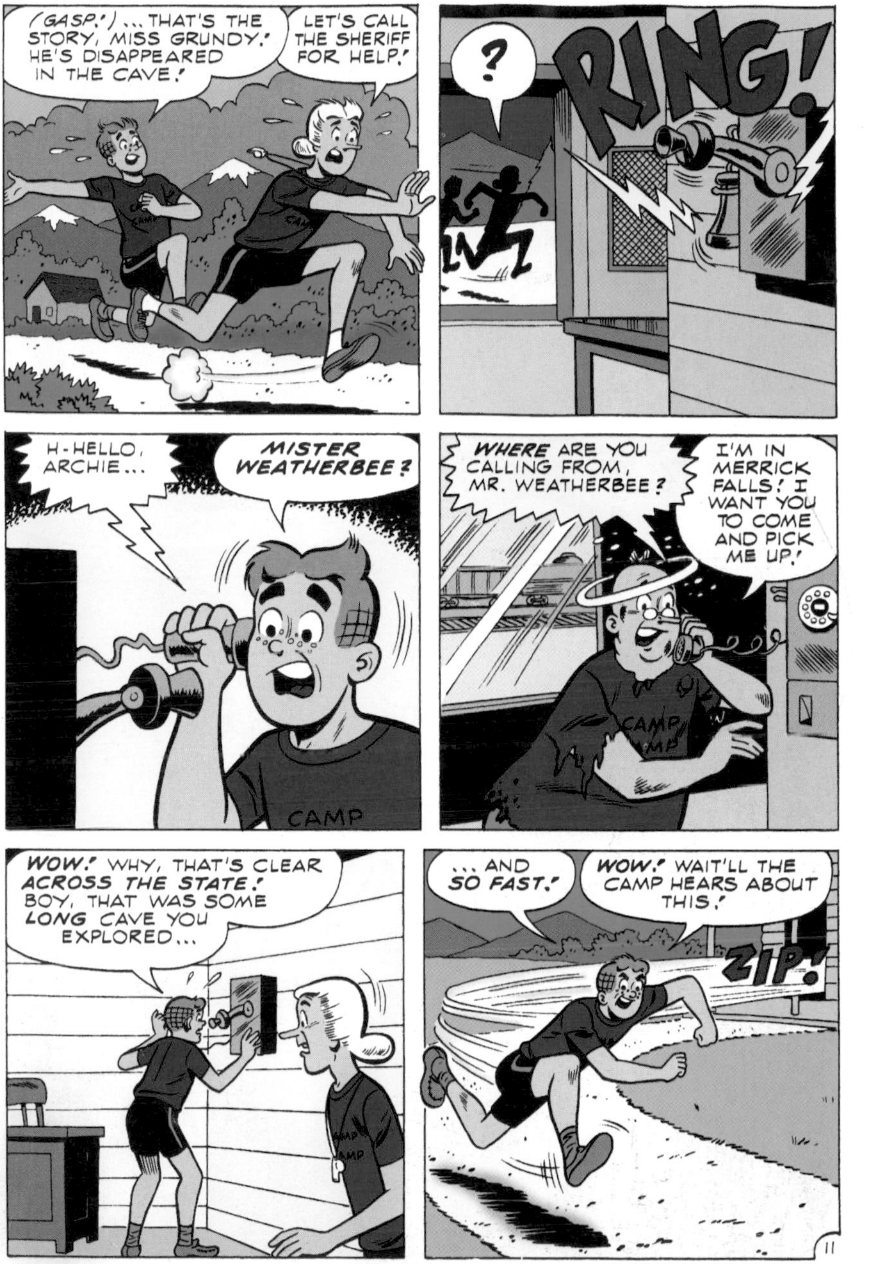
(GASP!) ... THAT'S THE STORY, MISS GRUNDY! HE'S DISAPPEARED IN THE CAVE!
LET'S CALL THE SHERIFF FOR HELP!
?
RING!
H-HELLO, ARCHIE...
MISTER WEATHERBEE?
CAMP
WHERE ARE YOU CALLING FROM, MR. WEATHERBEE?
I'M IN MERRICK FALLS! I WANT YOU TO COME AND PICK ME UP!
WOW! WHY, THAT'S CLEAR ACROSS THE STATE! BOY, THAT WAS SOME LONG CAVE YOU EXPLORED...
... AND SO FAST!
WOW! WAIT'LL THE CAMP HEARS ABOUT THIS!
ZIP!

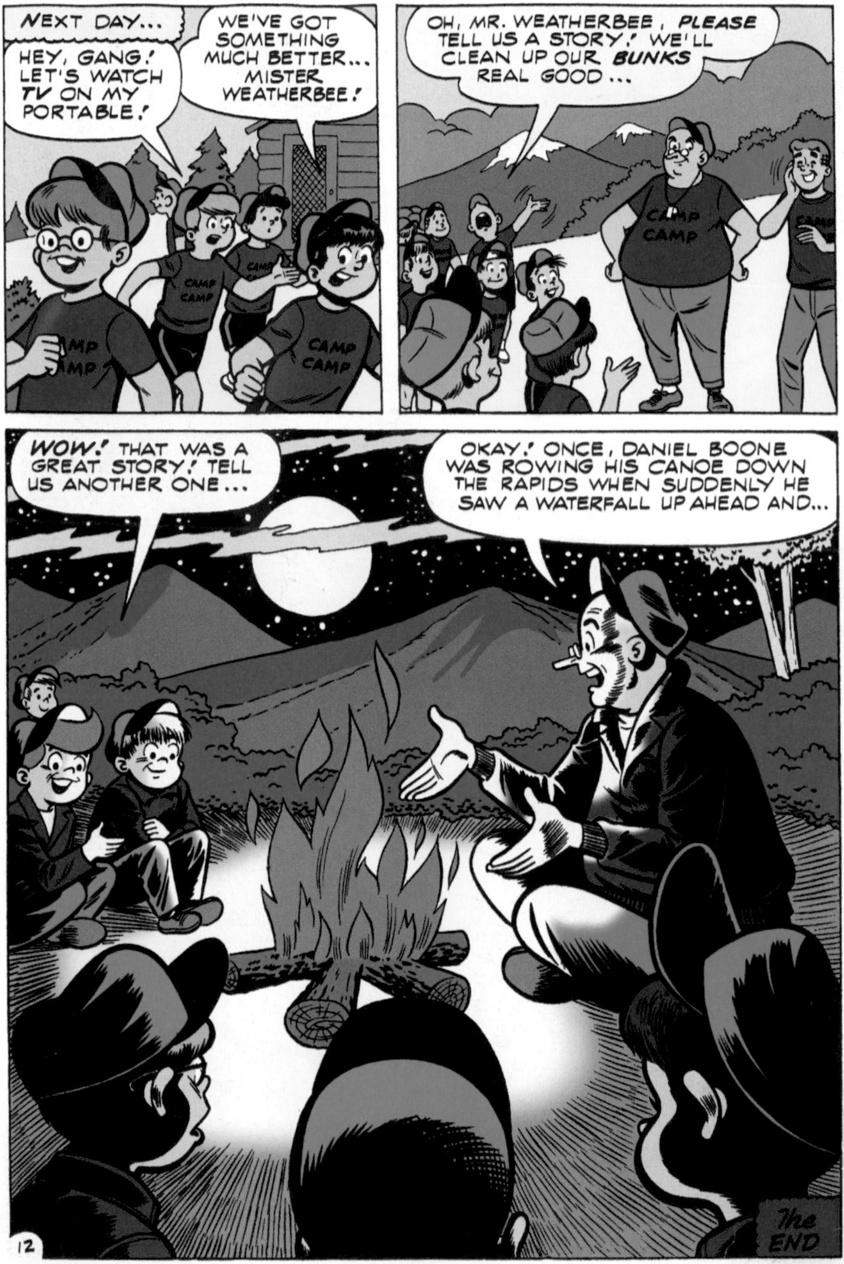
NEXT DAY...
HEY, GANG! LET'S WATCH TV ON MY PORTABLE!
WE'VE GOT SOMETHING MUCH BETTER... MISTER WEATHERBEE!
CAMP CAMP
OH, MR. WEATHERBEE, PLEASE TELL US A STORY! WE'LL CLEAN UP OUR BUNKS REAL GOOD...
CAMP CAMP
WOW! THAT WAS A GREAT STORY! TELL US ANOTHER ONE...
OKAY! ONCE, DANIEL BOONE WAS ROWING HIS CANOE DOWN THE RAPIDS WHEN SUDDENLY HE SAW A WATERFALL UP AHEAD AND...
The END

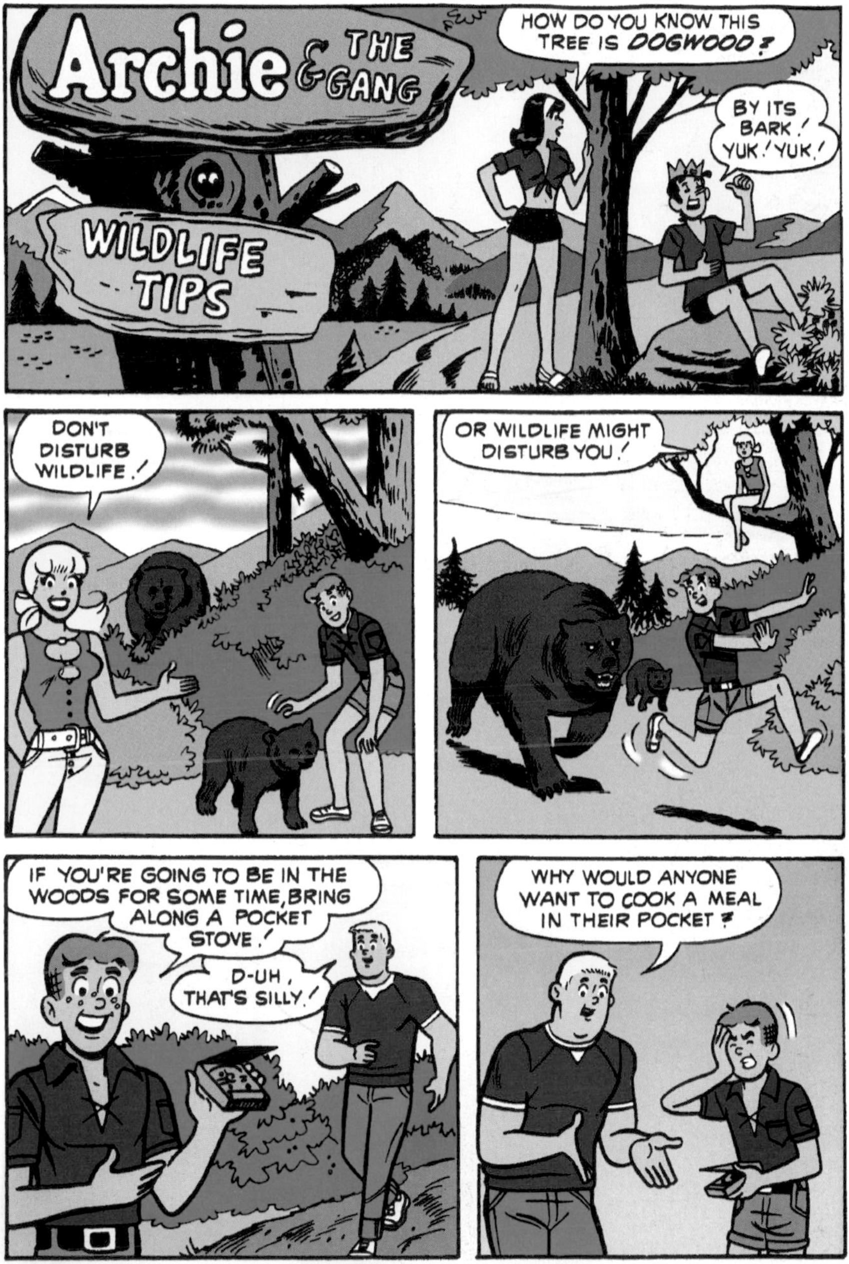

Archie & THE GANG
WILDLIFE TIPS
HOW DO YOU KNOW THIS TREE IS DOGWOOD?
BY ITS BARK! YUK! YUK!
DON'T DISTURB WILDLIFE!
OR WILDLIFE MIGHT DISTURB YOU!
IF YOU'RE GOING TO BE IN THE WOODS FOR SOME TIME, BRING ALONG A POCKET STOVE!
D-UH, THAT'S SILLY!
WHY WOULD ANYONE WANT TO COOK A MEAL IN THEIR POCKET?

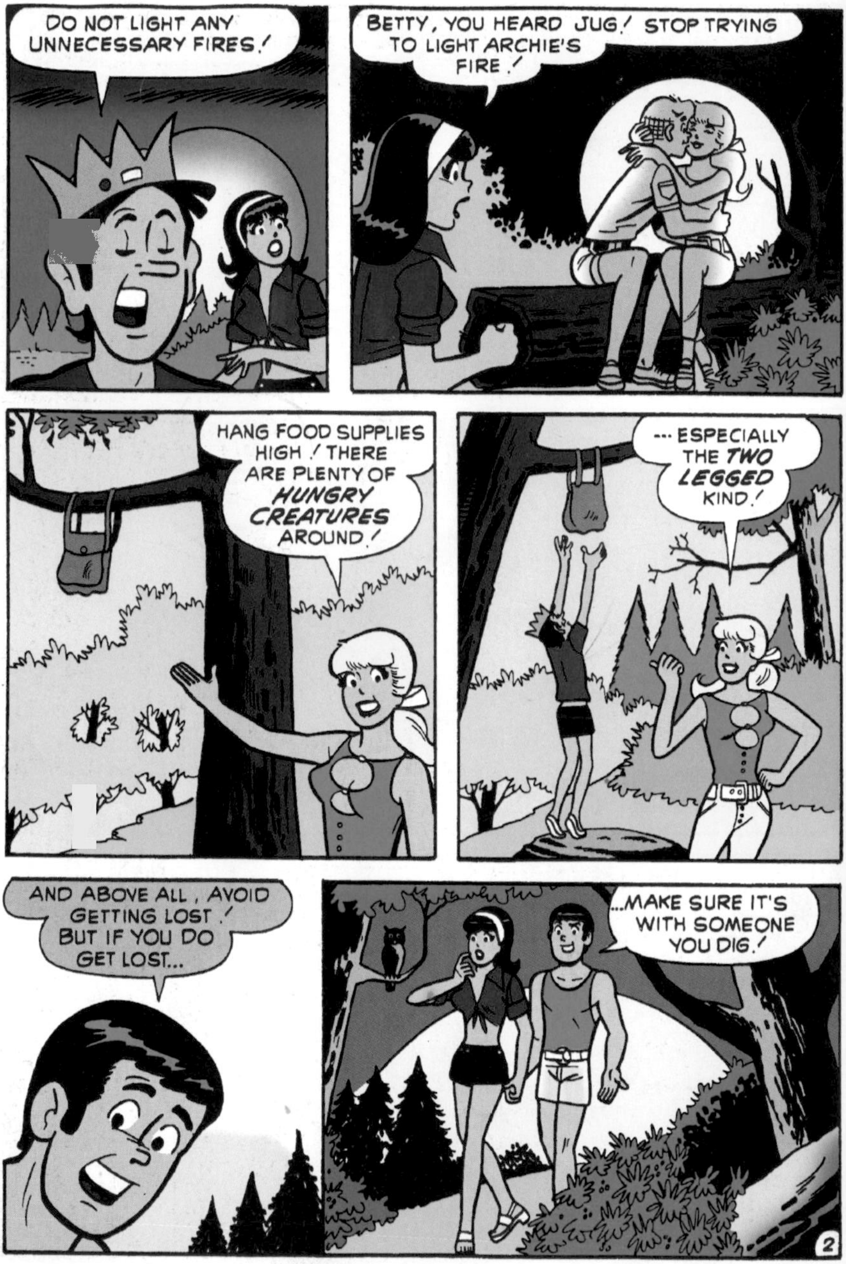
DO NOT LIGHT ANY UNNECESSARY FIRES!
BETTY, YOU HEARD JUG! STOP TRYING TO LIGHT ARCHIE'S FIRE!
HANG FOOD SUPPLIES HIGH! THERE ARE PLENTY OF HUNGRY CREATURES AROUND!
--- ESPECIALLY THE TWO LEGGED KIND!
AND ABOVE ALL, AVOID GETTING LOST! BUT IF YOU DO GET LOST...
...MAKE SURE IT'S WITH SOMEONE YOU DIG!
2

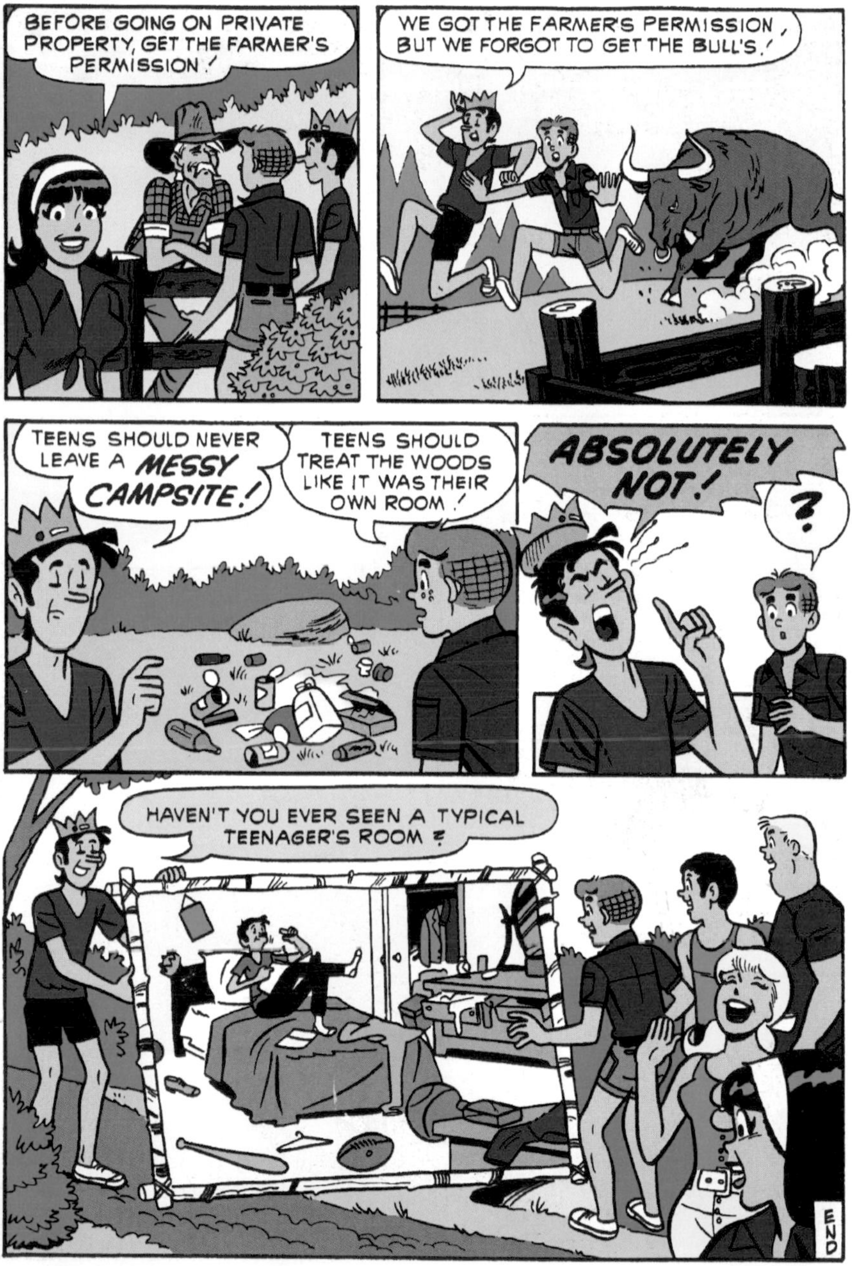
BEFORE GOING ON PRIVATE PROPERTY, GET THE FARMER'S PERMISSION!
WE GOT THE FARMER'S PERMISSION, BUT WE FORGOT TO GET THE BULL'S!
TEENS SHOULD NEVER LEAVE A MESSY CAMPSITE!
TEENS SHOULD TREAT THE WOODS LIKE IT WAS THEIR OWN ROOM!
ABSOLUTELY NOT!
?
HAVEN'T YOU EVER SEEN A TYPICAL TEENAGER'S ROOM?
END

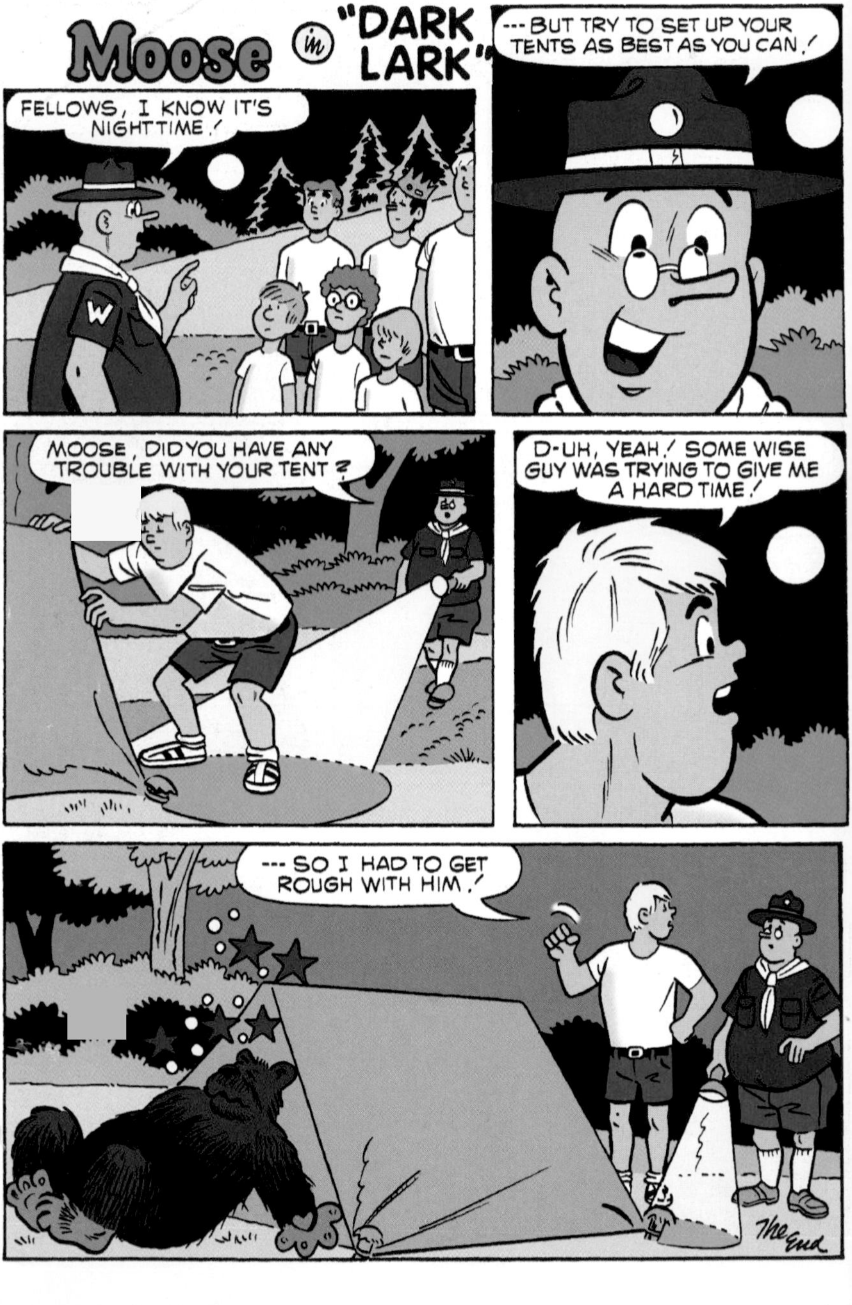
Moose in "DARK LARK"
FELLOWS, I KNOW IT'S NIGHTTIME!
--- BUT TRY TO SET UP YOUR TENTS AS BEST AS YOU CAN!
MOOSE, DID YOU HAVE ANY TROUBLE WITH YOUR TENT?
D-UH, YEAH! SOME WISE GUY WAS TRYING TO GIVE ME A HARD TIME!
--- SO I HAD TO GET ROUGH WITH HIM!
The End

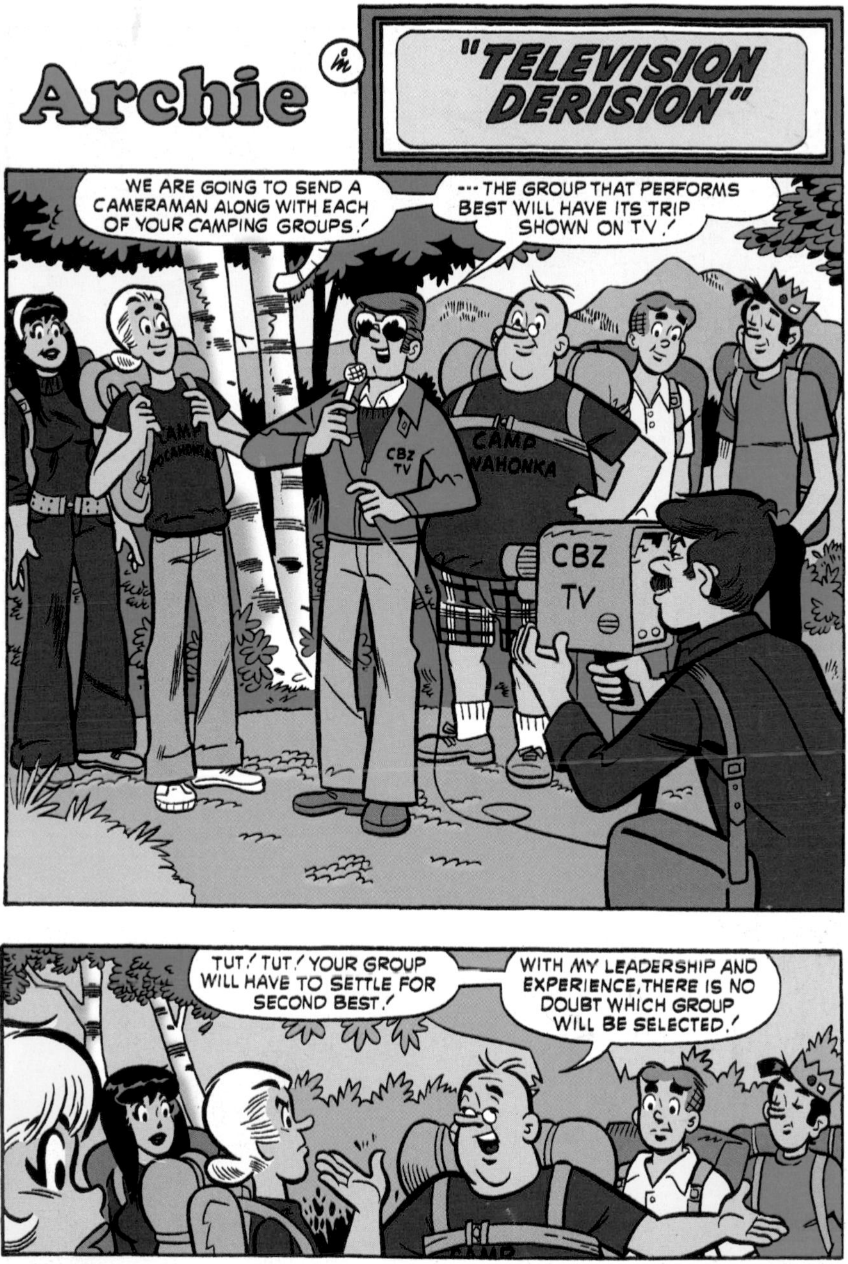
Archie in
"TELEVISION DERISION"
WE ARE GOING TO SEND A CAMERAMAN ALONG WITH EACH OF YOUR CAMPING GROUPS!
--- THE GROUP THAT PERFORMS BEST WILL HAVE ITS TRIP SHOWN ON TV!
CAMP POCAHONKA
CBZ TV
CAMP WAHONKA
CBZ TV
TUT! TUT! YOUR GROUP WILL HAVE TO SETTLE FOR SECOND BEST!
WITH MY LEADERSHIP AND EXPERIENCE, THERE IS NO DOUBT WHICH GROUP WILL BE SELECTED!

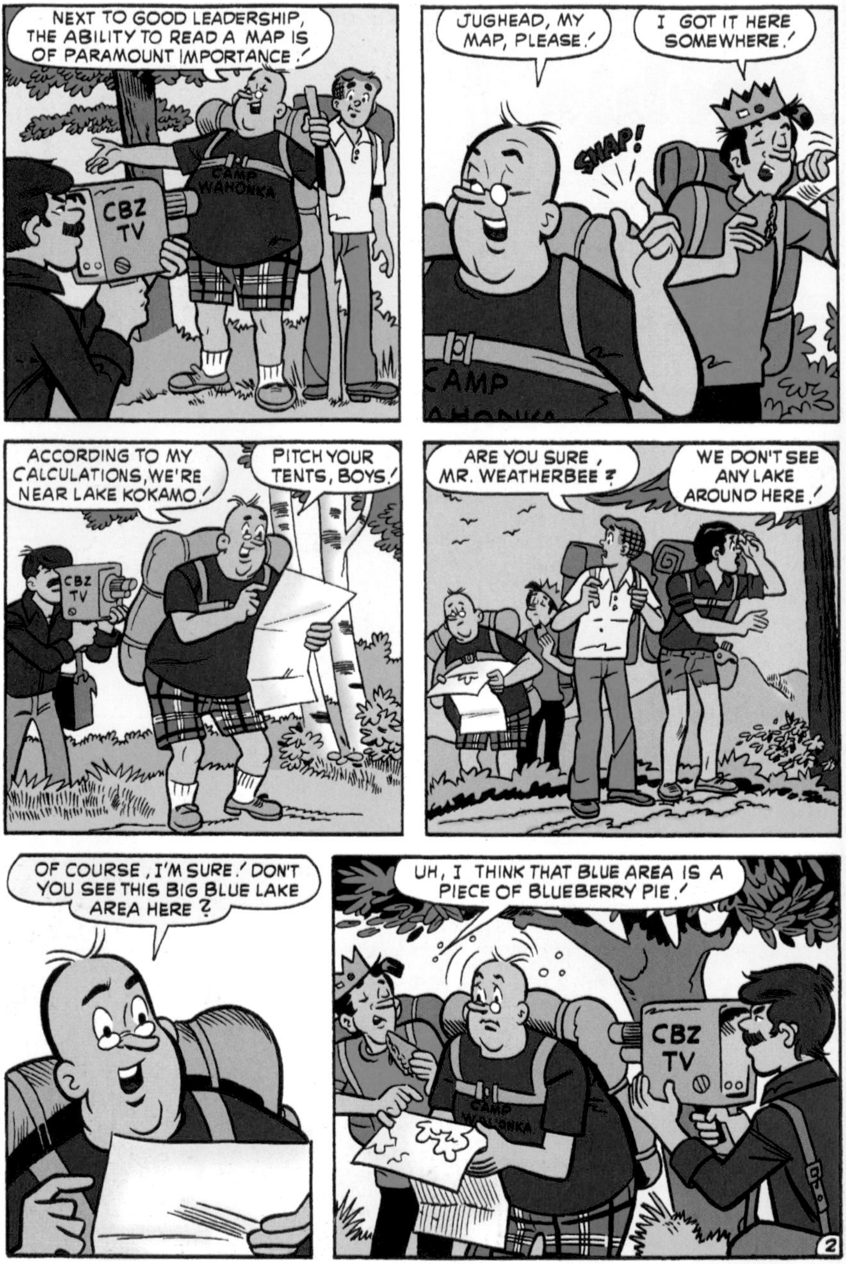
NEXT TO GOOD LEADERSHIP, THE ABILITY TO READ A MAP IS OF PARAMOUNT IMPORTANCE!
CBZ TV
CAMP WAHONKA
JUGHEAD, MY MAP, PLEASE!
I GOT IT HERE SOMEWHERE!
SNAP!
CAMP
ACCORDING TO MY CALCULATIONS, WE'RE NEAR LAKE KOKAMO!
PITCH YOUR TENTS, BOYS!
CBZ TV
ARE YOU SURE, MR. WEATHERBEE?
WE DON'T SEE ANY LAKE AROUND HERE!
OF COURSE, I'M SURE! DON'T YOU SEE THIS BIG BLUE LAKE AREA HERE?
UH, I THINK THAT BLUE AREA IS A PIECE OF BLUEBERRY PIE!
CBZ TV
CAMP WAHONKA
2

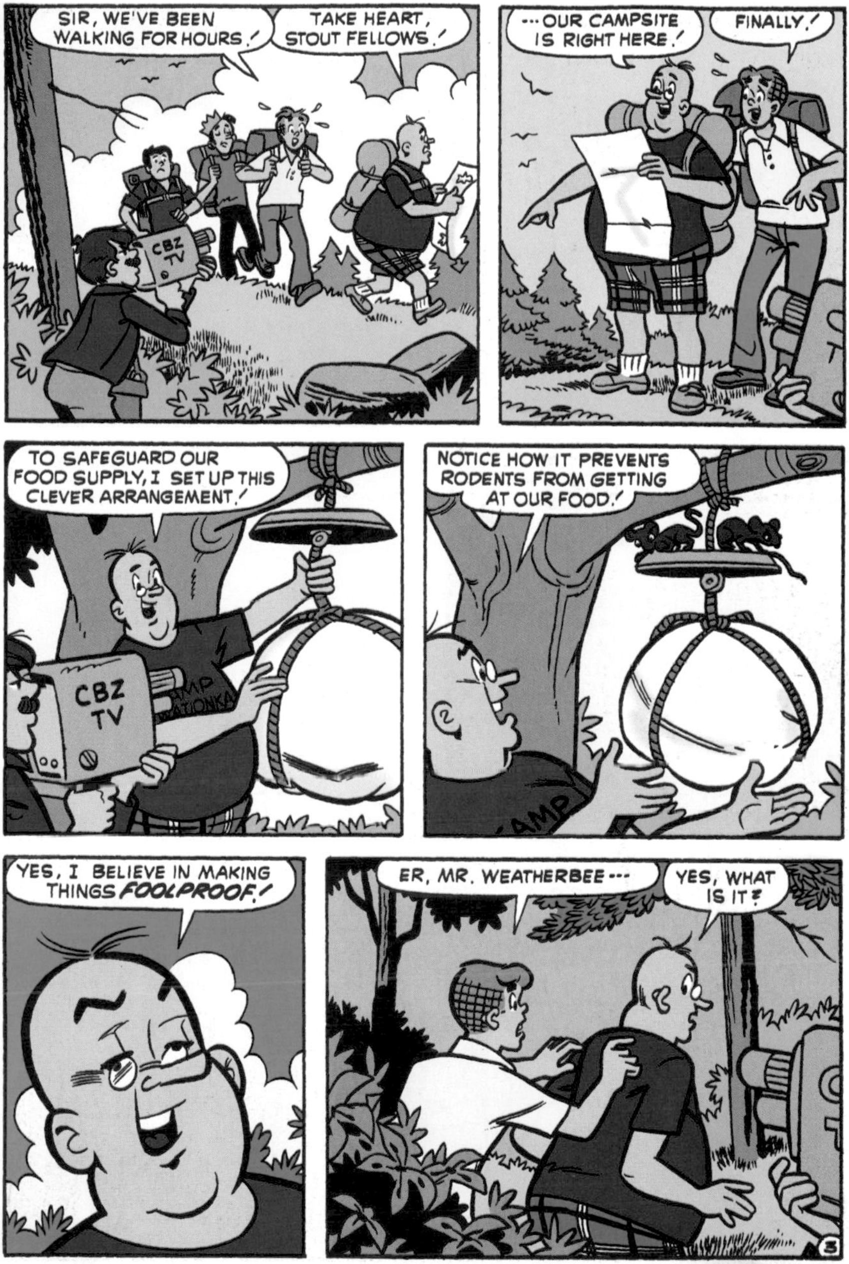
SIR, WE'VE BEEN WALKING FOR HOURS!
TAKE HEART, STOUT FELLOWS!
CBZ TV
...OUR CAMPSITE IS RIGHT HERE!
FINALLY!
TO SAFEGUARD OUR FOOD SUPPLY, I SET UP THIS CLEVER ARRANGEMENT!
CBZ TV
NOTICE HOW IT PREVENTS RODENTS FROM GETTING AT OUR FOOD!
YES, I BELIEVE IN MAKING THINGS FOOLPROOF!
ER, MR. WEATHERBEE---
YES, WHAT IS IT?
3

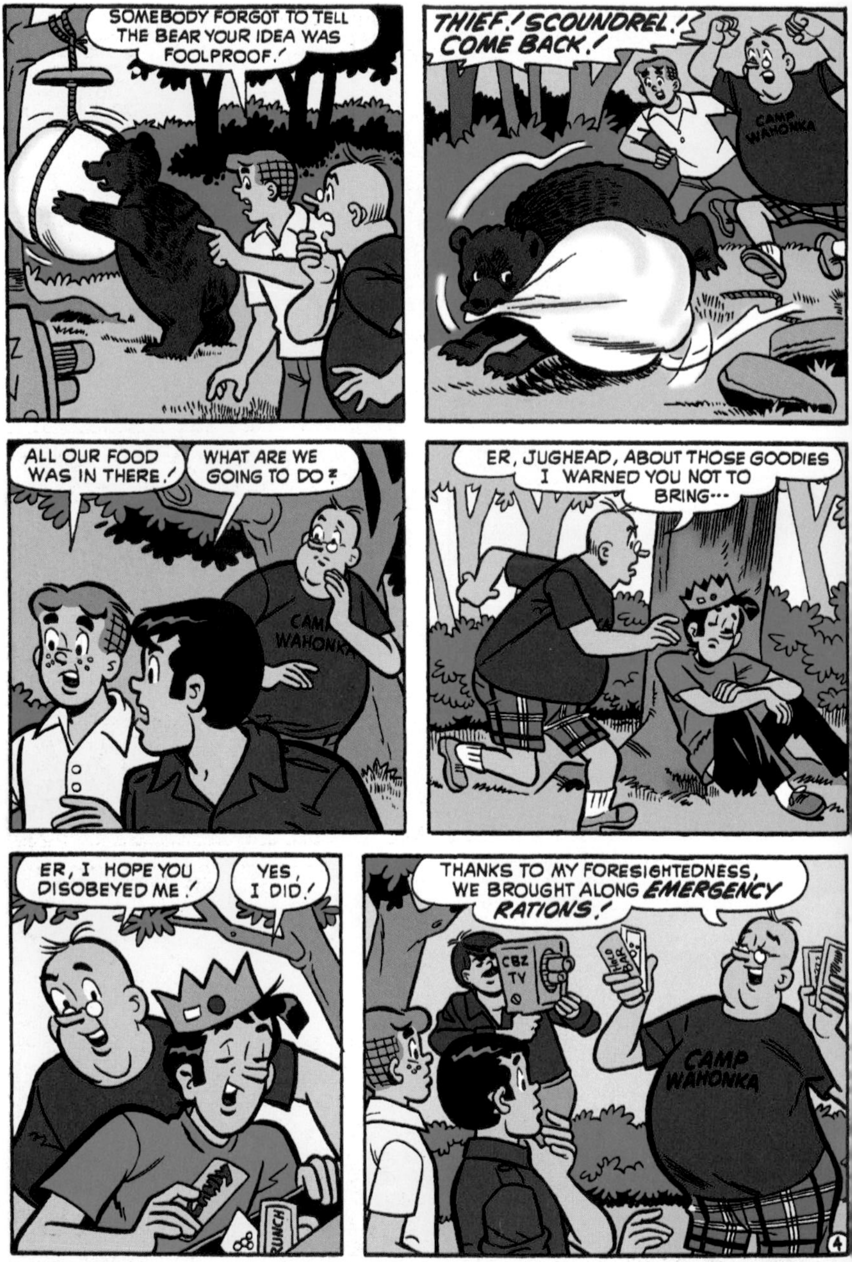
SOMEBODY FORGOT TO TELL THE BEAR YOUR IDEA WAS FOOLPROOF!
THIEF! SCOUNDREL! COME BACK!
CAMP WAHONKA
ALL OUR FOOD WAS IN THERE!
WHAT ARE WE GOING TO DO?
ER, JUGHEAD, ABOUT THOSE GOODIES I WARNED YOU NOT TO BRING---
ER, I HOPE YOU DISOBEYED ME!
YES, I DID!
CRUNCH
THANKS TO MY FORESIGHTEDNESS, WE BROUGHT ALONG *EMERGENCY RATIONS*!
CBZ TV
CAMP WAHONKA
4

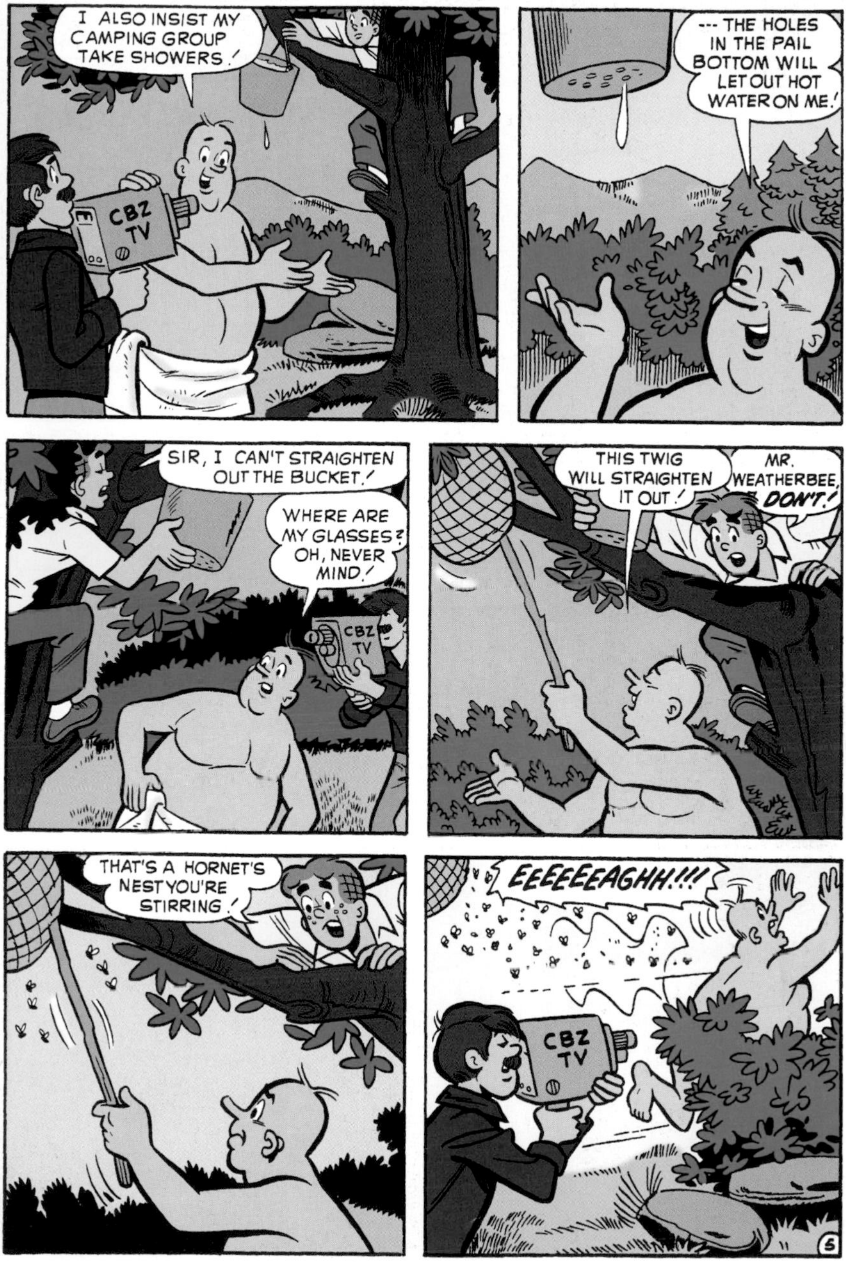
I ALSO INSIST MY CAMPING GROUP TAKE SHOWERS!
--- THE HOLES IN THE PAIL BOTTOM WILL LET OUT HOT WATER ON ME!
SIR, I CAN'T STRAIGHTEN OUT THE BUCKET!
WHERE ARE MY GLASSES? OH, NEVER MIND!
THIS TWIG WILL STRAIGHTEN IT OUT!
MR. WEATHERBEE, DON'T!
THAT'S A HORNET'S NEST YOU'RE STIRRING!
EEEEEEAGHH!!!!
CBZ TV
5

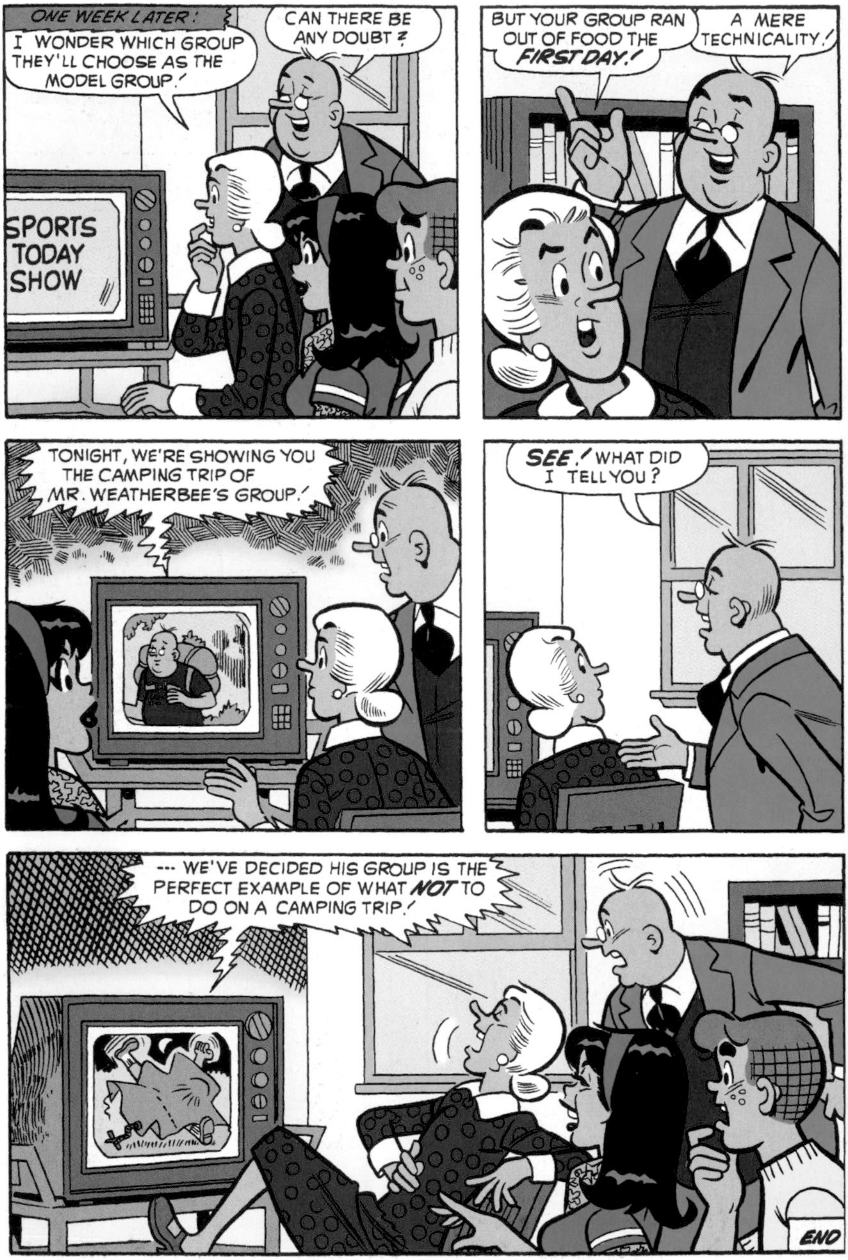
ONE WEEK LATER:
I WONDER WHICH GROUP THEY'LL CHOOSE AS THE MODEL GROUP!
CAN THERE BE ANY DOUBT?
SPORTS TODAY SHOW
BUT YOUR GROUP RAN OUT OF FOOD THE FIRST DAY!
A MERE TECHNICALITY!
TONIGHT, WE'RE SHOWING YOU THE CAMPING TRIP OF MR. WEATHERBEE'S GROUP!
SEE! WHAT DID I TELL YOU?
--- WE'VE DECIDED HIS GROUP IS THE PERFECT EXAMPLE OF WHAT NOT TO DO ON A CAMPING TRIP!
END

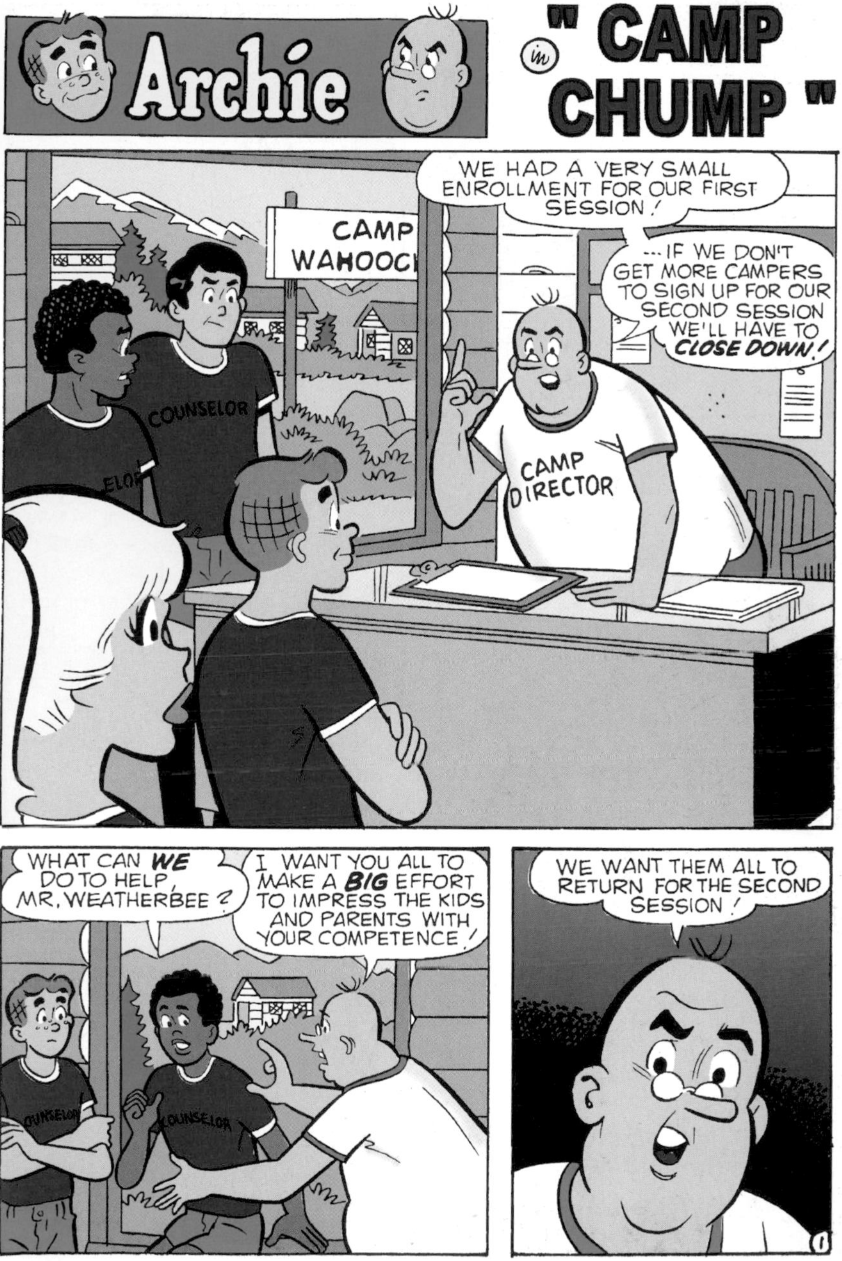

Archie
in "CAMP CHUMP"
WE HAD A VERY SMALL ENROLLMENT FOR OUR FIRST SESSION!
CAMP WAHOOCI
---IF WE DON'T GET MORE CAMPERS TO SIGN UP FOR OUR SECOND SESSION WE'LL HAVE TO CLOSE DOWN!
COUNSELOR
CAMP DIRECTOR
WHAT CAN WE DO TO HELP, MR. WEATHERBEE?
I WANT YOU ALL TO MAKE A BIG EFFORT TO IMPRESS THE KIDS AND PARENTS WITH YOUR COMPETENCE!
COUNSELOR
COUNSELOR
WE WANT THEM ALL TO RETURN FOR THE SECOND SESSION!
1

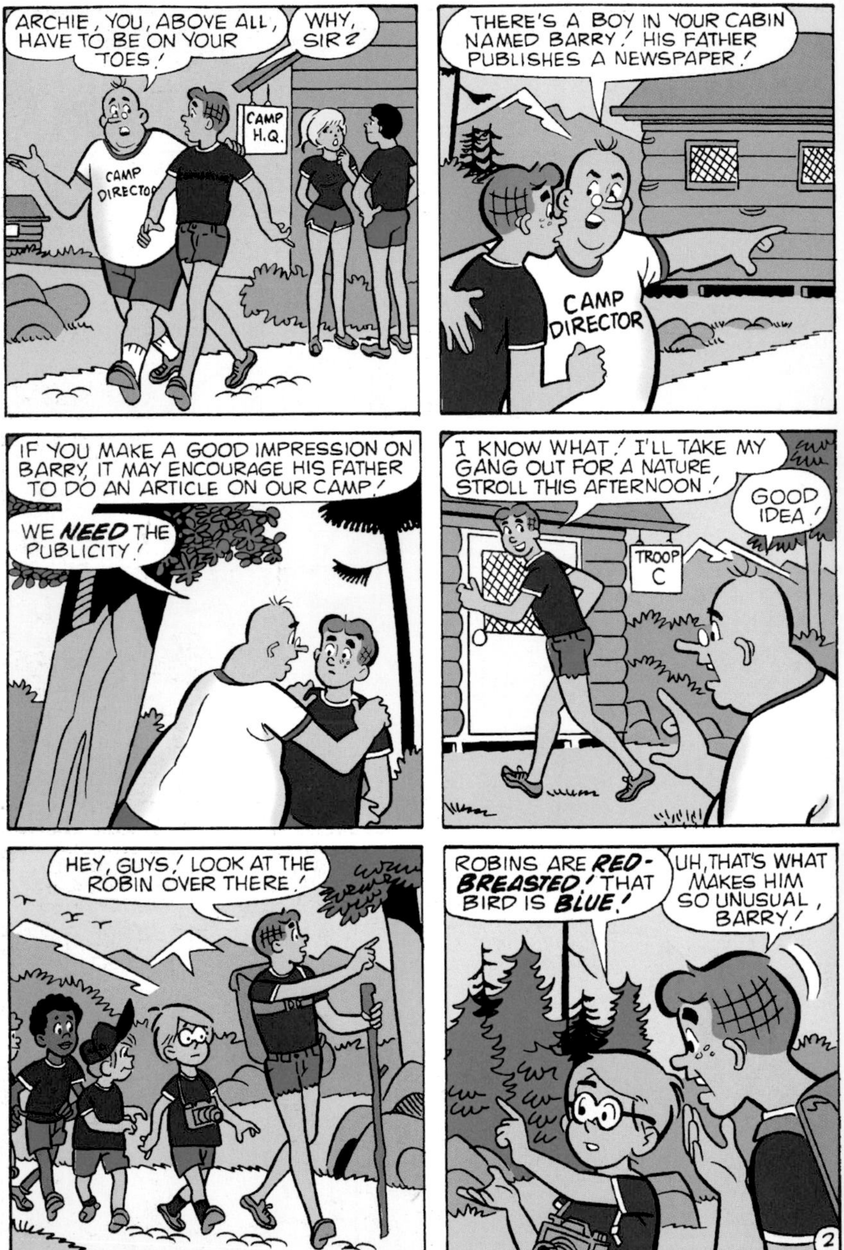
ARCHIE, YOU, ABOVE ALL, HAVE TO BE ON YOUR TOES!
WHY, SIR?
CAMP H.Q.
CAMP DIRECTOR
THERE'S A BOY IN YOUR CABIN NAMED BARRY! HIS FATHER PUBLISHES A NEWSPAPER!
CAMP DIRECTOR
IF YOU MAKE A GOOD IMPRESSION ON BARRY, IT MAY ENCOURAGE HIS FATHER TO DO AN ARTICLE ON OUR CAMP!
WE NEED THE PUBLICITY!
I KNOW WHAT! I'LL TAKE MY GANG OUT FOR A NATURE STROLL THIS AFTERNOON!
GOOD IDEA!
TROOP C
HEY, GUYS! LOOK AT THE ROBIN OVER THERE!
ROBINS ARE RED-BREASTED! THAT BIRD IS BLUE!
UH, THAT'S WHAT MAKES HIM SO UNUSUAL, BARRY!
2

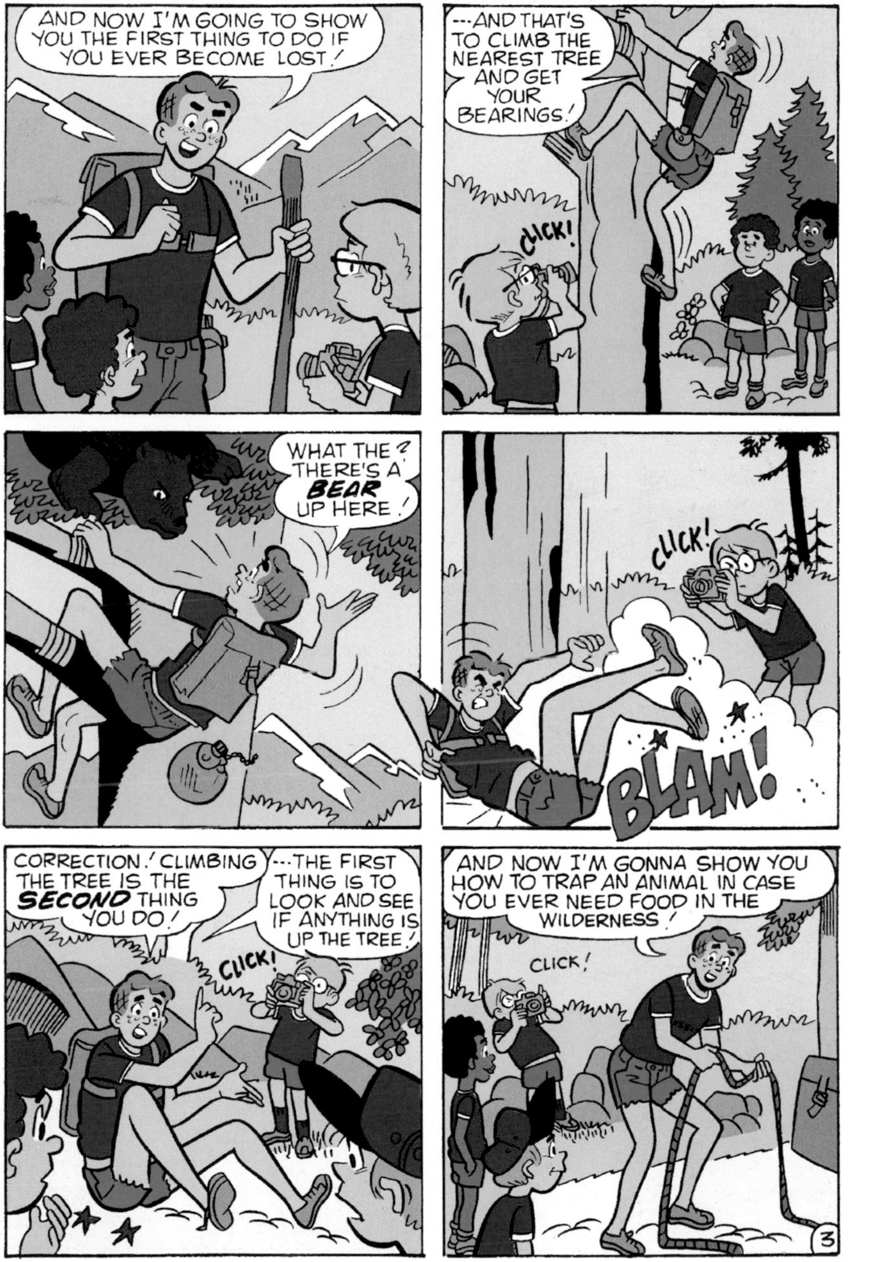
AND NOW I'M GOING TO SHOW YOU THE FIRST THING TO DO IF YOU EVER BECOME LOST!
---AND THAT'S TO CLIMB THE NEAREST TREE AND GET YOUR BEARINGS!
CLICK!
WHAT THE? THERE'S A BEAR UP HERE!
CLICK!
BLAM!
CORRECTION! CLIMBING THE TREE IS THE SECOND THING YOU DO!
---THE FIRST THING IS TO LOOK AND SEE IF ANYTHING IS UP THE TREE!
CLICK!
AND NOW I'M GONNA SHOW YOU HOW TO TRAP AN ANIMAL IN CASE YOU EVER NEED FOOD IN THE WILDERNESS!
CLICK!
3

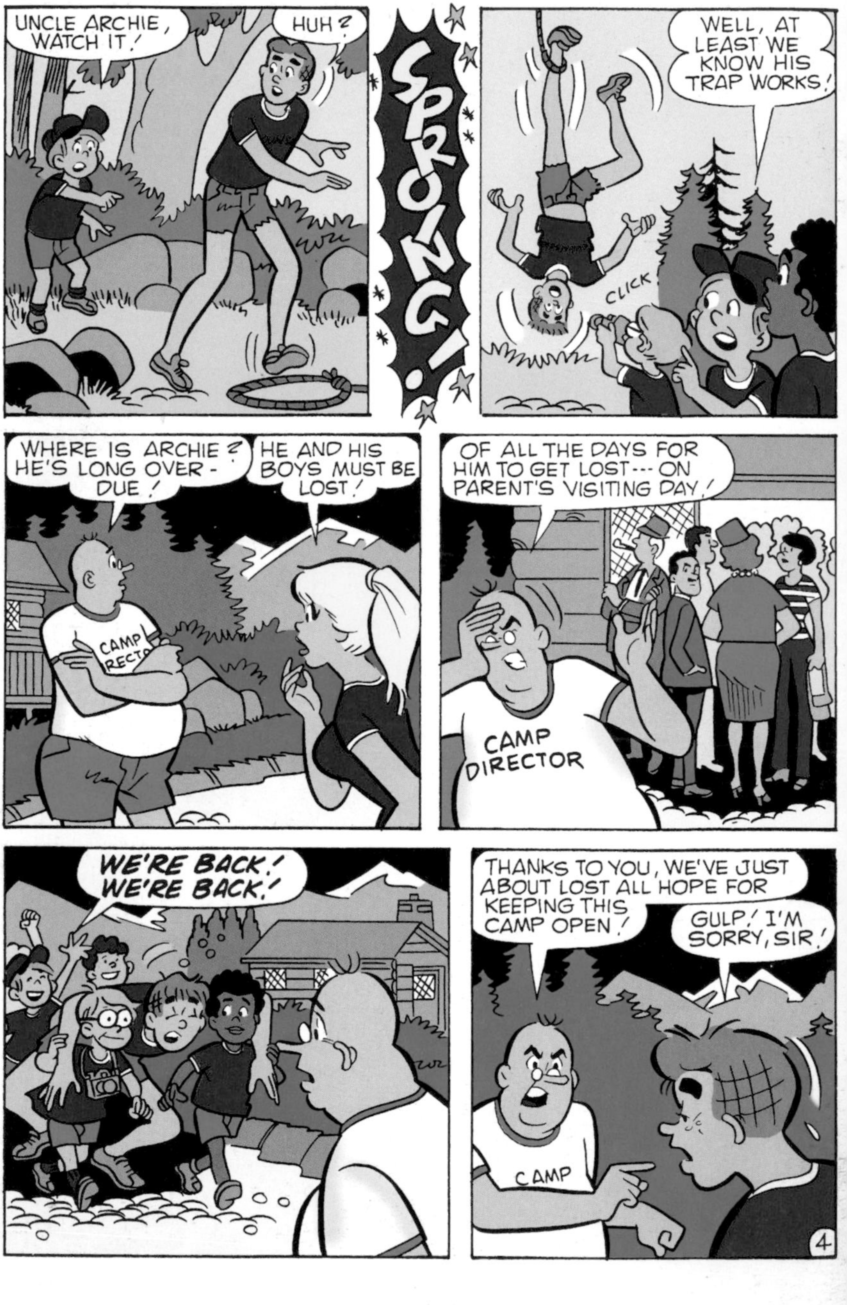
UNCLE ARCHIE, WATCH IT!
HUH?
SPROING!
WELL, AT LEAST WE KNOW HIS TRAP WORKS!
CLICK
WHERE IS ARCHIE? HE'S LONG OVER-DUE!
HE AND HIS BOYS MUST BE LOST!
CAMP DIRECTOR
OF ALL THE DAYS FOR HIM TO GET LOST--- ON PARENT'S VISITING DAY!
CAMP DIRECTOR
WE'RE BACK! WE'RE BACK!
THANKS TO YOU, WE'VE JUST ABOUT LOST ALL HOPE FOR KEEPING THIS CAMP OPEN!
GULP! I'M SORRY, SIR!
CAMP

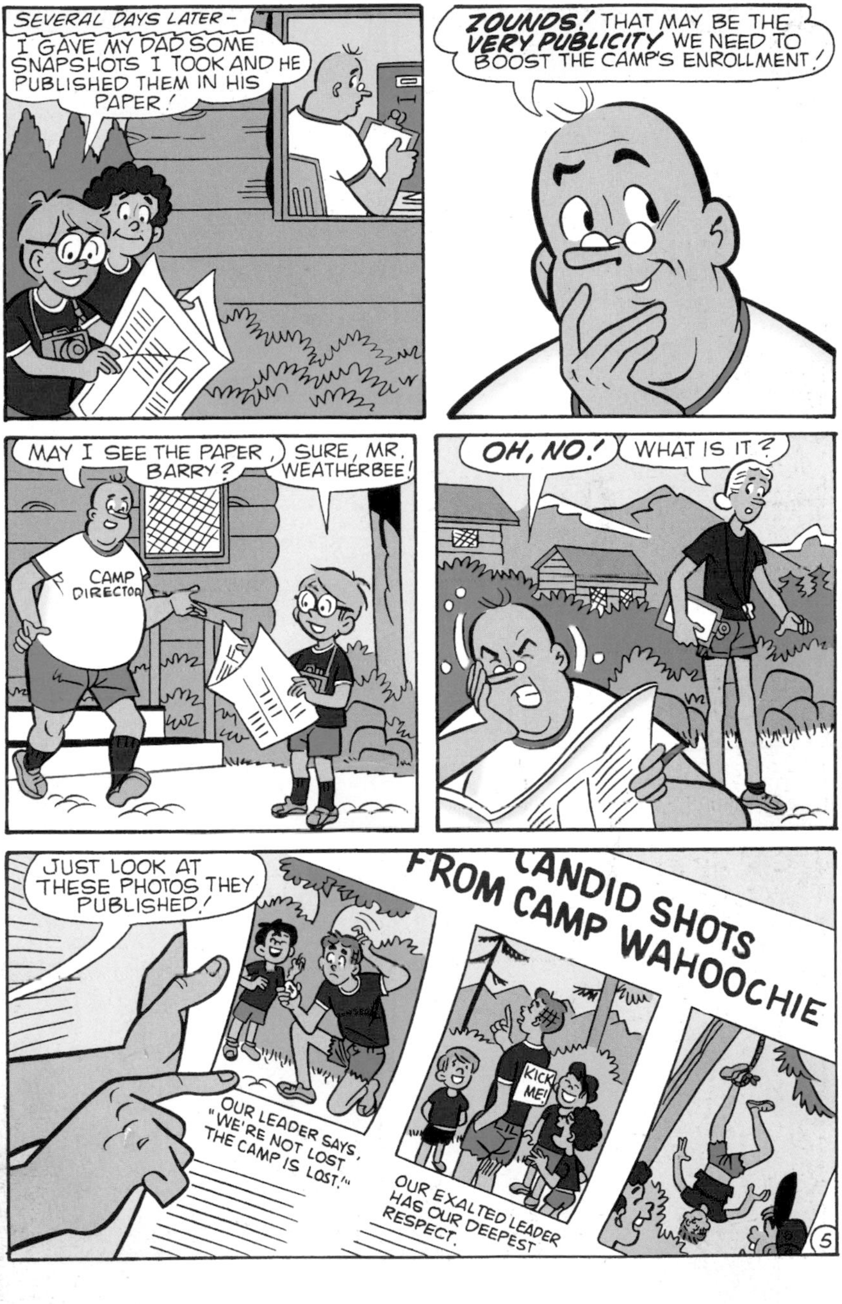

SEVERAL DAYS LATER –
I GAVE MY DAD SOME SNAPSHOTS I TOOK AND HE PUBLISHED THEM IN HIS PAPER!
ZOUNDS! THAT MAY BE THE VERY PUBLICITY WE NEED TO BOOST THE CAMP'S ENROLLMENT!
MAY I SEE THE PAPER, BARRY?
SURE, MR. WEATHERBEE!
CAMP DIRECTOR
OH, NO!
WHAT IS IT?
JUST LOOK AT THESE PHOTOS THEY PUBLISHED!
CANDID SHOTS FROM CAMP WAHOOCHIE
OUR LEADER SAYS, "WE'RE NOT LOST THE CAMP IS LOST."
KICK ME!
OUR EXALTED LEADER HAS OUR DEEPEST RESPECT.
5

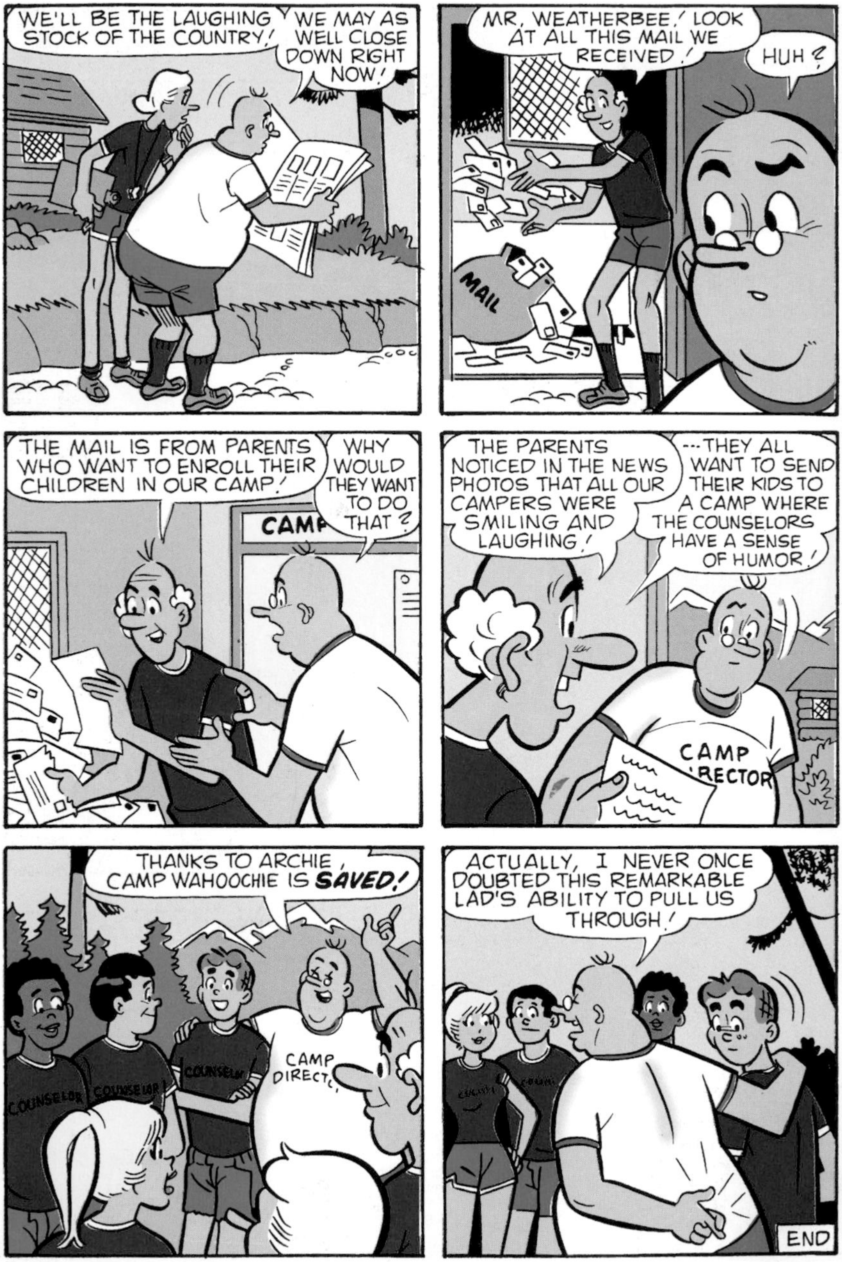
WE'LL BE THE LAUGHING STOCK OF THE COUNTRY!
WE MAY AS WELL CLOSE DOWN RIGHT NOW!
MR. WEATHERBEE! LOOK AT ALL THIS MAIL WE RECEIVED!
HUH?
MAIL
THE MAIL IS FROM PARENTS WHO WANT TO ENROLL THEIR CHILDREN IN OUR CAMP!
WHY WOULD THEY WANT TO DO THAT?
THE PARENTS NOTICED IN THE NEWS PHOTOS THAT ALL OUR CAMPERS WERE SMILING AND LAUGHING!
---THEY ALL WANT TO SEND THEIR KIDS TO A CAMP WHERE THE COUNSELORS HAVE A SENSE OF HUMOR!
THANKS TO ARCHIE, CAMP WAHOOCHIE IS SAVED!
COUNSELOR
CAMP DIRECT
ACTUALLY, I NEVER ONCE DOUBTED THIS REMARKABLE LAD'S ABILITY TO PULL US THROUGH!
END

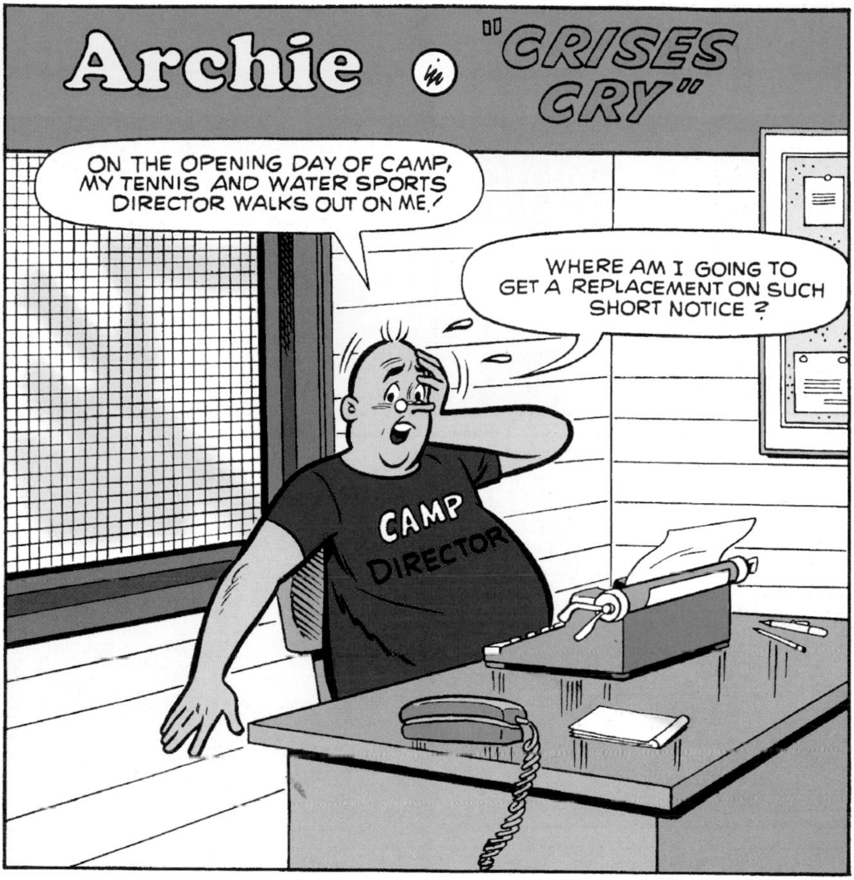
Archie in "CRISES CRY"
ON THE OPENING DAY OF CAMP, MY TENNIS AND WATER SPORTS DIRECTOR WALKS OUT ON ME!
WHERE AM I GOING TO GET A REPLACEMENT ON SUCH SHORT NOTICE ?
CAMP DIRECTOR

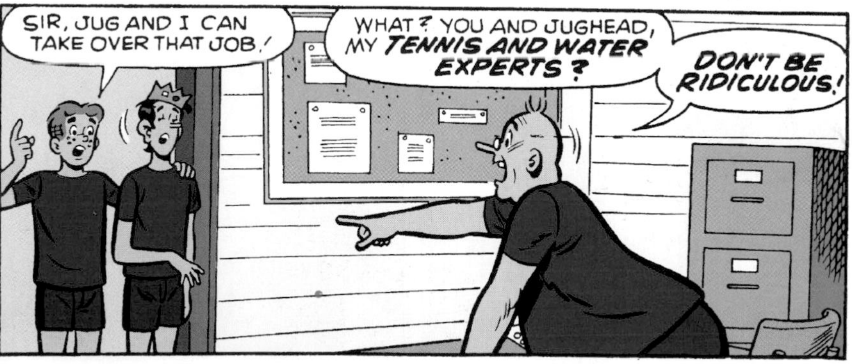
SIR, JUG AND I CAN TAKE OVER THAT JOB!
WHAT? YOU AND JUGHEAD, MY TENNIS AND WATER EXPERTS ?
DON'T BE RIDICULOUS!

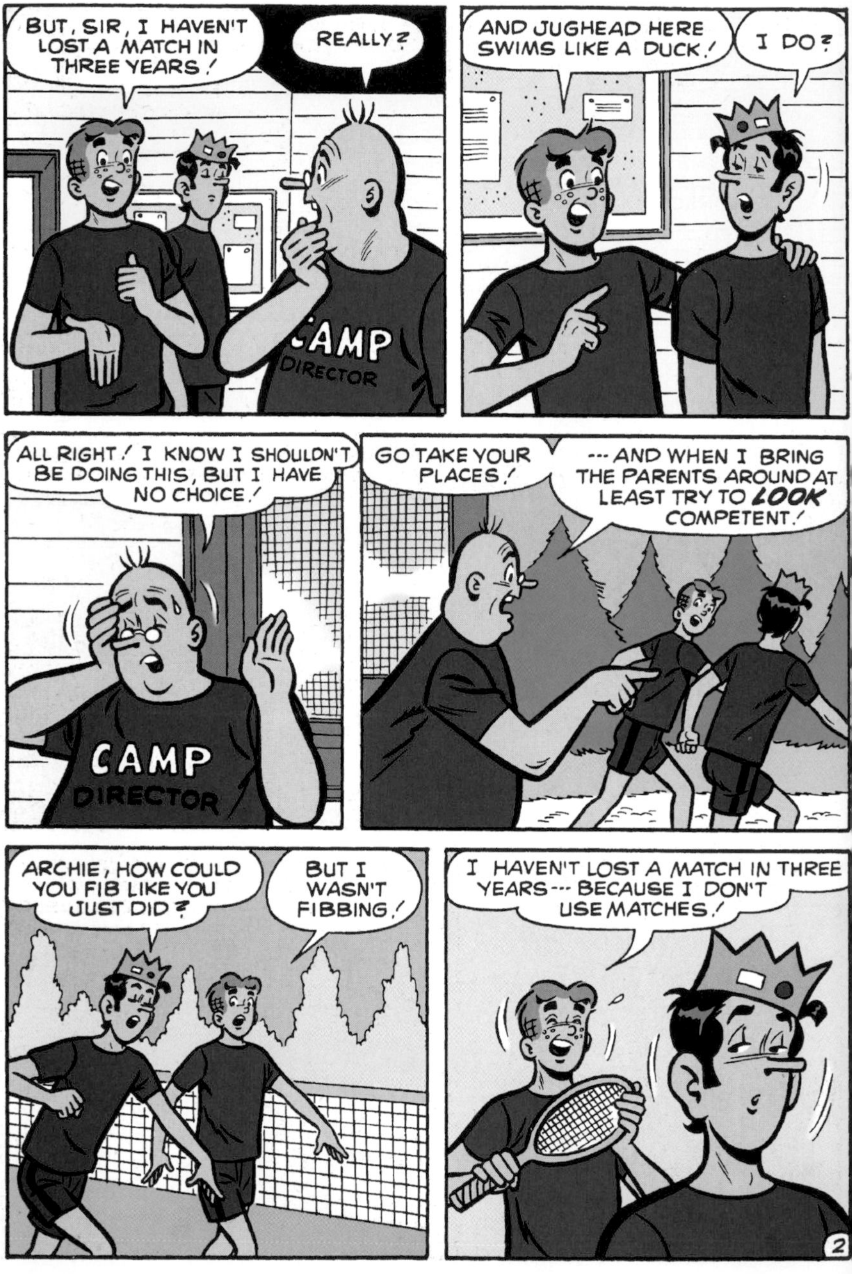

BUT, SIR, I HAVEN'T LOST A MATCH IN THREE YEARS!
REALLY?
AND JUGHEAD HERE SWIMS LIKE A DUCK!
I DO?
CAMP DIRECTOR
ALL RIGHT! I KNOW I SHOULDN'T BE DOING THIS, BUT I HAVE NO CHOICE!
CAMP DIRECTOR
GO TAKE YOUR PLACES!
--- AND WHEN I BRING THE PARENTS AROUND AT LEAST TRY TO LOOK COMPETENT!
ARCHIE, HOW COULD YOU FIB LIKE YOU JUST DID?
BUT I WASN'T FIBBING!
I HAVEN'T LOST A MATCH IN THREE YEARS --- BECAUSE I DON'T USE MATCHES!

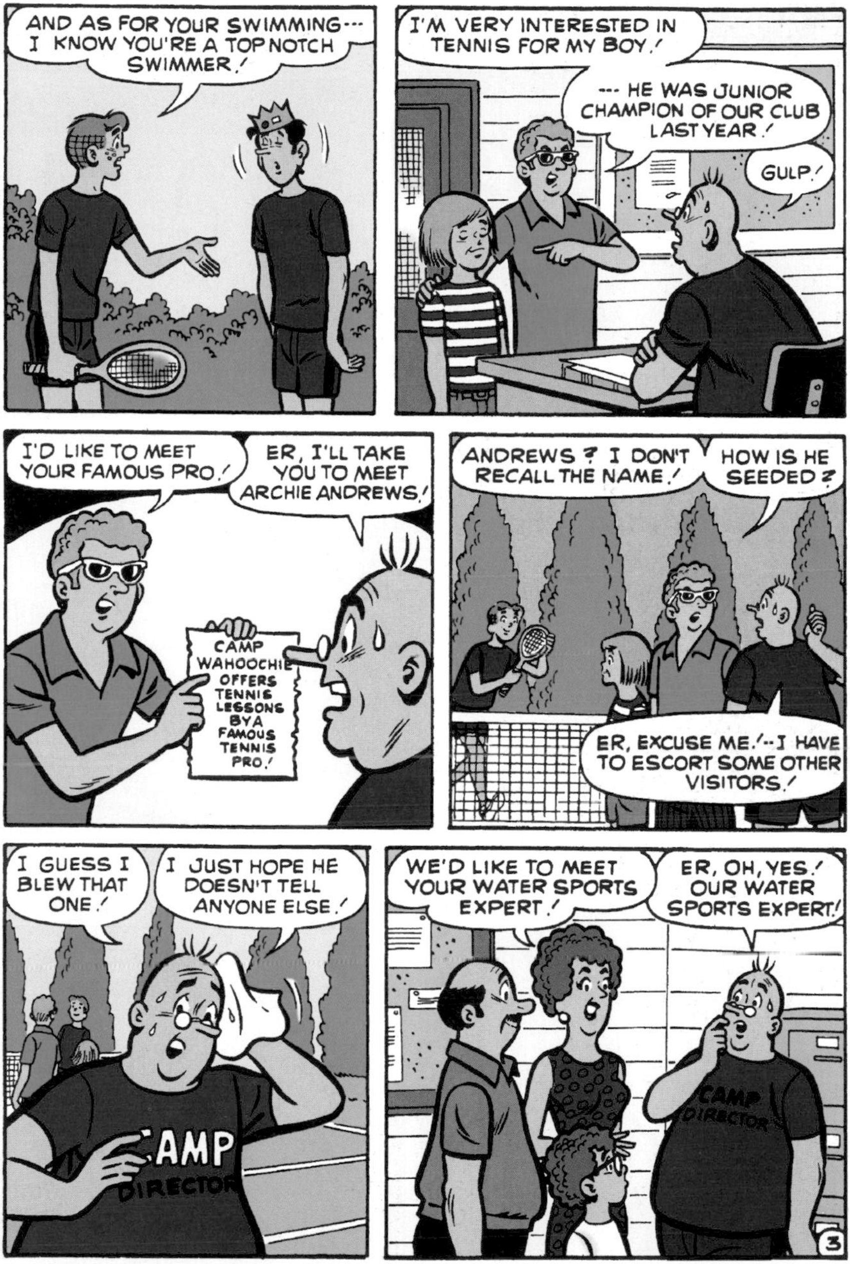

AND AS FOR YOUR SWIMMING--- I KNOW YOU'RE A TOP NOTCH SWIMMER!
I'M VERY INTERESTED IN TENNIS FOR MY BOY!
--- HE WAS JUNIOR CHAMPION OF OUR CLUB LAST YEAR!
GULP!
I'D LIKE TO MEET YOUR FAMOUS PRO!
ER, I'LL TAKE YOU TO MEET ARCHIE ANDREWS!
CAMP WAHOOCHIE OFFERS TENNIS LESSONS BY A FAMOUS TENNIS PRO!
ANDREWS? I DON'T RECALL THE NAME!
HOW IS HE SEEDED?
ER, EXCUSE ME!--I HAVE TO ESCORT SOME OTHER VISITORS!
I GUESS I BLEW THAT ONE!
I JUST HOPE HE DOESN'T TELL ANYONE ELSE!
CAMP DIRECTOR
WE'D LIKE TO MEET YOUR WATER SPORTS EXPERT!
ER, OH, YES! OUR WATER SPORTS EXPERT!
CAMP DIRECTOR
3

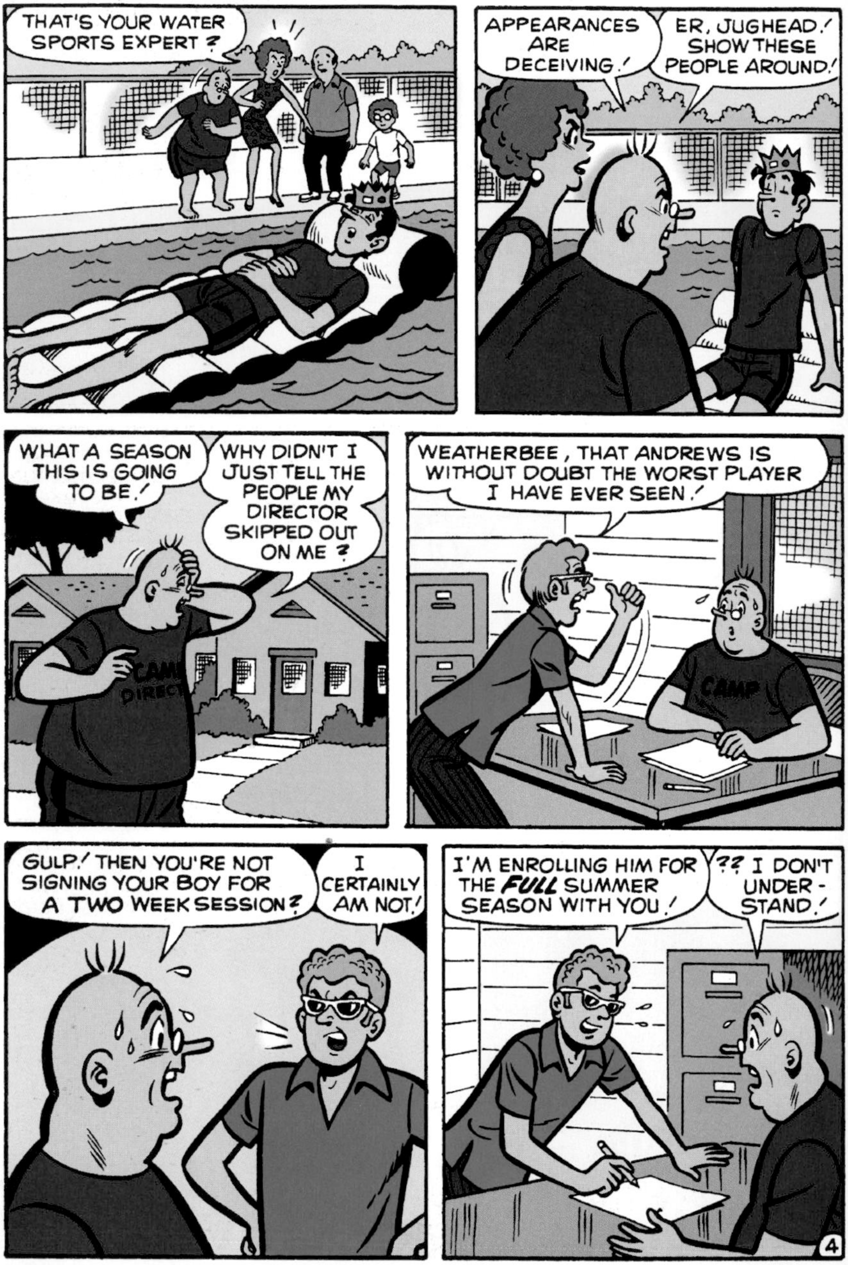
THAT'S YOUR WATER SPORTS EXPERT ?
APPEARANCES ARE DECEIVING!
ER, JUGHEAD! SHOW THESE PEOPLE AROUND!
WHAT A SEASON THIS IS GOING TO BE!
WHY DIDN'T I JUST TELL THE PEOPLE MY DIRECTOR SKIPPED OUT ON ME ?
CAMP DIRECT
WEATHERBEE, THAT ANDREWS IS WITHOUT DOUBT THE WORST PLAYER I HAVE EVER SEEN!
CAMP
GULP! THEN YOU'RE NOT SIGNING YOUR BOY FOR A TWO WEEK SESSION ?
I CERTAINLY AM NOT!
I'M ENROLLING HIM FOR THE FULL SUMMER SEASON WITH YOU!
?? I DON'T UNDER-STAND!
4

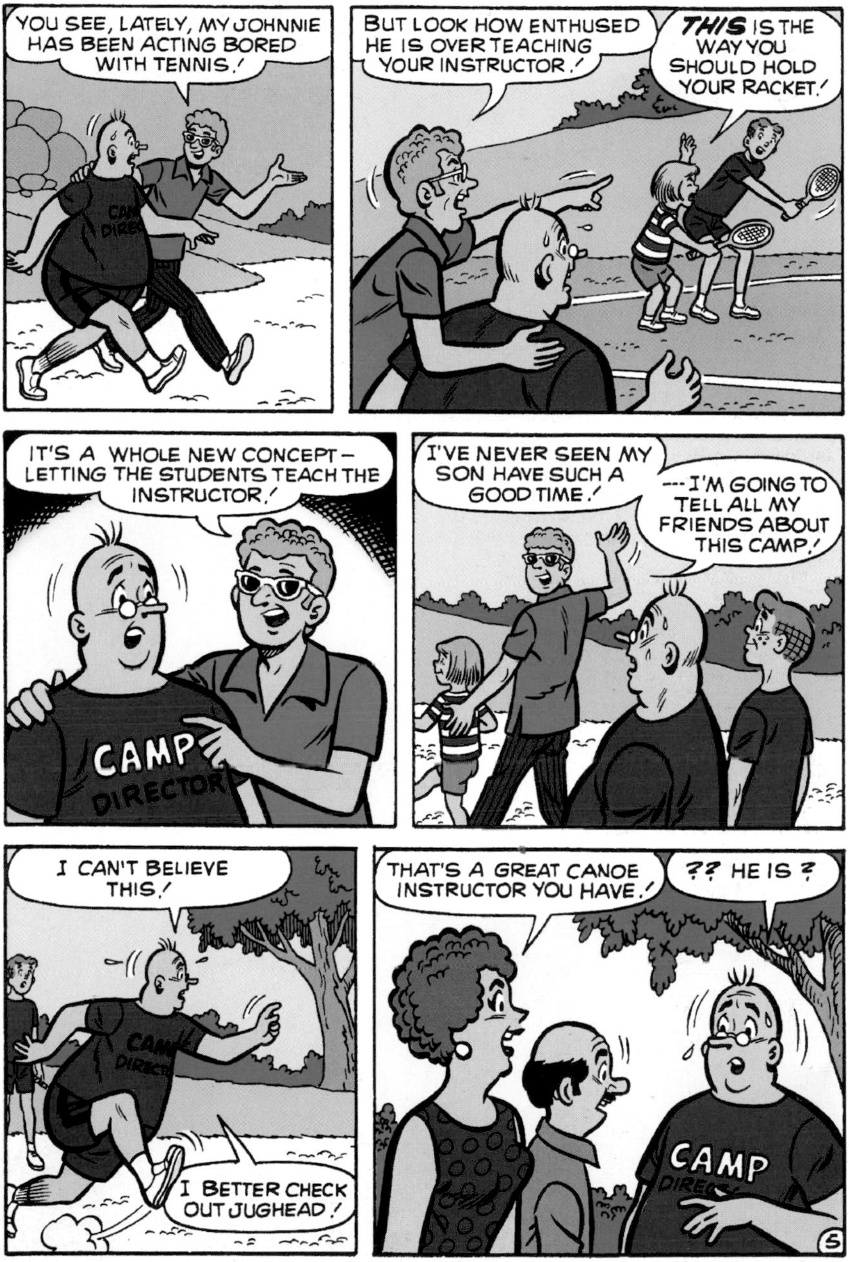
YOU SEE, LATELY, MY JOHNNIE HAS BEEN ACTING BORED WITH TENNIS!
BUT LOOK HOW ENTHUSED HE IS OVER TEACHING YOUR INSTRUCTOR!
THIS IS THE WAY YOU SHOULD HOLD YOUR RACKET!
IT'S A WHOLE NEW CONCEPT— LETTING THE STUDENTS TEACH THE INSTRUCTOR!
CAMP DIRECTOR
I'VE NEVER SEEN MY SON HAVE SUCH A GOOD TIME!
---I'M GOING TO TELL ALL MY FRIENDS ABOUT THIS CAMP!
I CAN'T BELIEVE THIS!
I BETTER CHECK OUT JUGHEAD!
THAT'S A GREAT CANOE INSTRUCTOR YOU HAVE!
?? HE IS ?
CAMP

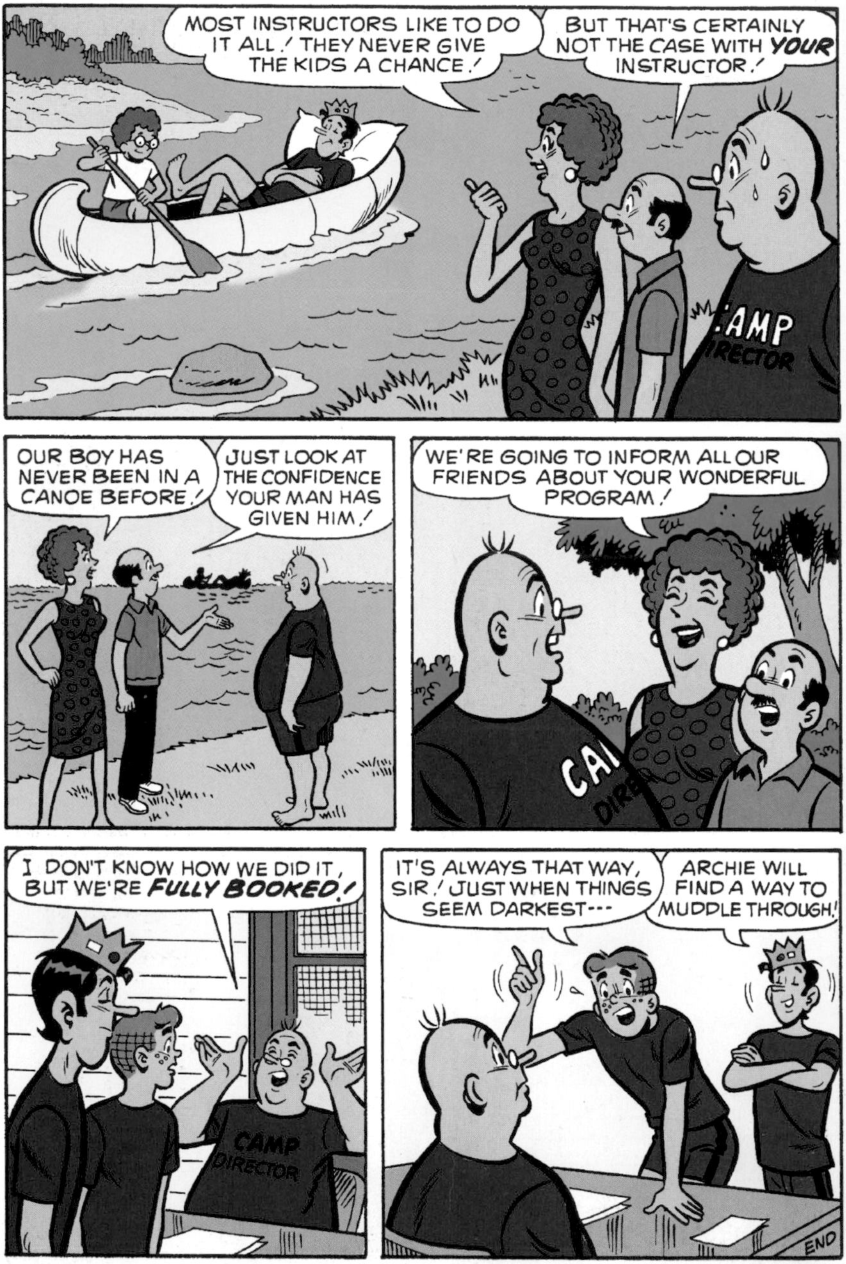
MOST INSTRUCTORS LIKE TO DO IT ALL! THEY NEVER GIVE THE KIDS A CHANCE!
BUT THAT'S CERTAINLY NOT THE CASE WITH *YOUR* INSTRUCTOR!
CAMP DIRECTOR
OUR BOY HAS NEVER BEEN IN A CANOE BEFORE!
JUST LOOK AT THE CONFIDENCE YOUR MAN HAS GIVEN HIM!
WE'RE GOING TO INFORM ALL OUR FRIENDS ABOUT YOUR WONDERFUL PROGRAM!
I DON'T KNOW HOW WE DID IT, BUT WE'RE *FULLY BOOKED!*
CAMP DIRECTOR
IT'S ALWAYS THAT WAY, SIR! JUST WHEN THINGS SEEM DARKEST---
ARCHIE WILL FIND A WAY TO MUDDLE THROUGH!
END

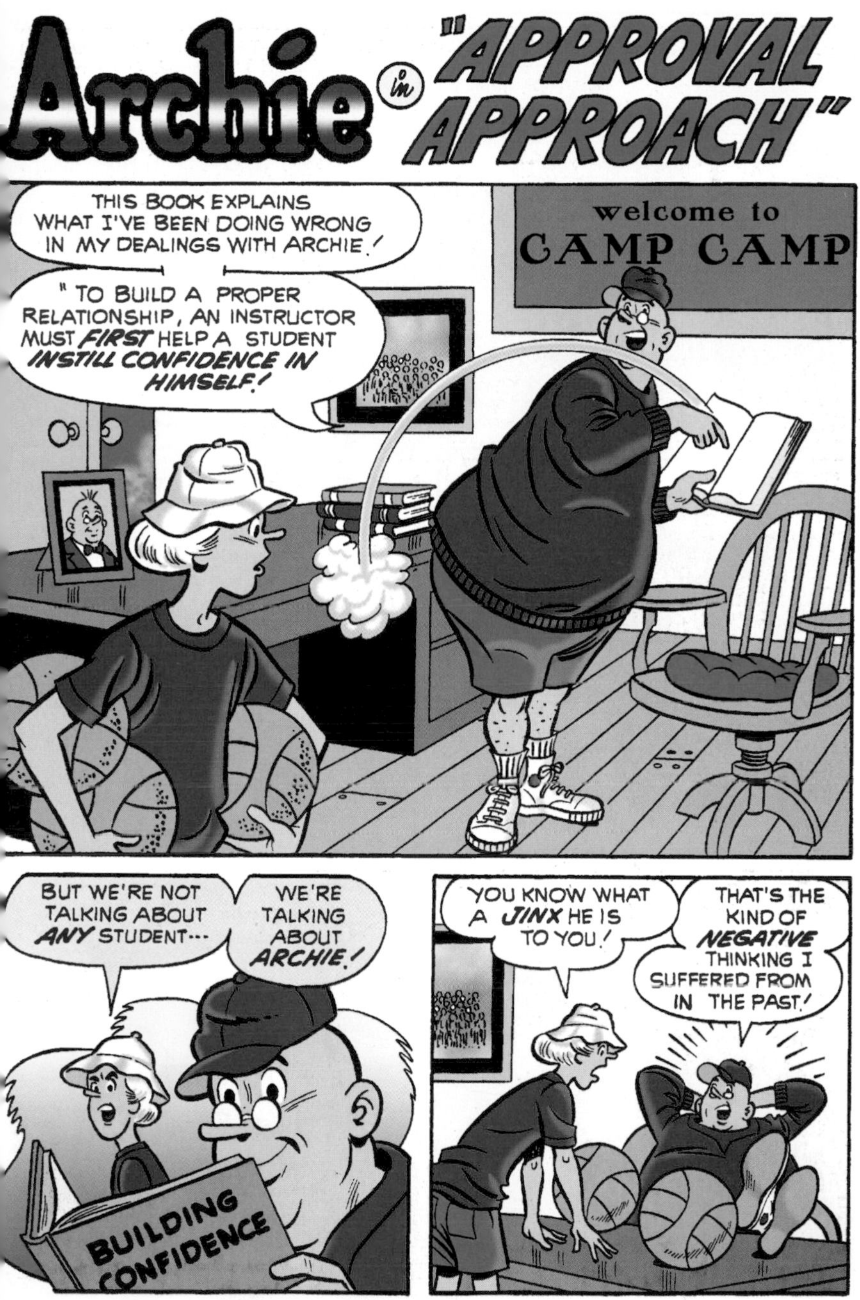

Archie in "APPROVAL APPROACH"
welcome to CAMP CAMP
THIS BOOK EXPLAINS WHAT I'VE BEEN DOING WRONG IN MY DEALINGS WITH ARCHIE!
" TO BUILD A PROPER RELATIONSHIP, AN INSTRUCTOR MUST FIRST HELP A STUDENT INSTILL CONFIDENCE IN HIMSELF!
BUT WE'RE NOT TALKING ABOUT ANY STUDENT---
WE'RE TALKING ABOUT ARCHIE!
BUILDING CONFIDENCE
YOU KNOW WHAT A JINX HE IS TO YOU!
THAT'S THE KIND OF NEGATIVE THINKING I SUFFERED FROM IN THE PAST!

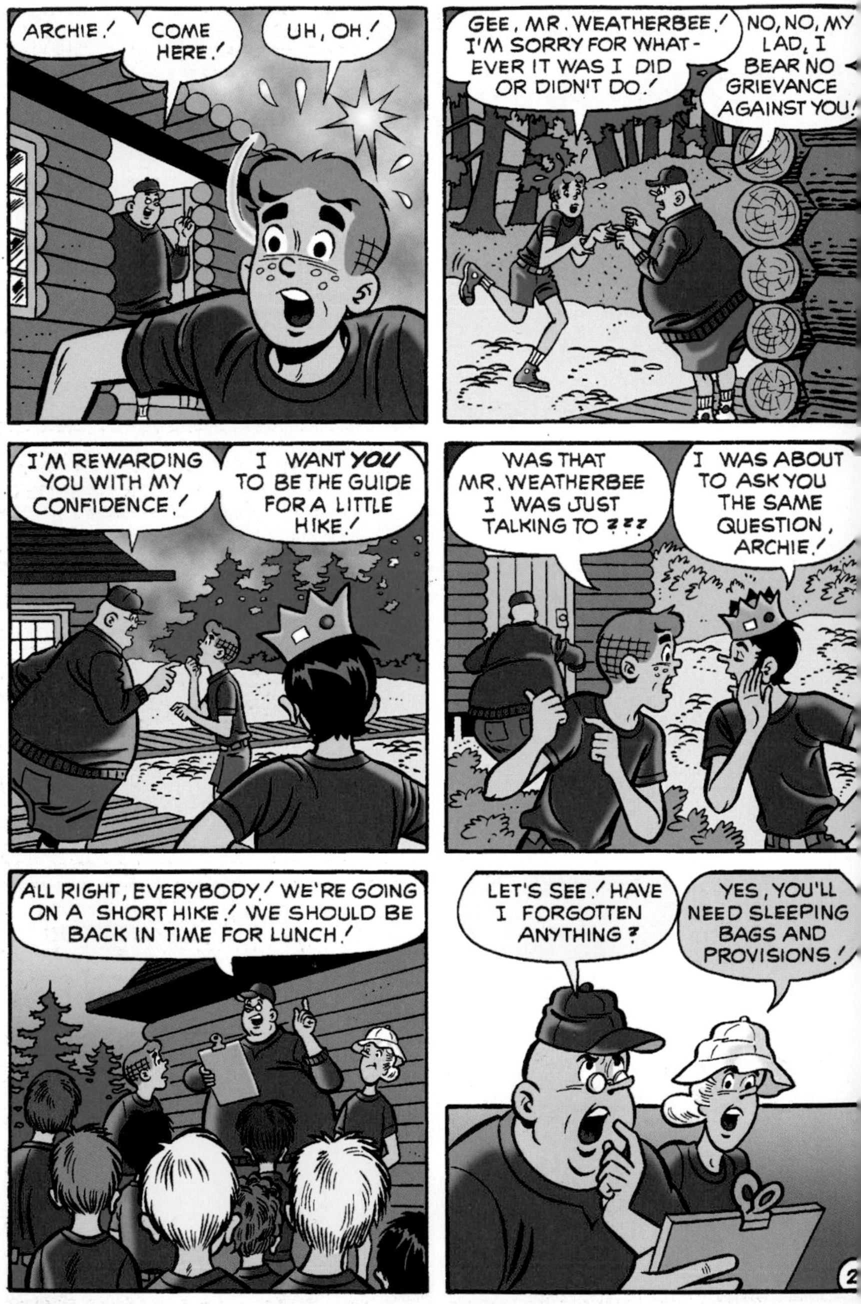
ARCHIE! COME HERE!
UH, OH!
GEE, MR. WEATHERBEE! I'M SORRY FOR WHAT-EVER IT WAS I DID OR DIDN'T DO!
NO, NO, MY LAD, I BEAR NO GRIEVANCE AGAINST YOU!
I'M REWARDING YOU WITH MY CONFIDENCE!
I WANT YOU TO BE THE GUIDE FOR A LITTLE HIKE!
WAS THAT MR. WEATHERBEE I WAS JUST TALKING TO ???
I WAS ABOUT TO ASK YOU THE SAME QUESTION, ARCHIE!
ALL RIGHT, EVERYBODY! WE'RE GOING ON A SHORT HIKE! WE SHOULD BE BACK IN TIME FOR LUNCH!
LET'S SEE! HAVE I FORGOTTEN ANYTHING?
YES, YOU'LL NEED SLEEPING BAGS AND PROVISIONS!
2

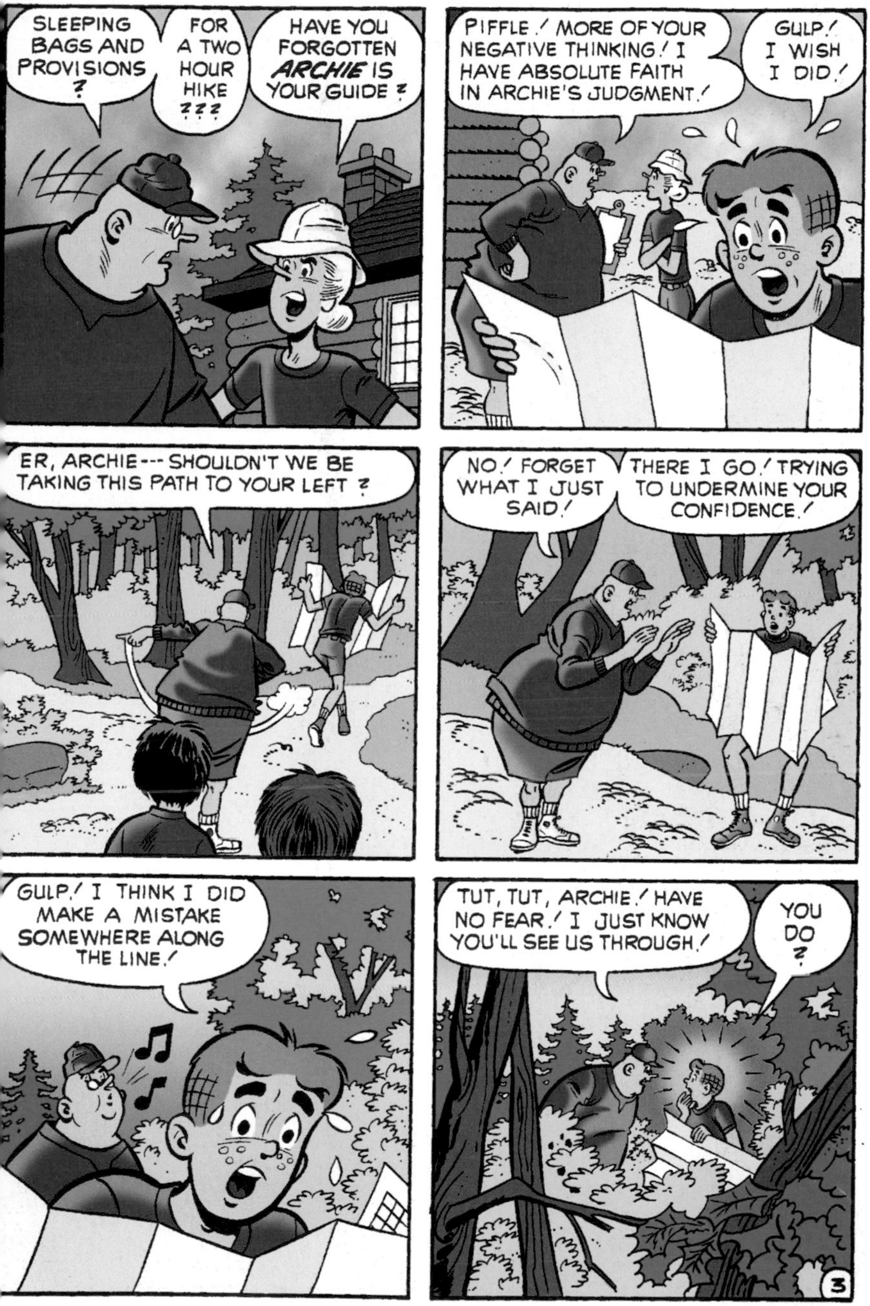
SLEEPING BAGS AND PROVISIONS?
FOR A TWO HOUR HIKE???
HAVE YOU FORGOTTEN ARCHIE IS YOUR GUIDE?
PIFFLE! MORE OF YOUR NEGATIVE THINKING! I HAVE ABSOLUTE FAITH IN ARCHIE'S JUDGMENT!
GULP! I WISH I DID!
ER, ARCHIE--- SHOULDN'T WE BE TAKING THIS PATH TO YOUR LEFT?
NO! FORGET WHAT I JUST SAID!
THERE I GO! TRYING TO UNDERMINE YOUR CONFIDENCE!
GULP! I THINK I DID MAKE A MISTAKE SOMEWHERE ALONG THE LINE!
TUT, TUT, ARCHIE! HAVE NO FEAR! I JUST KNOW YOU'LL SEE US THROUGH!
YOU DO?
3

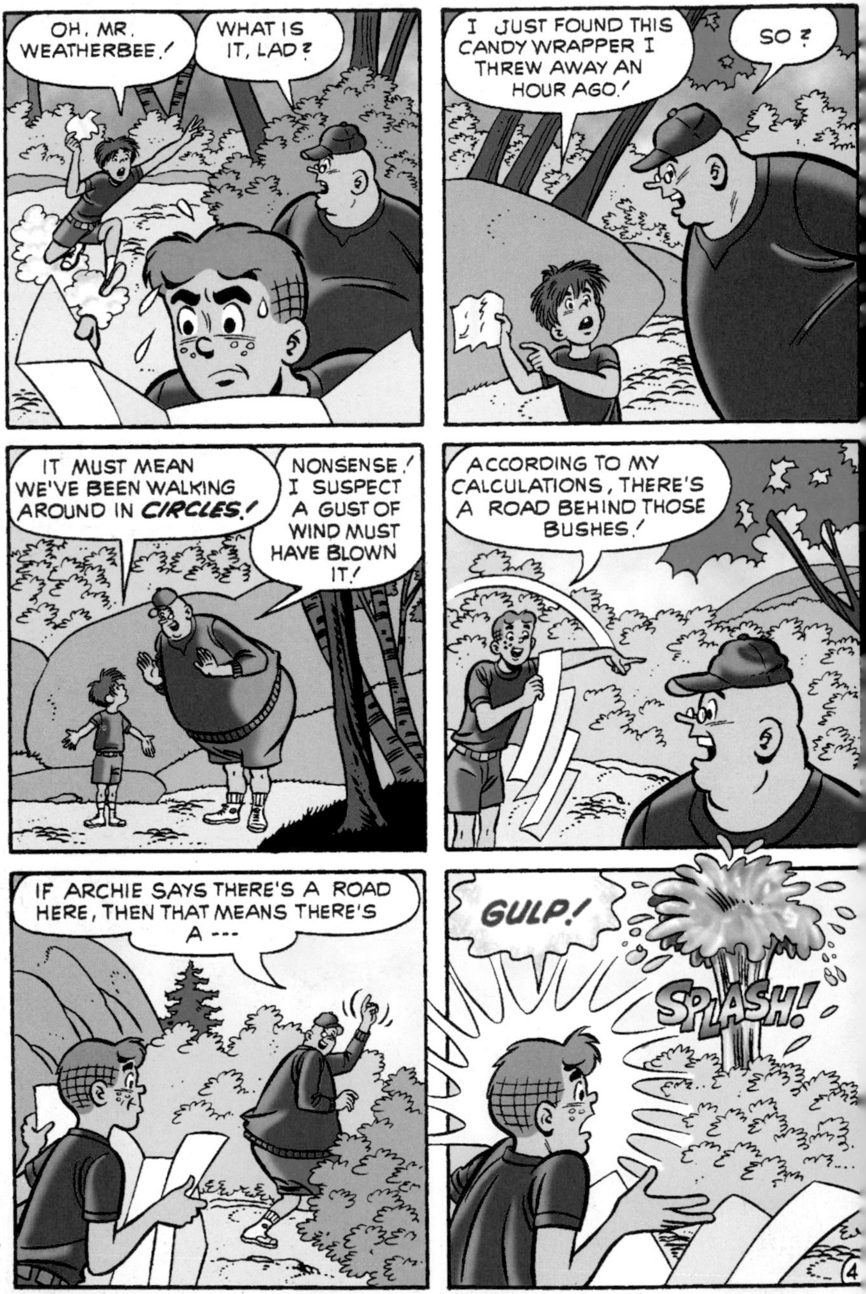
OH, MR. WEATHERBEE!
WHAT IS IT, LAD?
I JUST FOUND THIS CANDY WRAPPER I THREW AWAY AN HOUR AGO!
SO?
IT MUST MEAN WE'VE BEEN WALKING AROUND IN CIRCLES!
NONSENSE! I SUSPECT A GUST OF WIND MUST HAVE BLOWN IT!
ACCORDING TO MY CALCULATIONS, THERE'S A ROAD BEHIND THOSE BUSHES!
IF ARCHIE SAYS THERE'S A ROAD HERE, THEN THAT MEANS THERE'S A ---
GULP!
SPLASH!
4

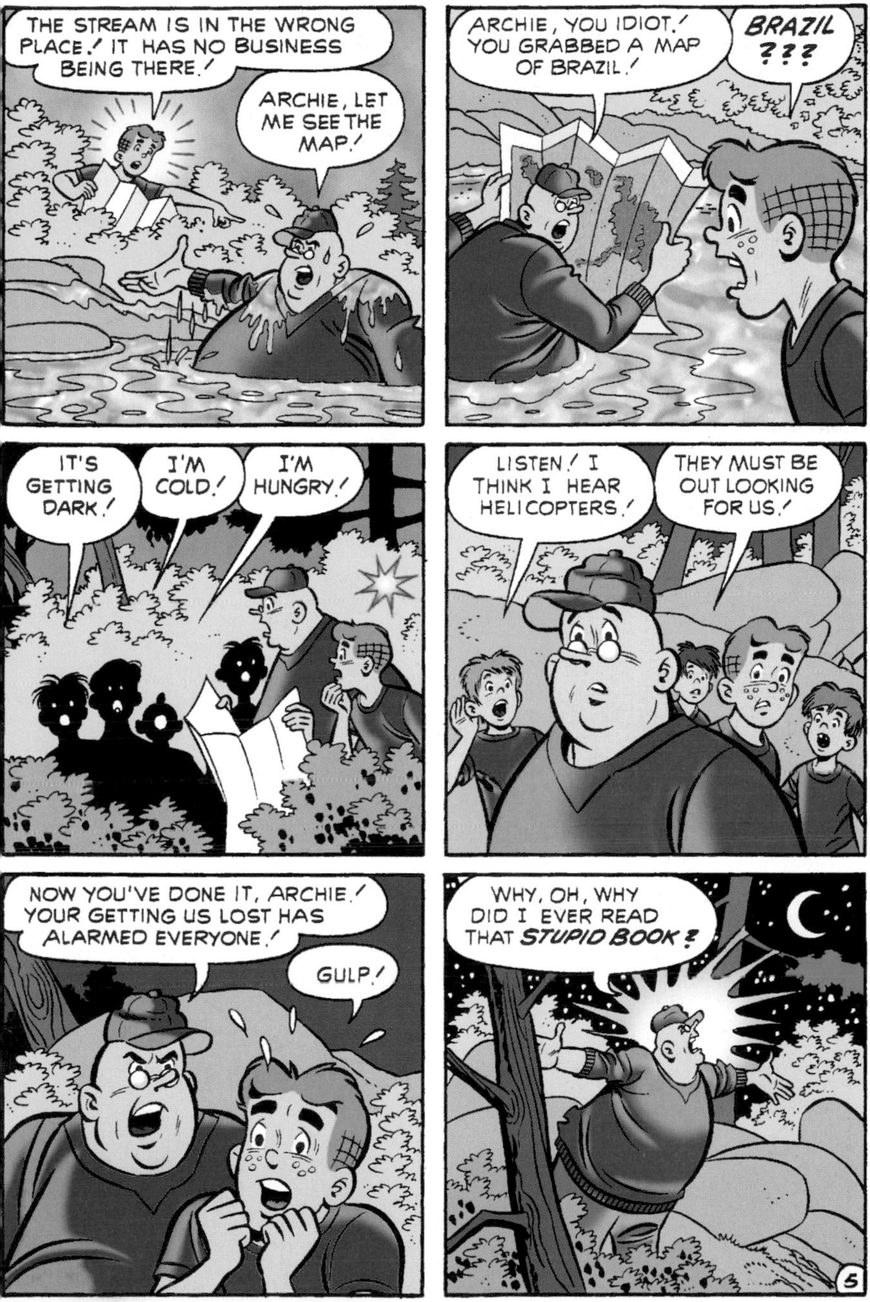
THE STREAM IS IN THE WRONG PLACE! IT HAS NO BUSINESS BEING THERE!
ARCHIE, LET ME SEE THE MAP!
ARCHIE, YOU IDIOT! YOU GRABBED A MAP OF BRAZIL!
BRAZIL ???
IT'S GETTING DARK!
I'M COLD!
I'M HUNGRY!
LISTEN! I THINK I HEAR HELICOPTERS!
THEY MUST BE OUT LOOKING FOR US!
NOW YOU'VE DONE IT, ARCHIE! YOUR GETTING US LOST HAS ALARMED EVERYONE!
GULP!
WHY, OH, WHY DID I EVER READ THAT STUPID BOOK?

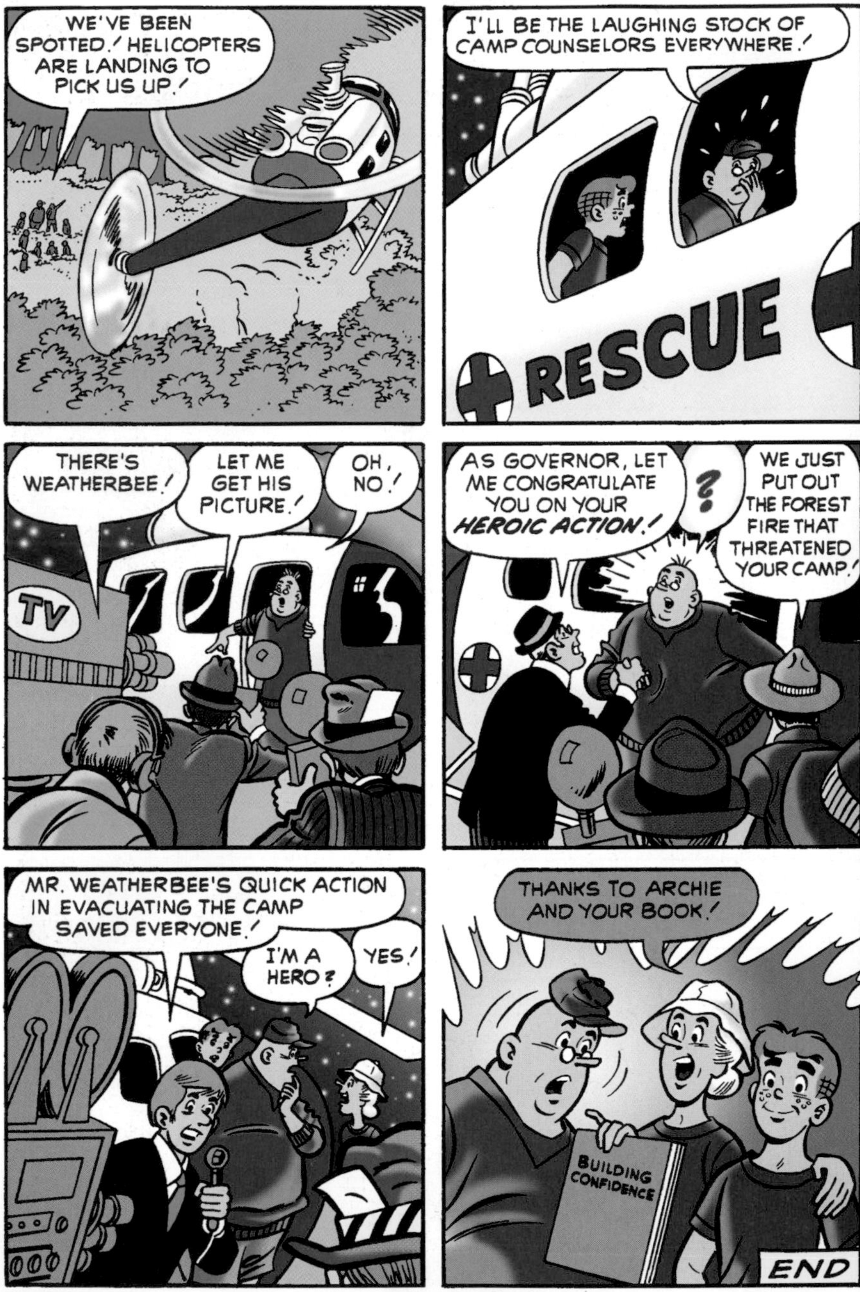
WE'VE BEEN SPOTTED! HELICOPTERS ARE LANDING TO PICK US UP!
I'LL BE THE LAUGHING STOCK OF CAMP COUNSELORS EVERYWHERE!
RESCUE
THERE'S WEATHERBEE!
LET ME GET HIS PICTURE!
OH, NO!
TV
AS GOVERNOR, LET ME CONGRATULATE YOU ON YOUR HEROIC ACTION!
?
WE JUST PUT OUT THE FOREST FIRE THAT THREATENED YOUR CAMP!
MR. WEATHERBEE'S QUICK ACTION IN EVACUATING THE CAMP SAVED EVERYONE!
I'M A HERO?
YES!
THANKS TO ARCHIE AND YOUR BOOK!
BUILDING CONFIDENCE
END

Archie in "CAMP CAPER"

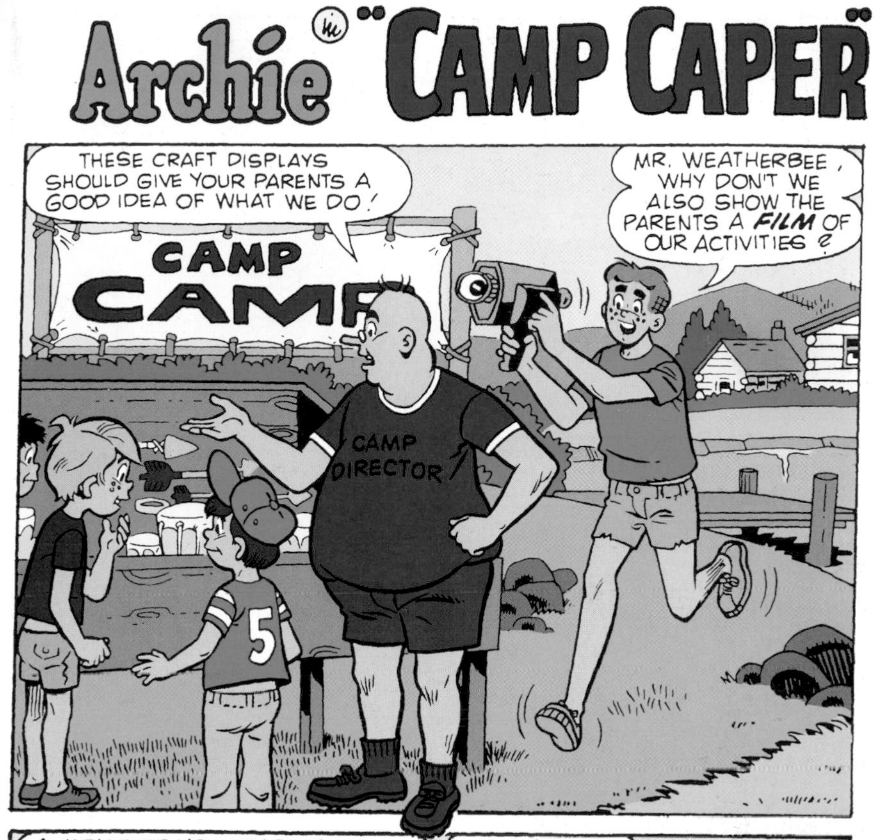
THESE CRAFT DISPLAYS SHOULD GIVE YOUR PARENTS A GOOD IDEA OF WHAT WE DO!
MR. WEATHERBEE, WHY DON'T WE ALSO SHOW THE PARENTS A FILM OF OUR ACTIVITIES?
CAMP
CAMP
CAMP DIRECTOR

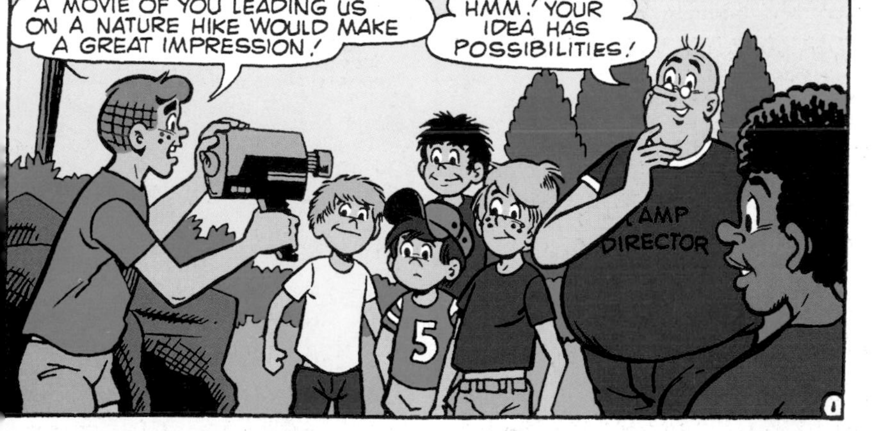
A MOVIE OF YOU LEADING US ON A NATURE HIKE WOULD MAKE A GREAT IMPRESSION!
HMM! YOUR IDEA HAS POSSIBILITIES!
5
5

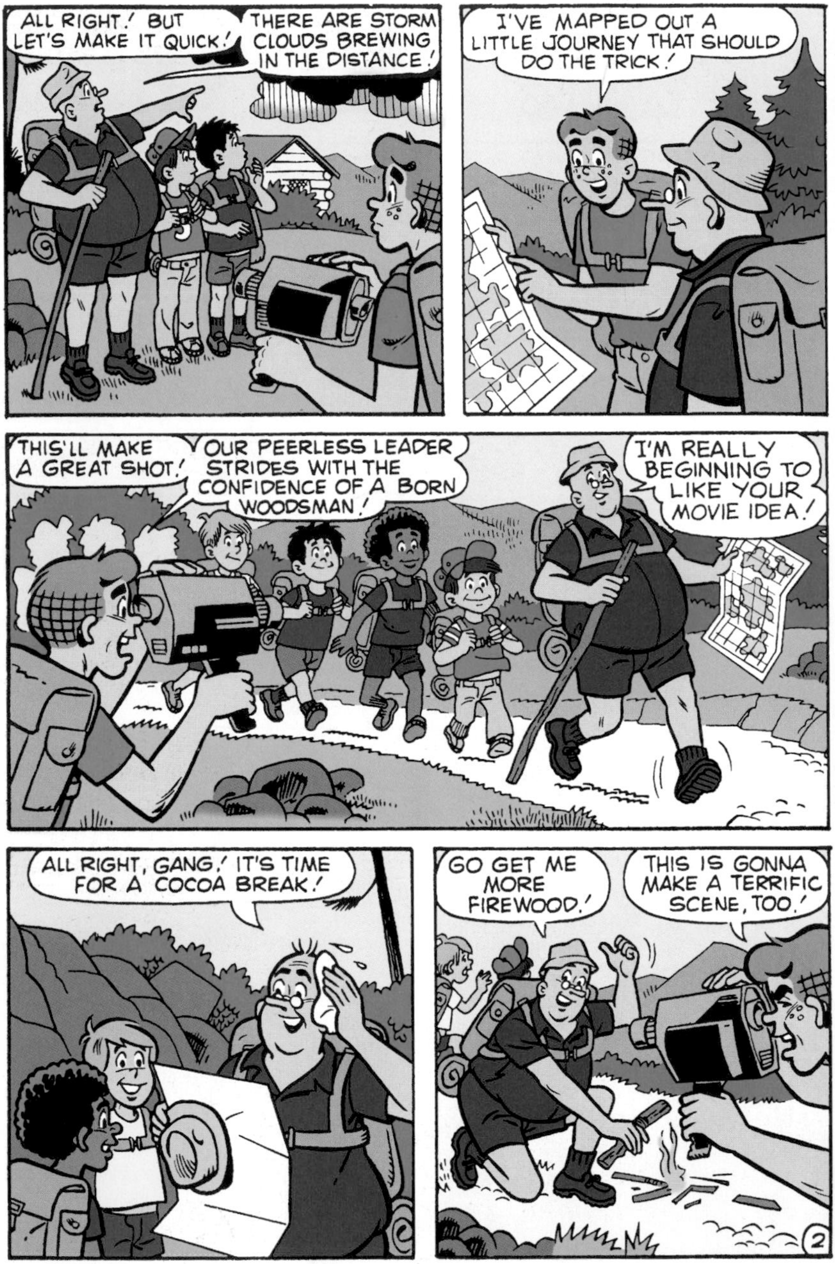
ALL RIGHT! BUT LET'S MAKE IT QUICK!
THERE ARE STORM CLOUDS BREWING IN THE DISTANCE!
I'VE MAPPED OUT A LITTLE JOURNEY THAT SHOULD DO THE TRICK!
THIS'LL MAKE A GREAT SHOT!
OUR PEERLESS LEADER STRIDES WITH THE CONFIDENCE OF A BORN WOODSMAN!
I'M REALLY BEGINNING TO LIKE YOUR MOVIE IDEA!
ALL RIGHT, GANG! IT'S TIME FOR A COCOA BREAK!
GO GET ME MORE FIREWOOD!
THIS IS GONNA MAKE A TERRIFIC SCENE, TOO!
2

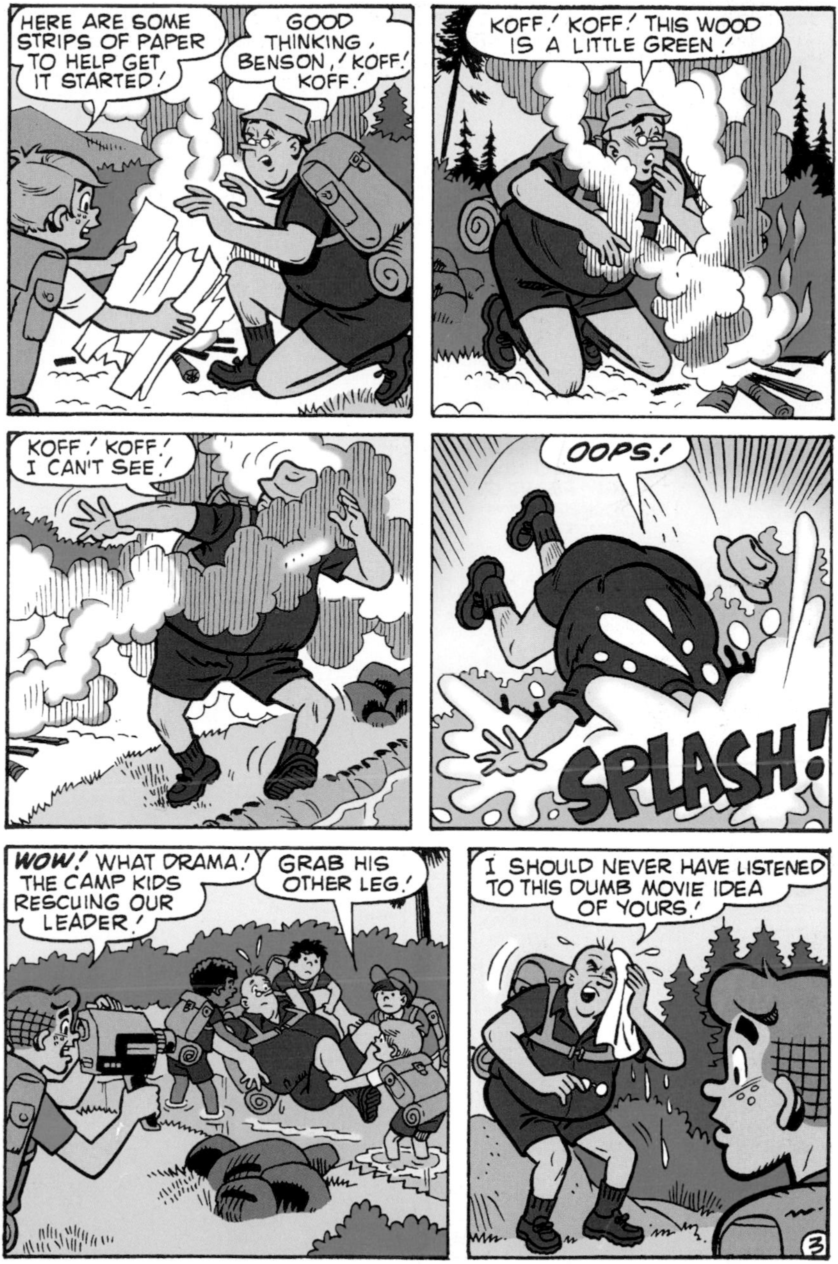
HERE ARE SOME STRIPS OF PAPER TO HELP GET IT STARTED!
GOOD THINKING, BENSON! KOFF! KOFF!
KOFF! KOFF! THIS WOOD IS A LITTLE GREEN!
KOFF! KOFF! I CAN'T SEE!
OOPS!
SPLASH!
WOW! WHAT DRAMA! THE CAMP KIDS RESCUING OUR LEADER!
GRAB HIS OTHER LEG!
I SHOULD NEVER HAVE LISTENED TO THIS DUMB MOVIE IDEA OF YOURS!
3

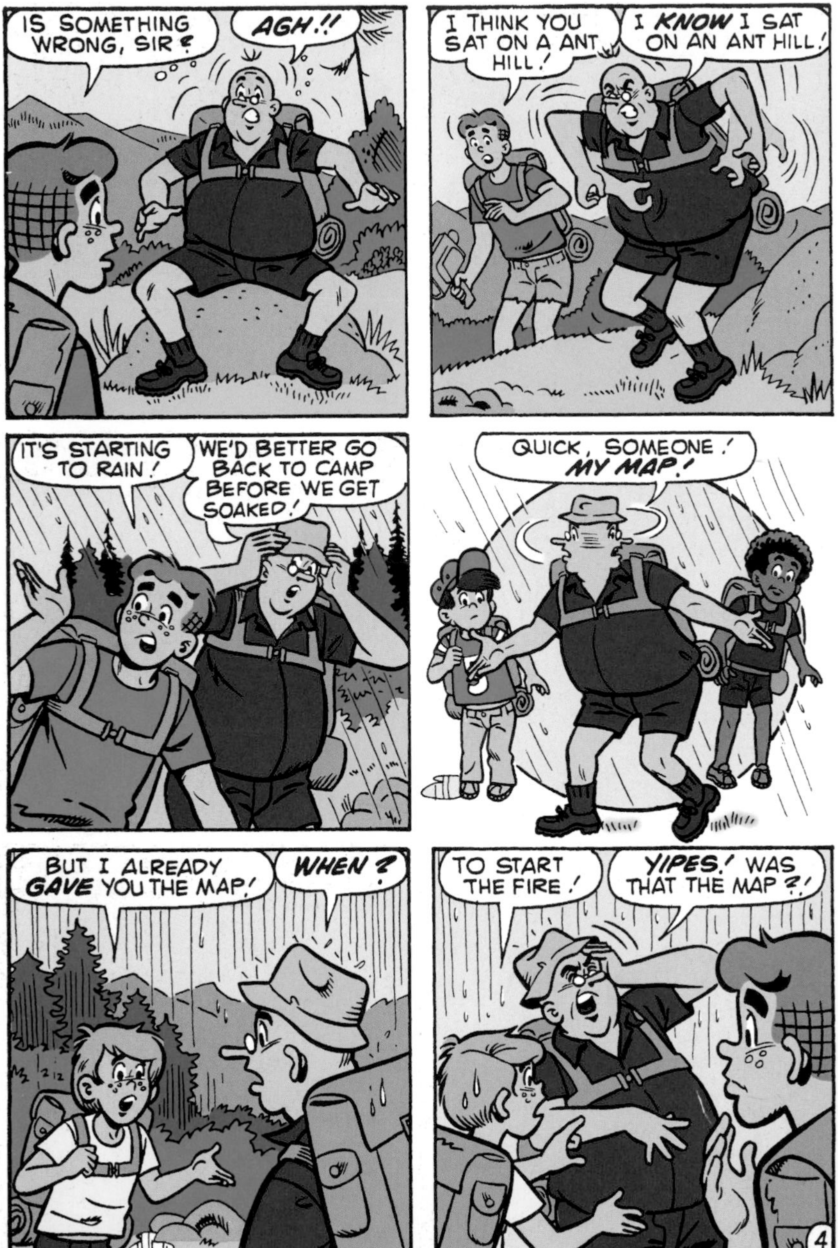
IS SOMETHING WRONG, SIR?
AGH!!
I THINK YOU SAT ON A ANT HILL!
I KNOW I SAT ON AN ANT HILL!
IT'S STARTING TO RAIN!
WE'D BETTER GO BACK TO CAMP BEFORE WE GET SOAKED!
QUICK, SOMEONE! MY MAP!
BUT I ALREADY GAVE YOU THE MAP!
WHEN?
TO START THE FIRE!
YIPES! WAS THAT THE MAP?!
4

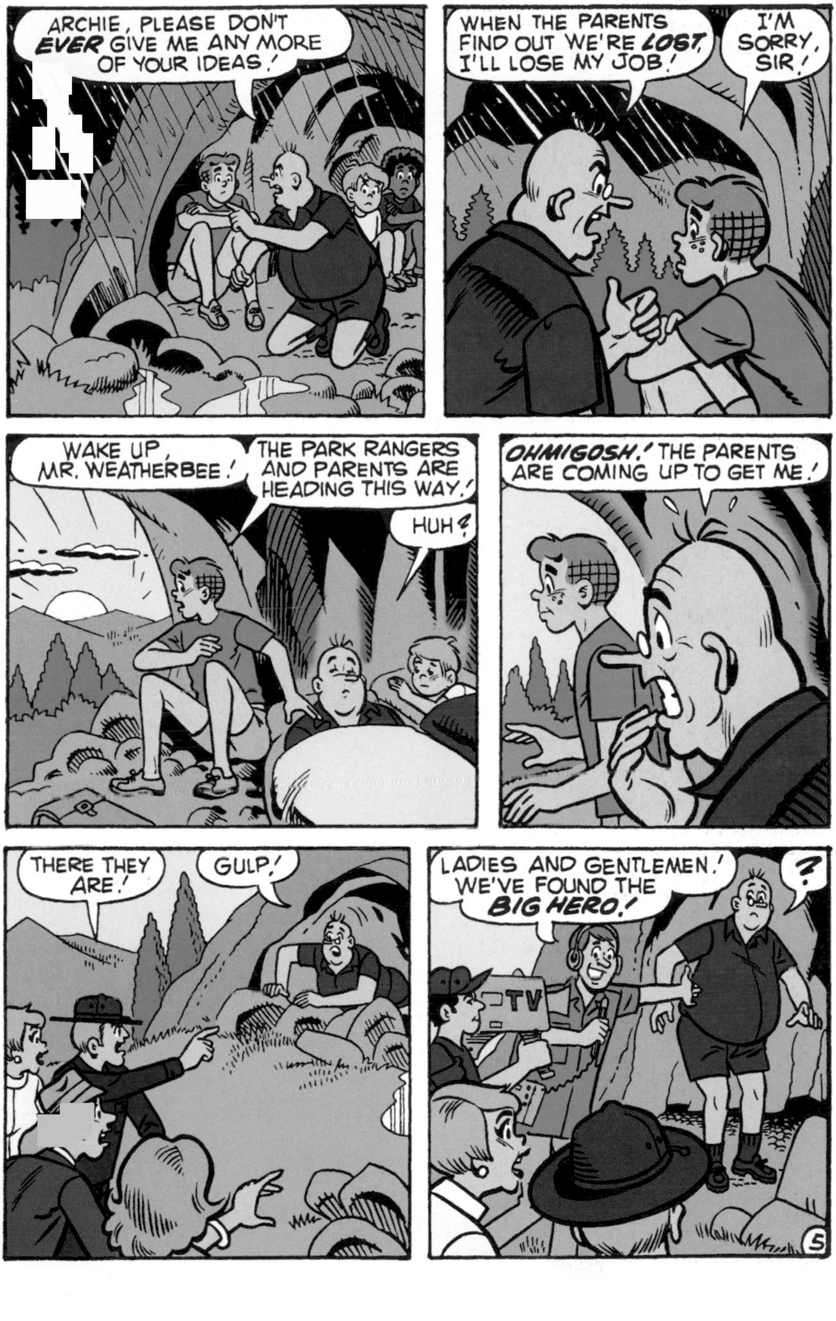
ARCHIE, PLEASE DON'T EVER GIVE ME ANY MORE OF YOUR IDEAS!
WHEN THE PARENTS FIND OUT WE'RE LOST, I'LL LOSE MY JOB!
I'M SORRY, SIR!
WAKE UP, MR. WEATHERBEE!
THE PARK RANGERS AND PARENTS ARE HEADING THIS WAY!
HUH?
OHMIGOSH! THE PARENTS ARE COMING UP TO GET ME!
THERE THEY ARE!
GULP!
LADIES AND GENTLEMEN! WE'VE FOUND THE BIG HERO!
?
TV
5

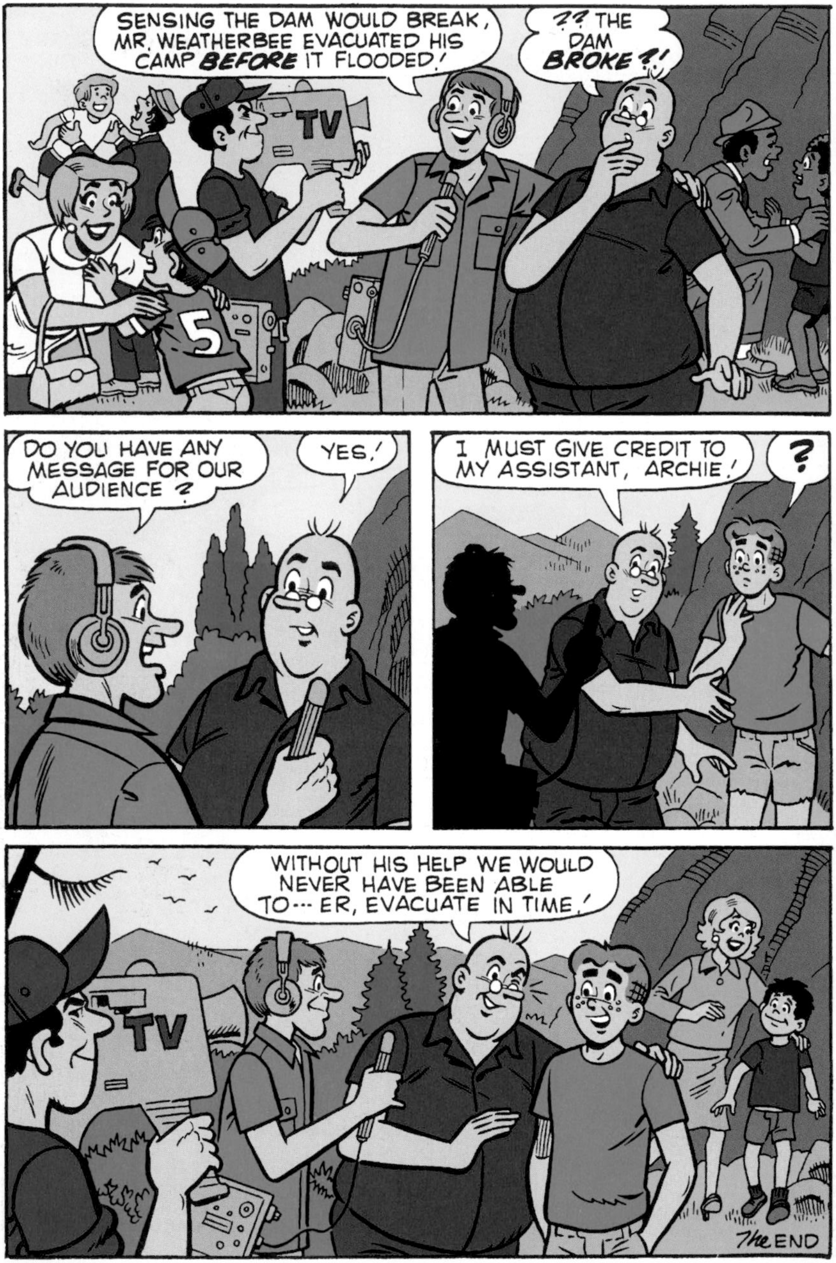
SENSING THE DAM WOULD BREAK, MR. WEATHERBEE EVACUATED HIS CAMP BEFORE IT FLOODED!
?? THE DAM BROKE ?!
TV
5
DO YOU HAVE ANY MESSAGE FOR OUR AUDIENCE ?
YES!
I MUST GIVE CREDIT TO MY ASSISTANT, ARCHIE!
?
WITHOUT HIS HELP WE WOULD NEVER HAVE BEEN ABLE TO--- ER, EVACUATE IN TIME!
TV
The END

Archie in VALIANT VICTORY

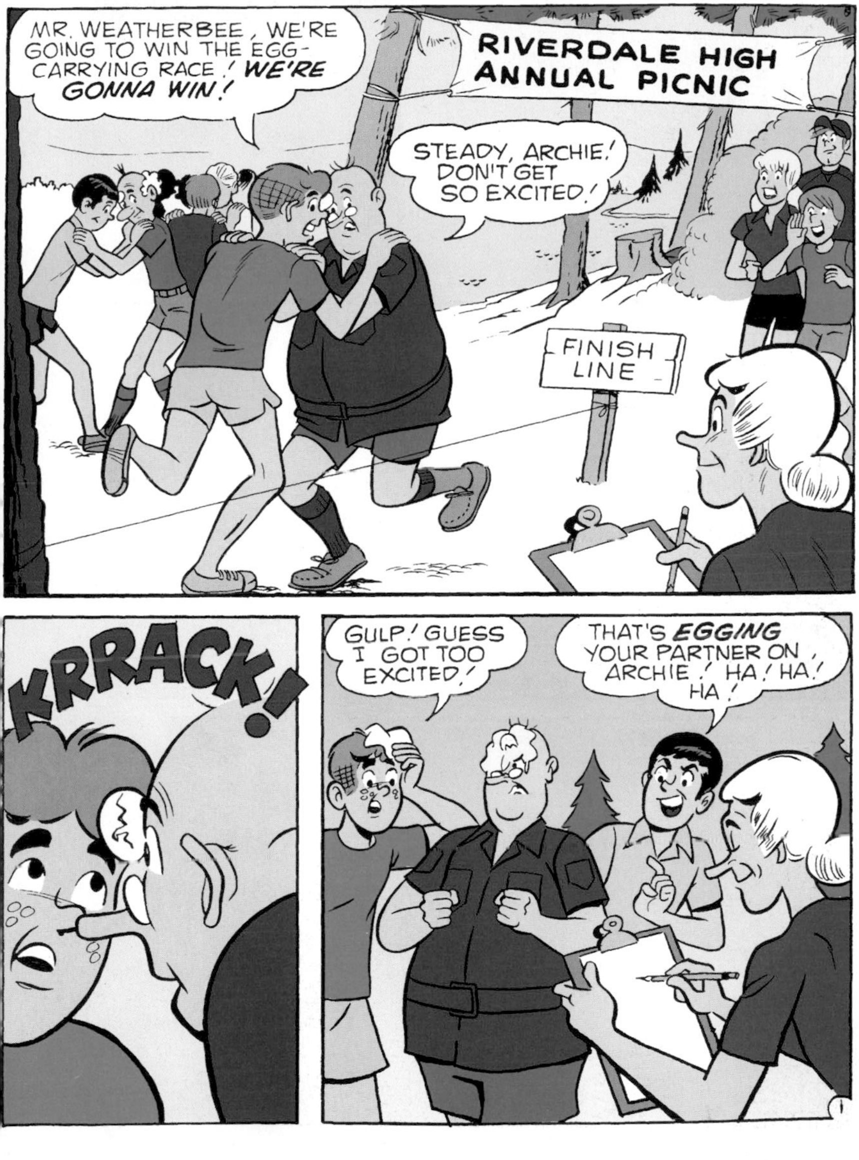
RIVERDALE HIGH ANNUAL PICNIC
MR. WEATHERBEE, WE'RE GOING TO WIN THE EGG-CARRYING RACE! WE'RE GONNA WIN!
STEADY, ARCHIE! DON'T GET SO EXCITED!
FINISH LINE
KRRACK!
GULP! GUESS I GOT TOO EXCITED!
THAT'S EGGING YOUR PARTNER ON, ARCHIE! HA! HA! HA!
1

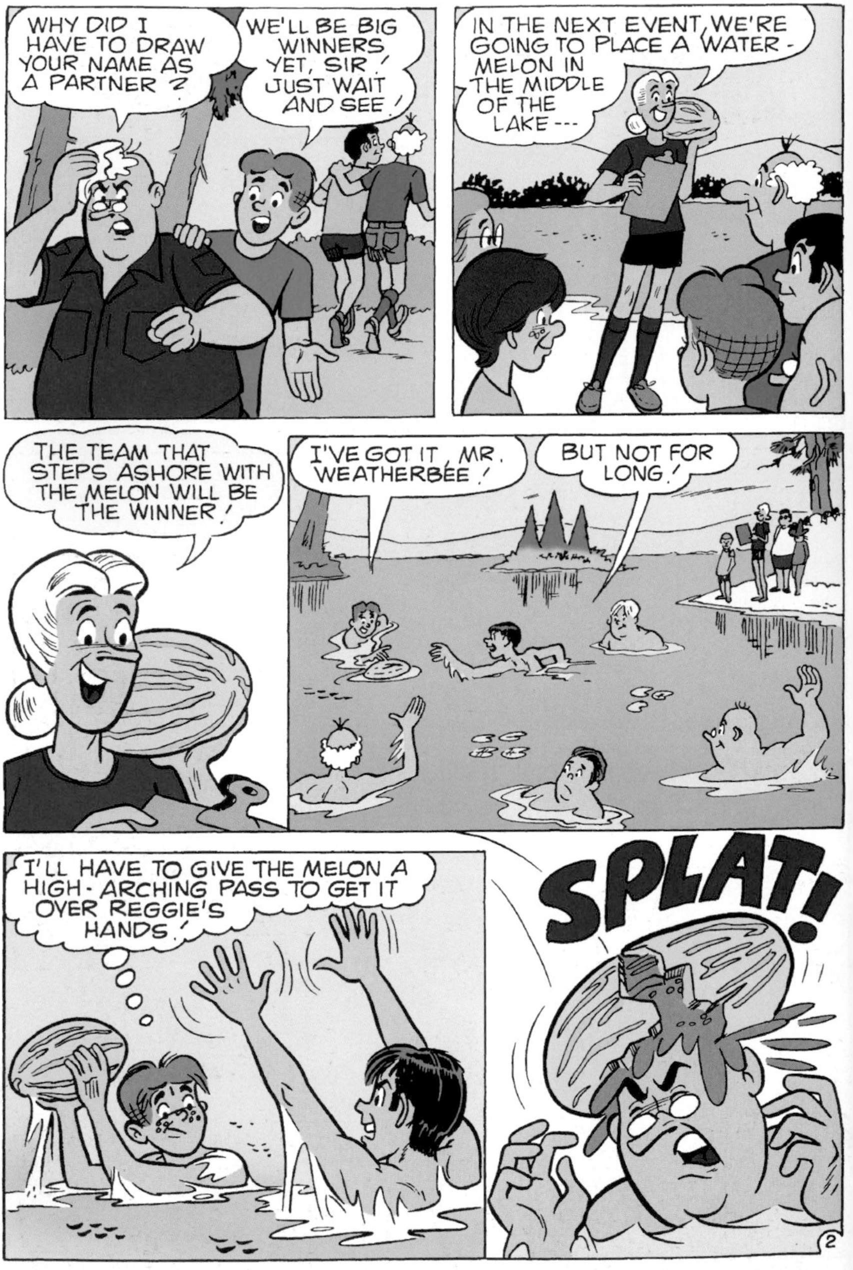
WHY DID I HAVE TO DRAW YOUR NAME AS A PARTNER ?
WE'LL BE BIG WINNERS YET, SIR ! JUST WAIT AND SEE !
IN THE NEXT EVENT, WE'RE GOING TO PLACE A WATER-MELON IN THE MIDDLE OF THE LAKE ---
THE TEAM THAT STEPS ASHORE WITH THE MELON WILL BE THE WINNER !
I'VE GOT IT, MR. WEATHERBEE !
BUT NOT FOR LONG !
I'LL HAVE TO GIVE THE MELON A HIGH-ARCHING PASS TO GET IT OVER REGGIE'S HANDS !
SPLAT!

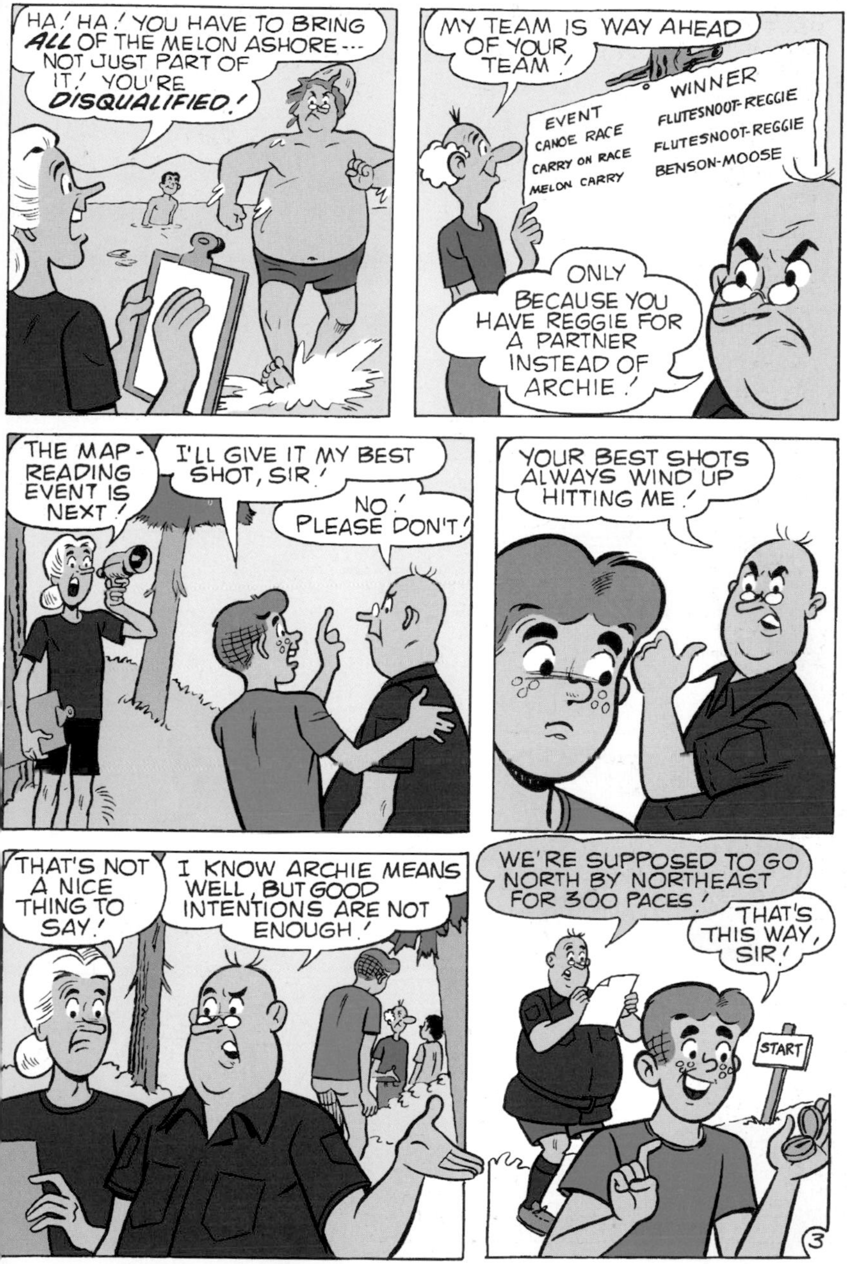
HA! HA! YOU HAVE TO BRING ALL OF THE MELON ASHORE--- NOT JUST PART OF IT! YOU'RE DISQUALIFIED!
MY TEAM IS WAY AHEAD OF YOUR TEAM!
EVENT WINNER
CANOE RACE FLUTESNOOT-REGGIE
CARRY ON RACE FLUTESNOOT-REGGIE
MELON CARRY BENSON-MOOSE
ONLY BECAUSE YOU HAVE REGGIE FOR A PARTNER INSTEAD OF ARCHIE!
THE MAP-READING EVENT IS NEXT!
I'LL GIVE IT MY BEST SHOT, SIR!
NO! PLEASE DON'T!
YOUR BEST SHOTS ALWAYS WIND UP HITTING ME!
THAT'S NOT A NICE THING TO SAY!
I KNOW ARCHIE MEANS WELL, BUT GOOD INTENTIONS ARE NOT ENOUGH!
WE'RE SUPPOSED TO GO NORTH BY NORTHEAST FOR 300 PACES!
THAT'S THIS WAY, SIR!
START
3

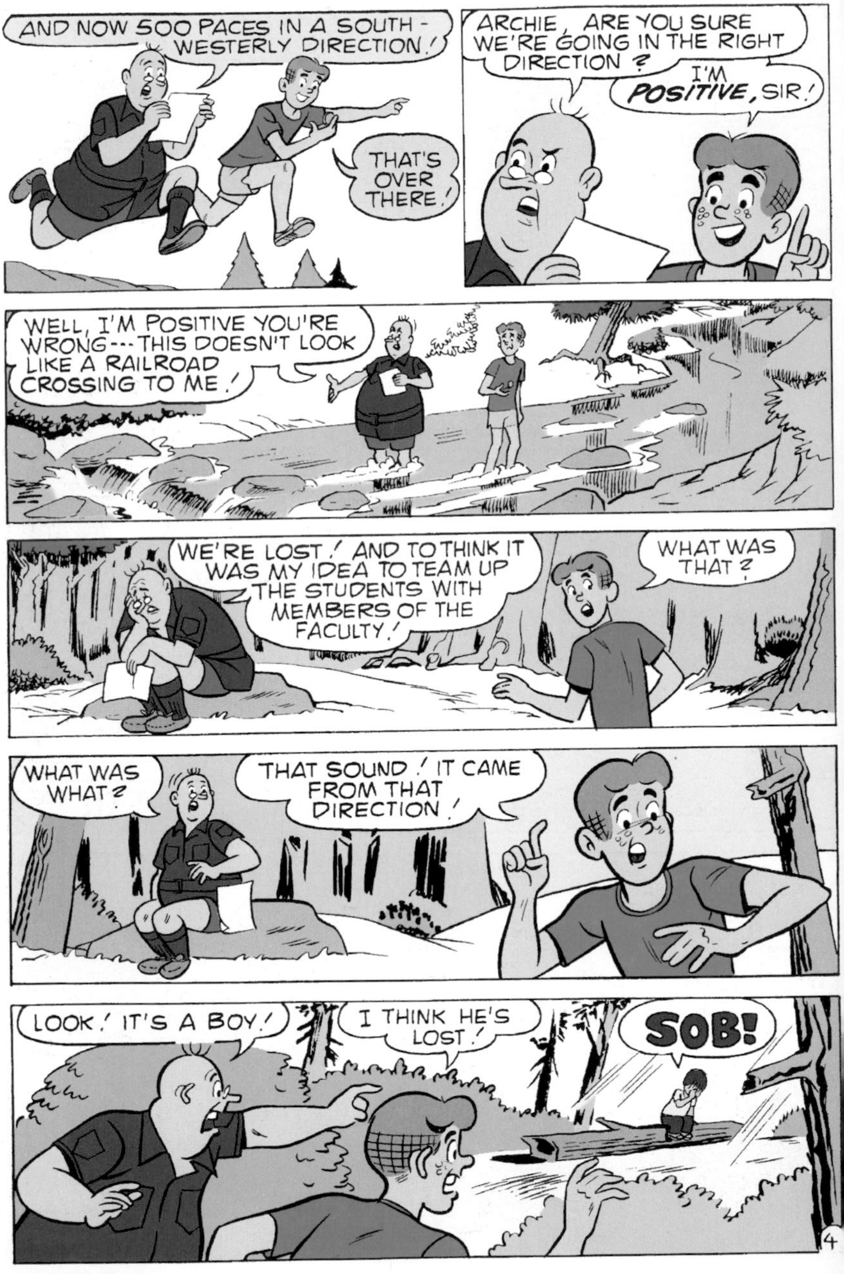
AND NOW 500 PACES IN A SOUTH-WESTERLY DIRECTION!
THAT'S OVER THERE!
ARCHIE, ARE YOU SURE WE'RE GOING IN THE RIGHT DIRECTION?
I'M *POSITIVE*, SIR!
WELL, I'M POSITIVE YOU'RE WRONG--- THIS DOESN'T LOOK LIKE A RAILROAD CROSSING TO ME!
WE'RE LOST! AND TO THINK IT WAS MY IDEA TO TEAM UP THE STUDENTS WITH MEMBERS OF THE FACULTY!
WHAT WAS THAT?
WHAT WAS WHAT?
THAT SOUND! IT CAME FROM THAT DIRECTION!
LOOK! IT'S A BOY!
I THINK HE'S LOST!
SOB!

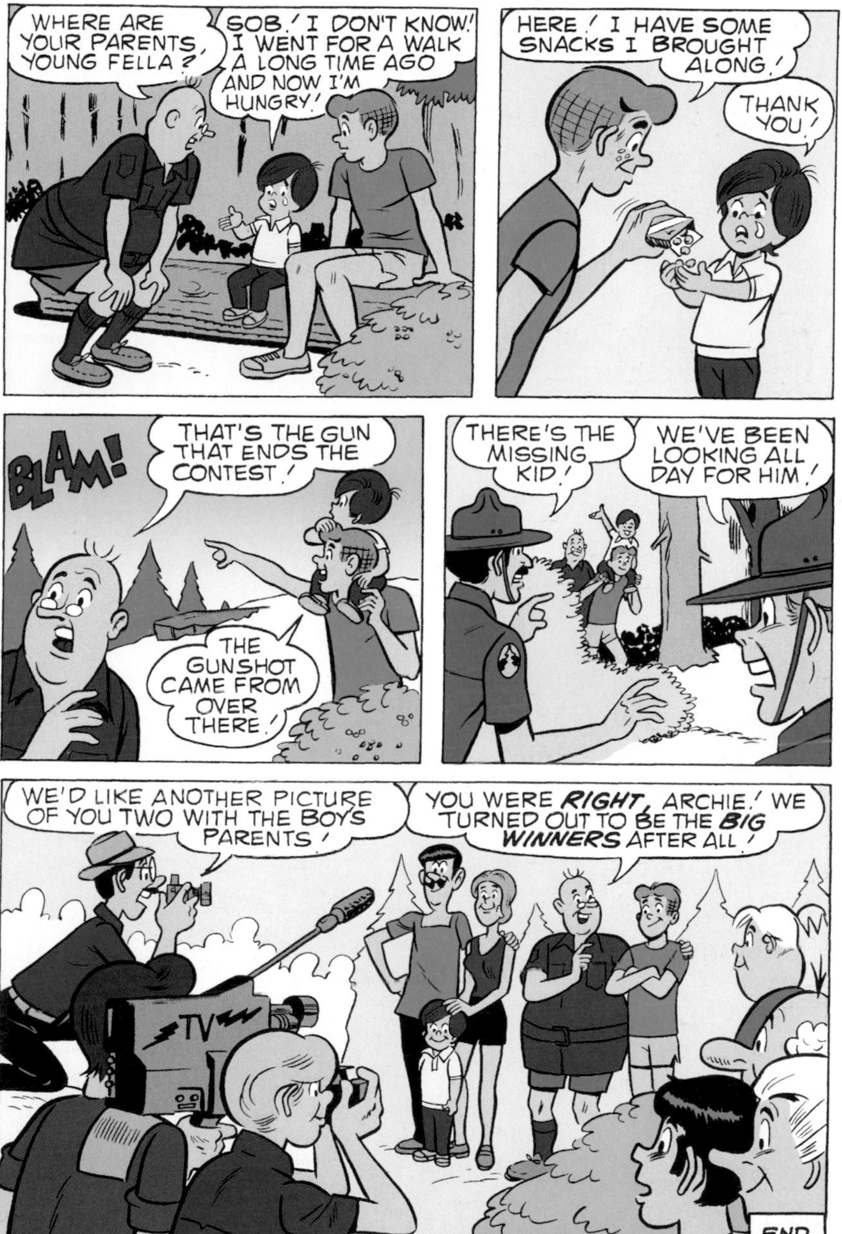
WHERE ARE YOUR PARENTS, YOUNG FELLA?
SOB! I DON'T KNOW! I WENT FOR A WALK A LONG TIME AGO AND NOW I'M HUNGRY!
HERE! I HAVE SOME SNACKS I BROUGHT ALONG!
THANK YOU!
BLAM!
THAT'S THE GUN THAT ENDS THE CONTEST!
THE GUNSHOT CAME FROM OVER THERE!
THERE'S THE MISSING KID!
WE'VE BEEN LOOKING ALL DAY FOR HIM!
WE'D LIKE ANOTHER PICTURE OF YOU TWO WITH THE BOYS PARENTS!
YOU WERE RIGHT, ARCHIE! WE TURNED OUT TO BE THE BIG WINNERS AFTER ALL!
TV
END.

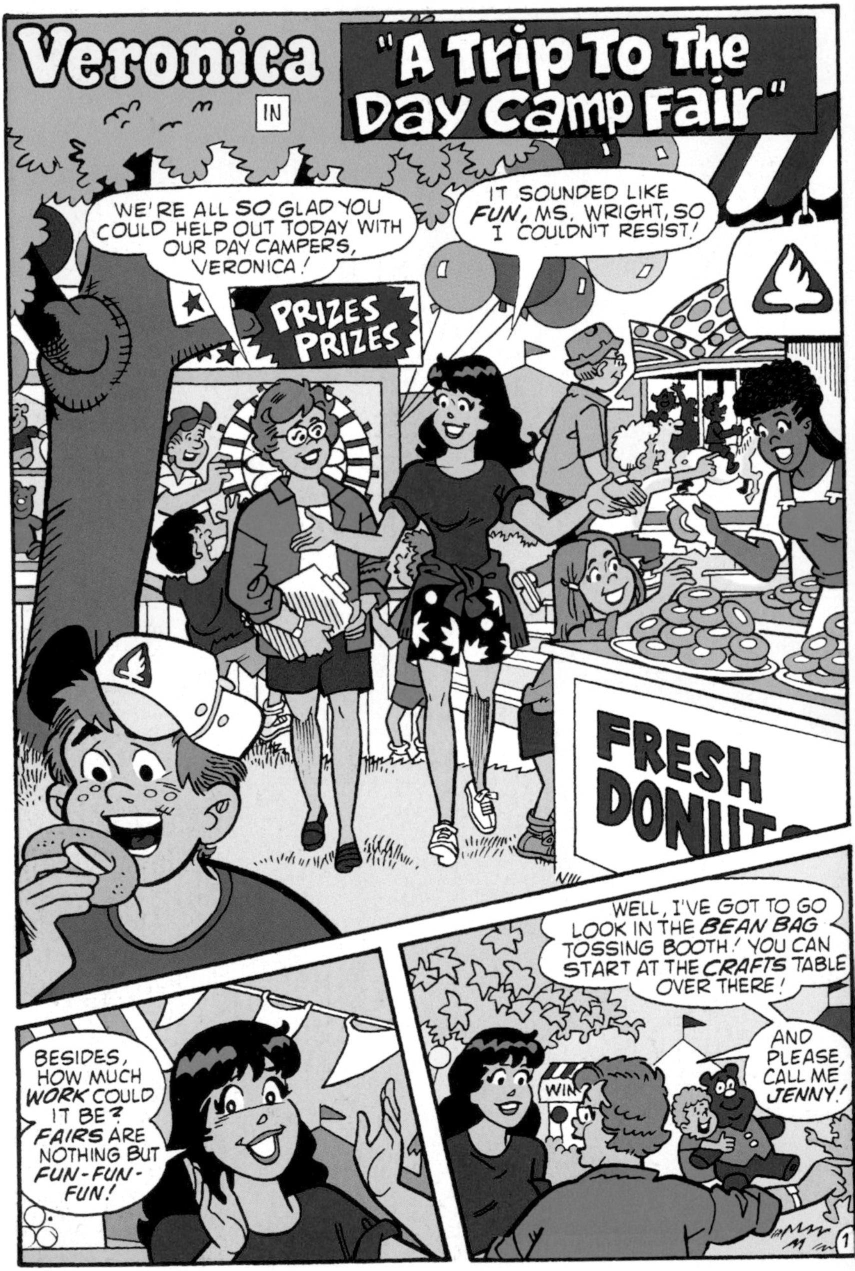
Veronica
IN
"A Trip To The Day Camp Fair"
WE'RE ALL SO GLAD YOU COULD HELP OUT TODAY WITH OUR DAY CAMPERS, VERONICA!
IT SOUNDED LIKE FUN, MS. WRIGHT, SO I COULDN'T RESIST!
PRIZES PRIZES
FRESH DONUT
BESIDES, HOW MUCH WORK COULD IT BE? FAIRS ARE NOTHING BUT FUN-FUN-FUN!
WELL, I'VE GOT TO GO LOOK IN THE BEAN BAG TOSSING BOOTH! YOU CAN START AT THE CRAFTS TABLE OVER THERE!
AND PLEASE, CALL ME JENNY!
WIN

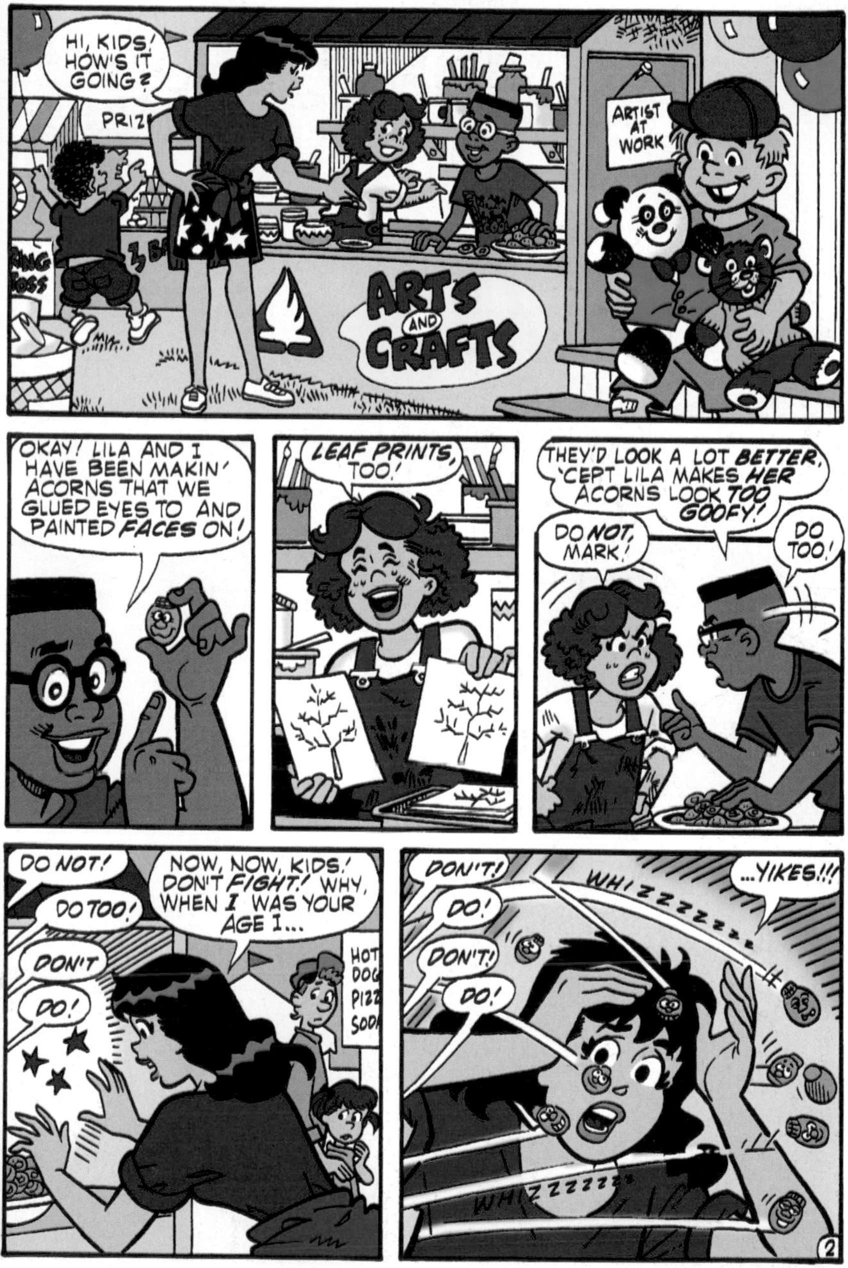
HI, KIDS! HOW'S IT GOING?
PRIZ
ARTIST AT WORK
ARTS AND CRAFTS
OKAY! LILA AND I HAVE BEEN MAKIN' ACORNS THAT WE GLUED EYES TO AND PAINTED FACES ON!
LEAF PRINTS, TOO!
THEY'D LOOK A LOT BETTER, 'CEPT LILA MAKES HER ACORNS LOOK TOO GOOFY!
DO NOT, MARK!
DO TOO!
DO NOT!
DO TOO!
NOW, NOW, KIDS! DON'T FIGHT! WHY, WHEN I WAS YOUR AGE I...
DON'T
DO!
HOT DOG PIZZ SODA
DON'T!
DO!
DON'T!
DO!
WHIZZZZZZZ
...YIKES!!!
WHIZZZZZZZ
2

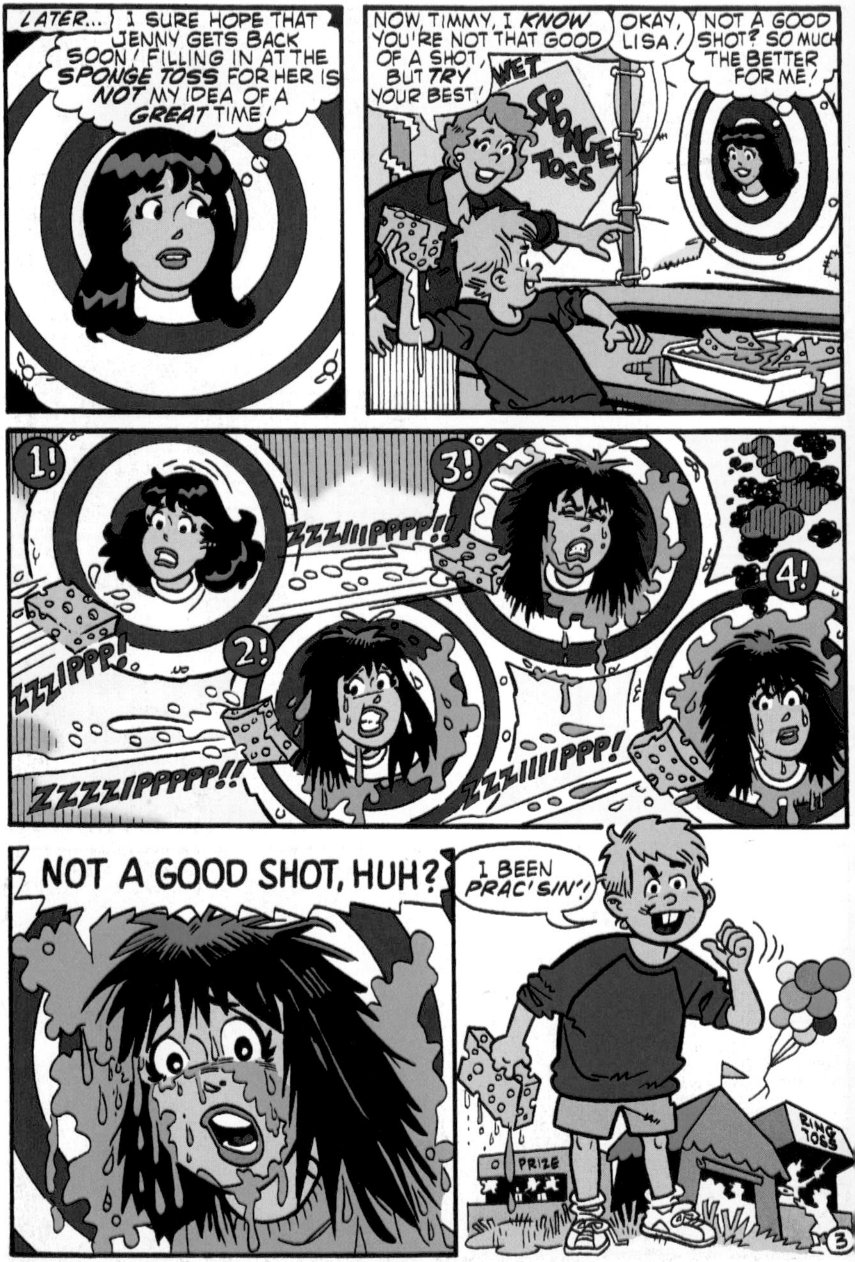

LATER...
I SURE HOPE THAT JENNY GETS BACK SOON! FILLING IN AT THE SPONGE TOSS FOR HER IS NOT MY IDEA OF A GREAT TIME!
NOW, TIMMY, I KNOW YOU'RE NOT THAT GOOD OF A SHOT, BUT TRY YOUR BEST!
WET SPONGE TOSS
OKAY, LISA!
NOT A GOOD SHOT? SO MUCH THE BETTER FOR ME!
1!
ZZZIPPP!
2!
ZZZZIPPPPPP!!
3!
ZZZIIIPPPP!!
4!
ZZZIIIIPPP!
NOT A GOOD SHOT, HUH?
I BEEN PRAC'SIN'!
PRIZE
RING TOSS

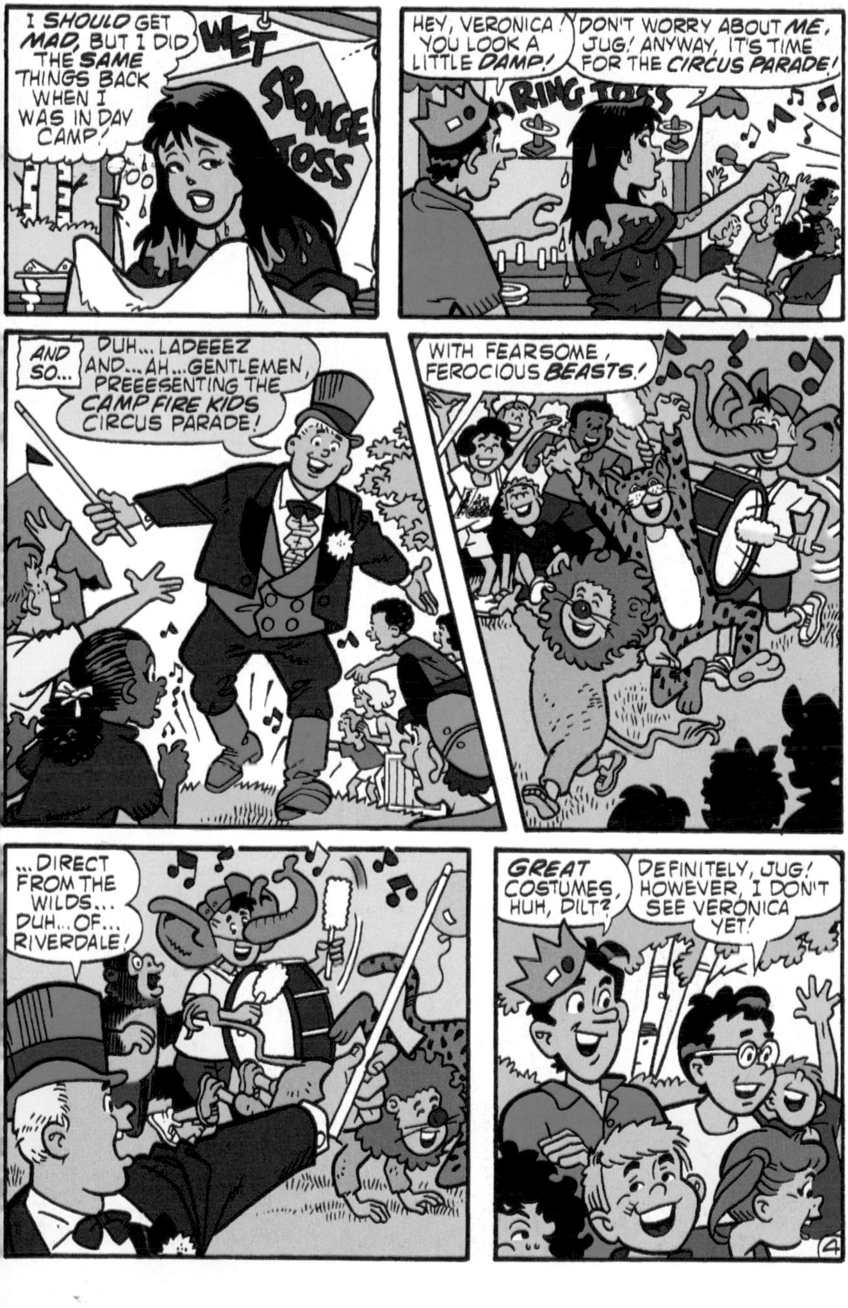
I SHOULD GET MAD, BUT I DID THE SAME THINGS BACK WHEN I WAS IN DAY CAMP!
WET SPONGE TOSS
HEY, VERONICA! YOU LOOK A LITTLE DAMP!
DON'T WORRY ABOUT ME, JUG! ANYWAY, IT'S TIME FOR THE CIRCUS PARADE!
RING TOSS
AND SO...
DUH... LADEEEZ AND... AH... GENTLEMEN, PREEEESENTING THE CAMP FIRE KIDS CIRCUS PARADE!
WITH FEARSOME, FEROCIOUS BEASTS!
...DIRECT FROM THE WILDS... DUH... OF... RIVERDALE!
GREAT COSTUMES, HUH, DILT?
DEFINITELY, JUG! HOWEVER, I DON'T SEE VERONICA YET!
4

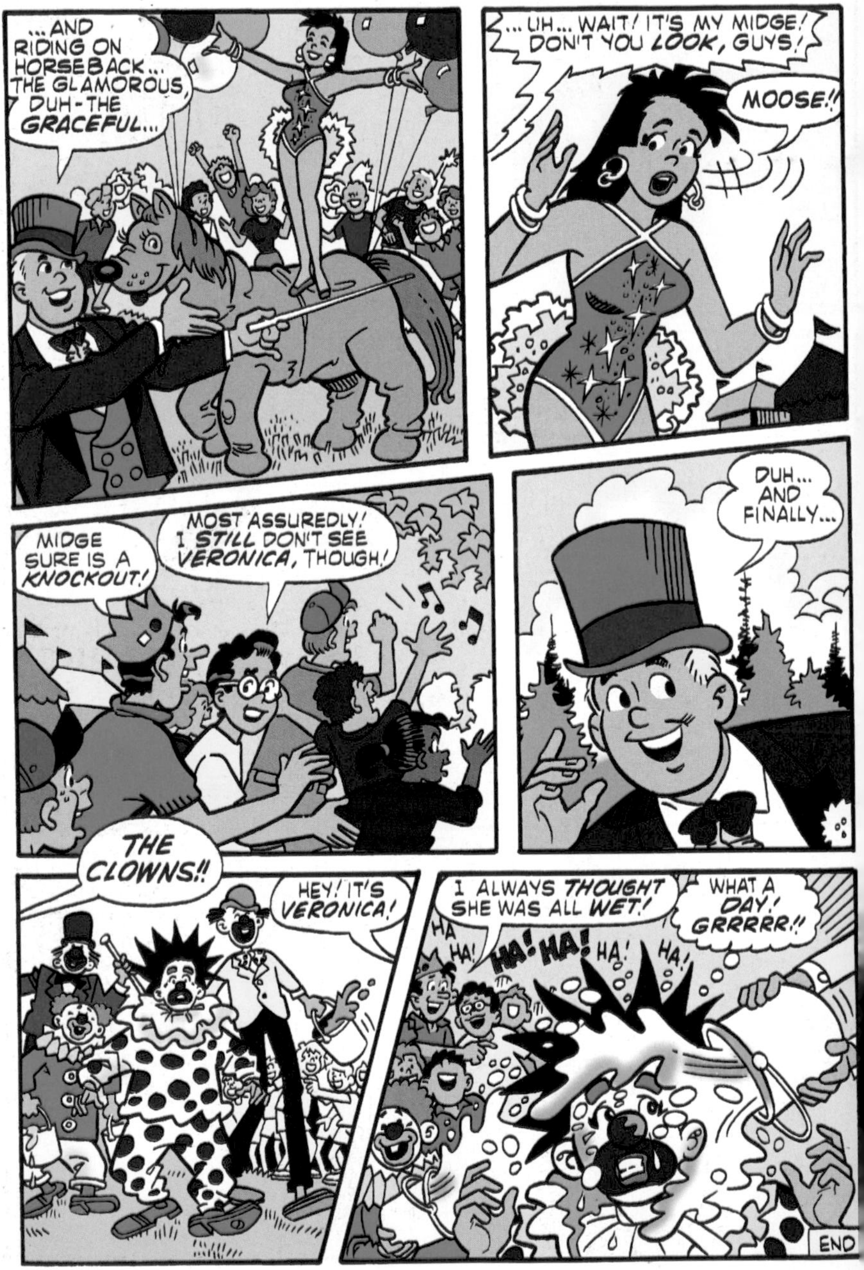
...AND RIDING ON HORSEBACK... THE GLAMOROUS, DUH-THE GRACEFUL...
...UH... WAIT! IT'S MY MIDGE! DON'T YOU LOOK, GUYS!
MOOSE!!
MIDGE SURE IS A KNOCKOUT!
MOST ASSUREDLY! I STILL DON'T SEE VERONICA, THOUGH!
DUH... AND FINALLY...
THE CLOWNS!!
HEY! IT'S VERONICA!
I ALWAYS THOUGHT SHE WAS ALL WET!
WHAT A DAY! GRRRRR!!
HA HA!
HA! HA!
HA!
HA!
END

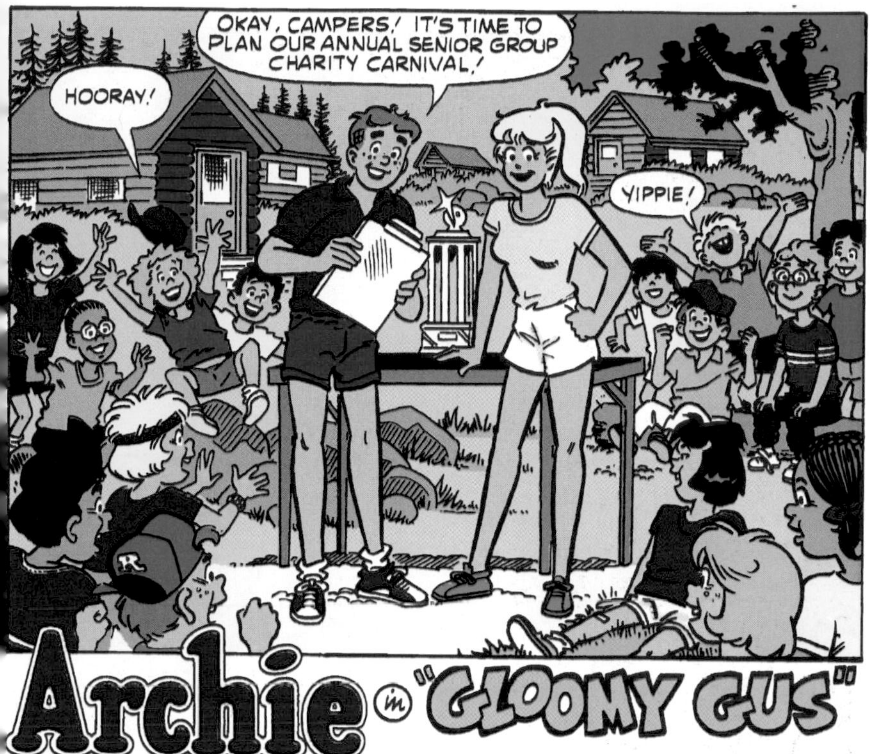
OKAY, CAMPERS! IT'S TIME TO PLAN OUR ANNUAL SENIOR GROUP CHARITY CARNIVAL!
HOORAY!
YIPPIE!

Archie in "GLOOMY GUS"

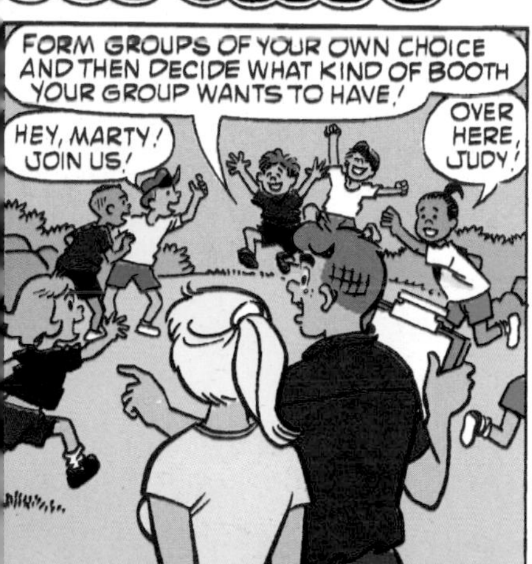
FORM GROUPS OF YOUR OWN CHOICE AND THEN DECIDE WHAT KIND OF BOOTH YOUR GROUP WANTS TO HAVE!
HEY, MARTY! JOIN US!
OVER HERE, JUDY!

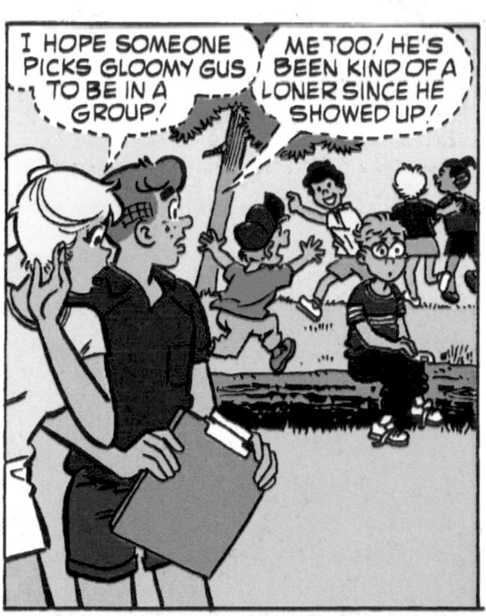
I HOPE SOMEONE PICKS GLOOMY GUS TO BE IN A GROUP!
ME TOO! HE'S BEEN KIND OF A LONER SINCE HE SHOWED UP!

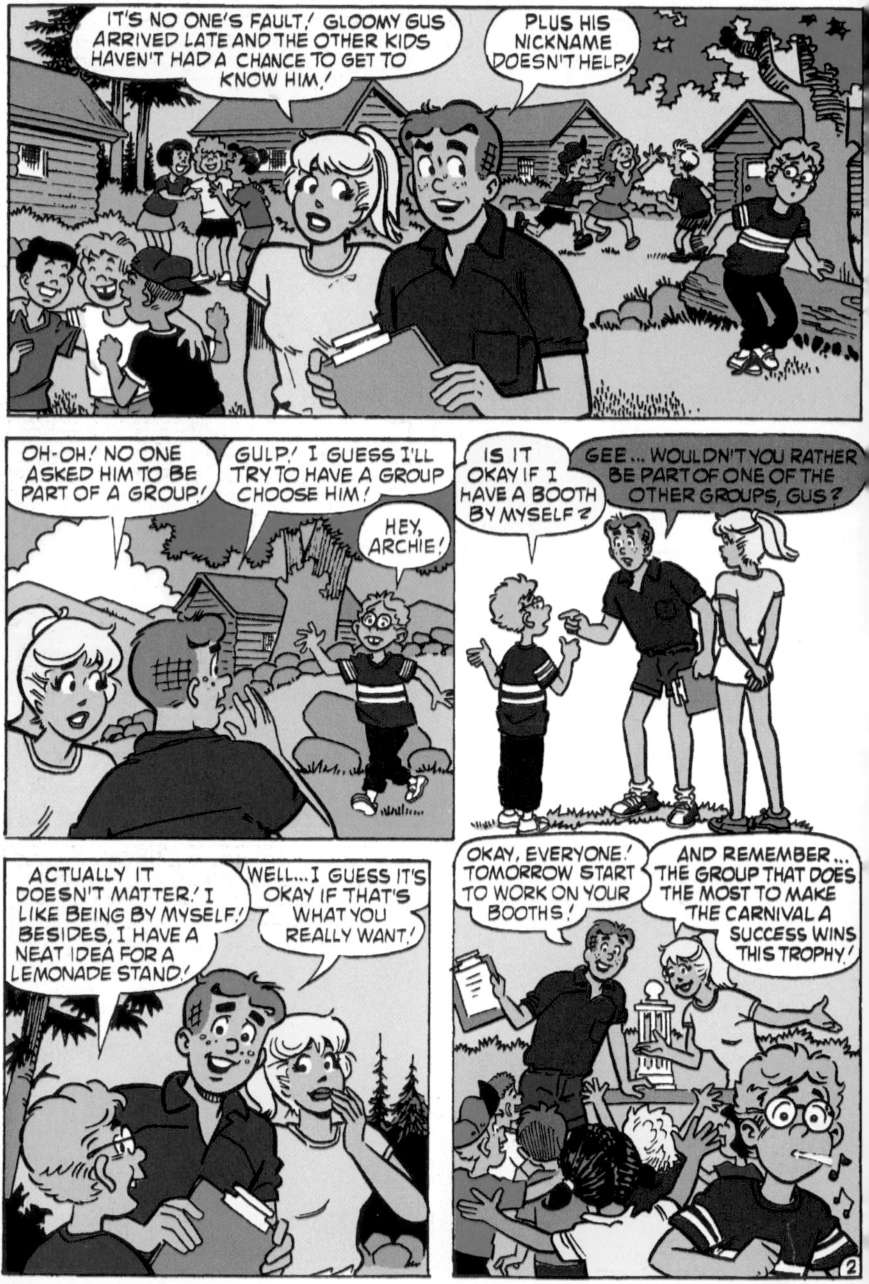
IT'S NO ONE'S FAULT! GLOOMY GUS ARRIVED LATE AND THE OTHER KIDS HAVEN'T HAD A CHANCE TO GET TO KNOW HIM!
PLUS HIS NICKNAME DOESN'T HELP!
OH-OH! NO ONE ASKED HIM TO BE PART OF A GROUP!
GULP! I GUESS I'LL TRY TO HAVE A GROUP CHOOSE HIM!
HEY, ARCHIE!
IS IT OKAY IF I HAVE A BOOTH BY MYSELF?
GEE... WOULDN'T YOU RATHER BE PART OF ONE OF THE OTHER GROUPS, GUS?
ACTUALLY IT DOESN'T MATTER! I LIKE BEING BY MYSELF! BESIDES, I HAVE A NEAT IDEA FOR A LEMONADE STAND!
WELL... I GUESS IT'S OKAY IF THAT'S WHAT YOU REALLY WANT!
OKAY, EVERYONE! TOMORROW START TO WORK ON YOUR BOOTHS!
AND REMEMBER... THE GROUP THAT DOES THE MOST TO MAKE THE CARNIVAL A SUCCESS WINS THIS TROPHY!
2

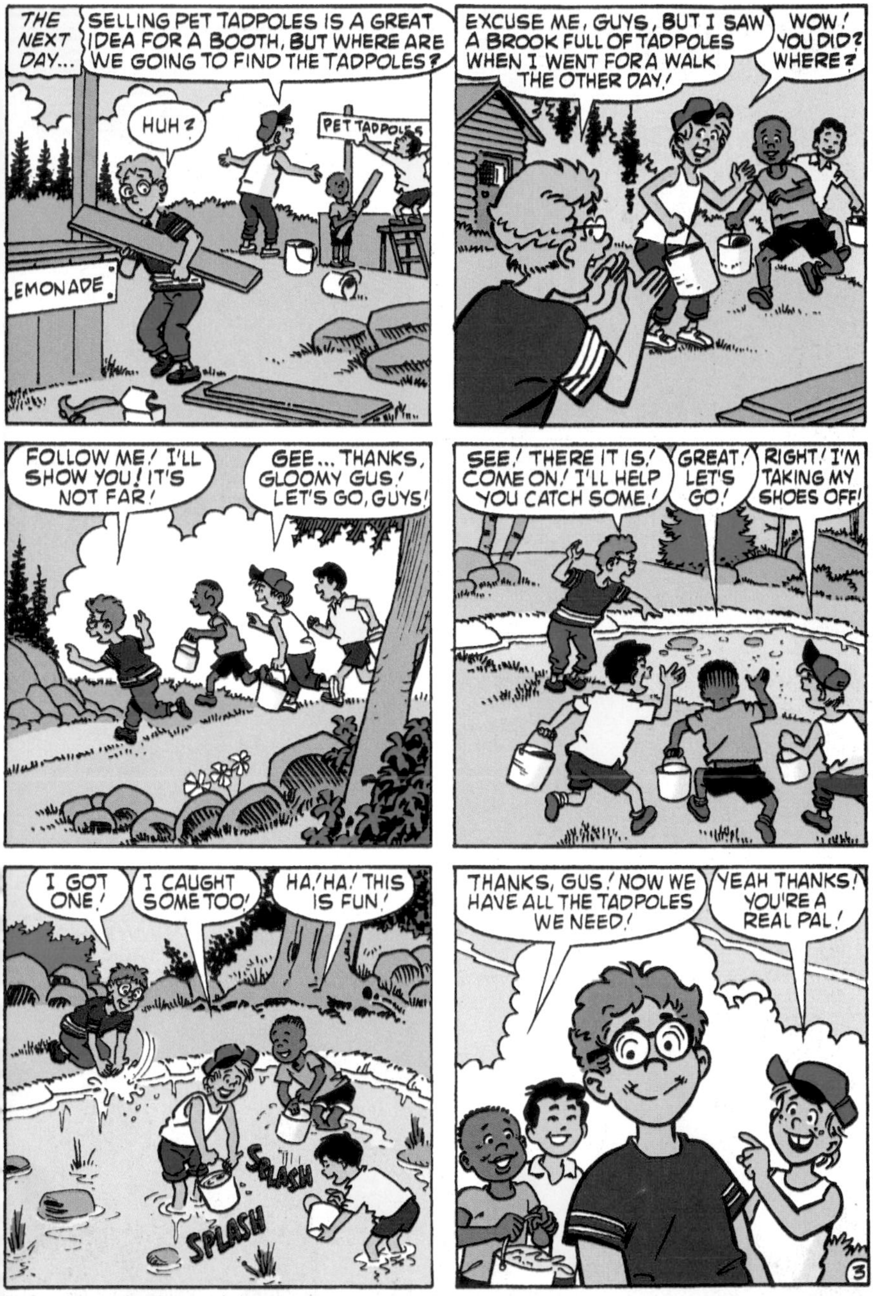
THE NEXT DAY...
SELLING PET TADPOLES IS A GREAT IDEA FOR A BOOTH, BUT WHERE ARE WE GOING TO FIND THE TADPOLES?
HUH?
PET TADPOLES
LEMONADE
EXCUSE ME, GUYS, BUT I SAW A BROOK FULL OF TADPOLES WHEN I WENT FOR A WALK THE OTHER DAY!
WOW! YOU DID? WHERE?
FOLLOW ME! I'LL SHOW YOU! IT'S NOT FAR!
GEE... THANKS, GLOOMY GUS! LET'S GO, GUYS!
SEE! THERE IT IS! COME ON! I'LL HELP YOU CATCH SOME!
GREAT! LET'S GO!
RIGHT! I'M TAKING MY SHOES OFF!
I GOT ONE!
I CAUGHT SOME TOO!
HA! HA! THIS IS FUN!
SPLASH
SPLASH
THANKS, GUS! NOW WE HAVE ALL THE TADPOLES WE NEED!
YEAH THANKS! YOU'RE A REAL PAL!

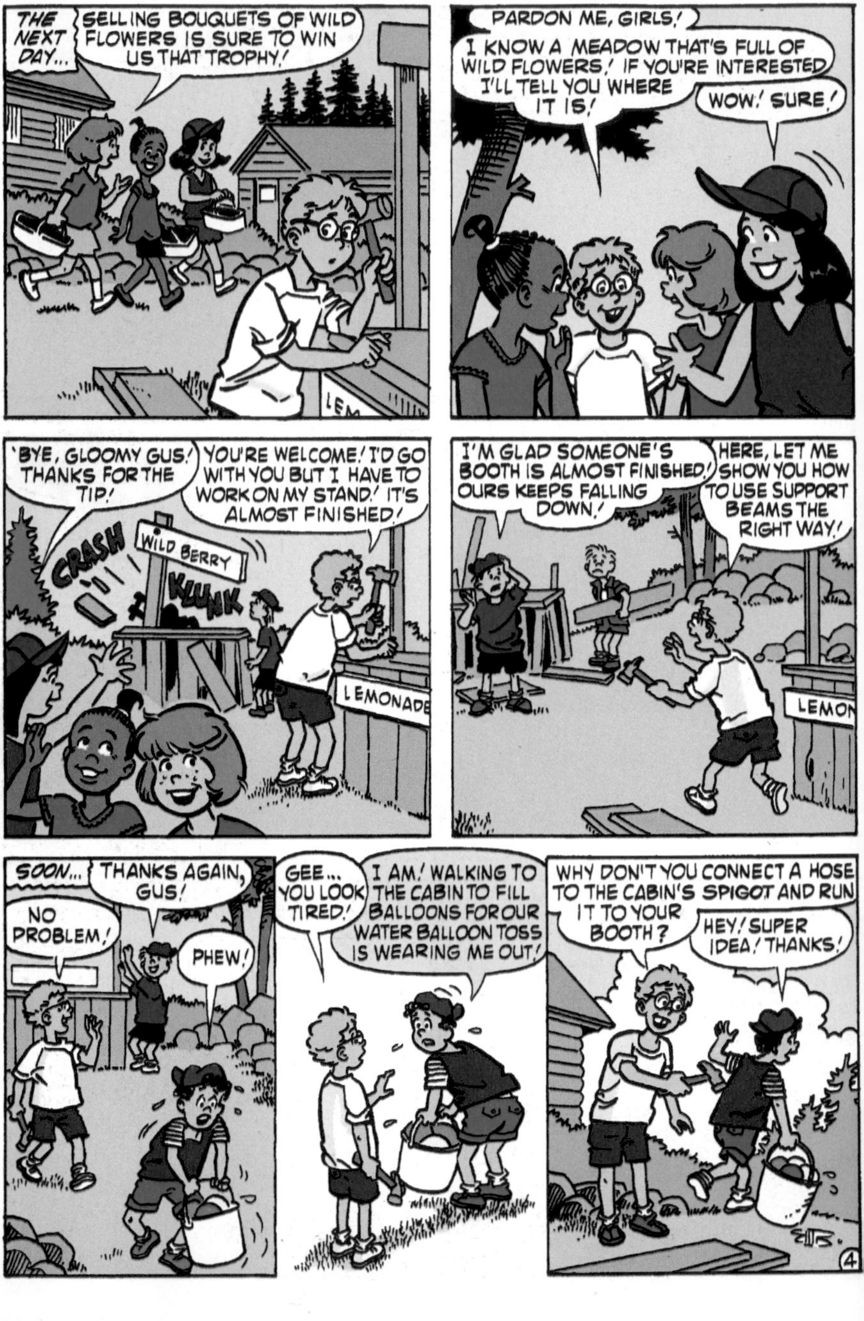
THE NEXT DAY...
SELLING BOUQUETS OF WILD FLOWERS IS SURE TO WIN US THAT TROPHY!
LEM
PARDON ME, GIRLS!
I KNOW A MEADOW THAT'S FULL OF WILD FLOWERS! IF YOU'RE INTERESTED I'LL TELL YOU WHERE IT IS!
WOW! SURE!
'BYE, GLOOMY GUS! THANKS FOR THE TIP!
YOU'RE WELCOME! I'D GO WITH YOU BUT I HAVE TO WORK ON MY STAND! IT'S ALMOST FINISHED!
CRASH
WILD BERRY
KLUNK
LEMONADE
I'M GLAD SOMEONE'S BOOTH IS ALMOST FINISHED! OURS KEEPS FALLING DOWN!
HERE, LET ME SHOW YOU HOW TO USE SUPPORT BEAMS THE RIGHT WAY!
LEMON
SOON...
THANKS AGAIN, GUS!
NO PROBLEM!
PHEW!
GEE... YOU LOOK TIRED!
I AM! WALKING TO THE CABIN TO FILL BALLOONS FOR OUR WATER BALLOON TOSS IS WEARING ME OUT!
WHY DON'T YOU CONNECT A HOSE TO THE CABIN'S SPIGOT AND RUN IT TO YOUR BOOTH?
HEY! SUPER IDEA! THANKS!

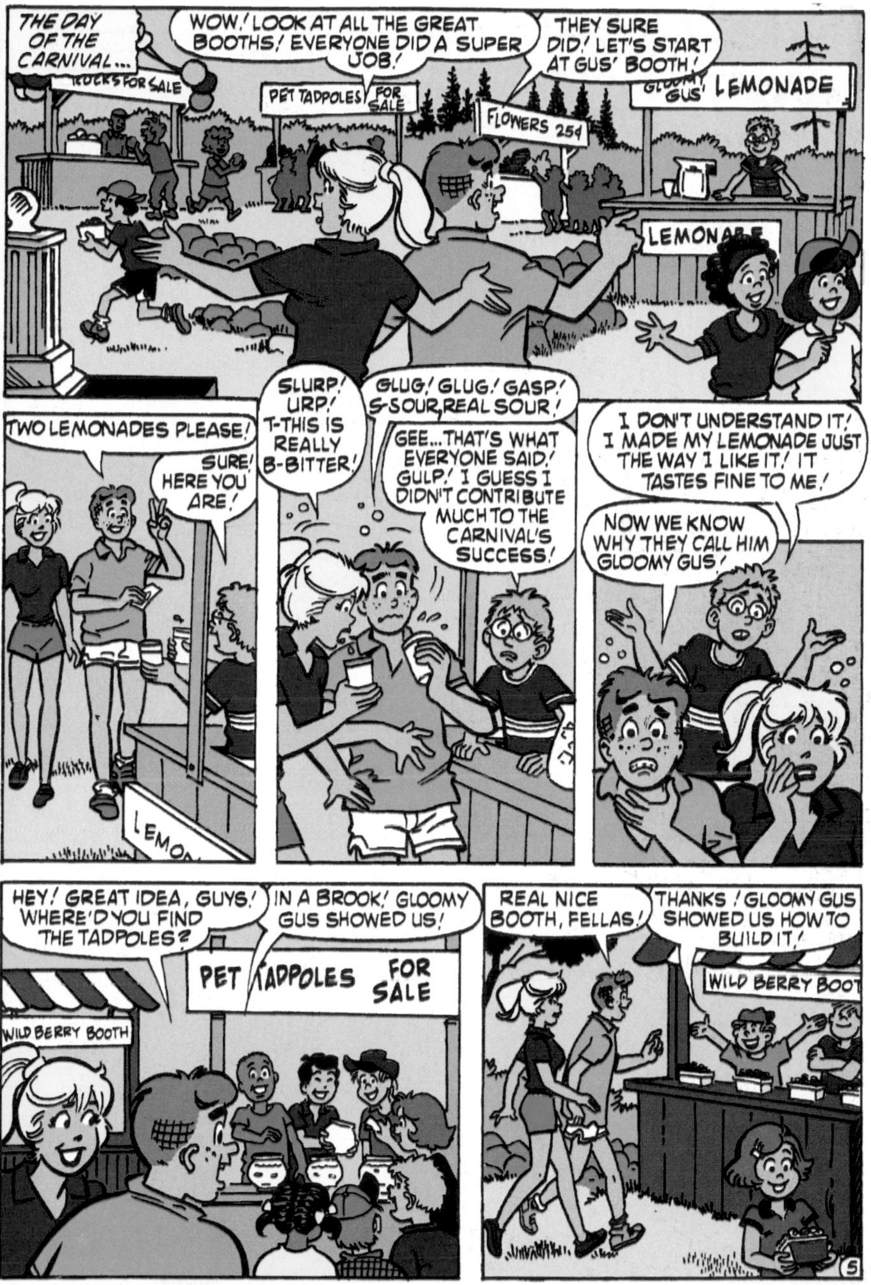
THE DAY OF THE CARNIVAL...
WOW! LOOK AT ALL THE GREAT BOOTHS! EVERYONE DID A SUPER JOB!
THEY SURE DID! LET'S START AT GUS' BOOTH!
ROCKS FOR SALE
PET TADPOLES FOR SALE
FLOWERS 25¢
GLOOMY GUS' LEMONADE
LEMONADE
TWO LEMONADES PLEASE!
SURE! HERE YOU ARE!
SLURP! URP! T-THIS IS REALLY B-BITTER!
GLUG! GLUG! GASP! S-SOUR, REAL SOUR!
GEE...THAT'S WHAT EVERYONE SAID! GULP! I GUESS I DIDN'T CONTRIBUTE MUCH TO THE CARNIVAL'S SUCCESS!
I DON'T UNDERSTAND IT! I MADE MY LEMONADE JUST THE WAY I LIKE IT! IT TASTES FINE TO ME!
NOW WE KNOW WHY THEY CALL HIM GLOOMY GUS!
HEY! GREAT IDEA, GUYS! WHERE'D YOU FIND THE TADPOLES?
IN A BROOK! GLOOMY GUS SHOWED US!
PET TADPOLES FOR SALE
WILD BERRY BOOTH
REAL NICE BOOTH, FELLAS!
THANKS! GLOOMY GUS SHOWED US HOW TO BUILD IT!
WILD BERRY BOOT

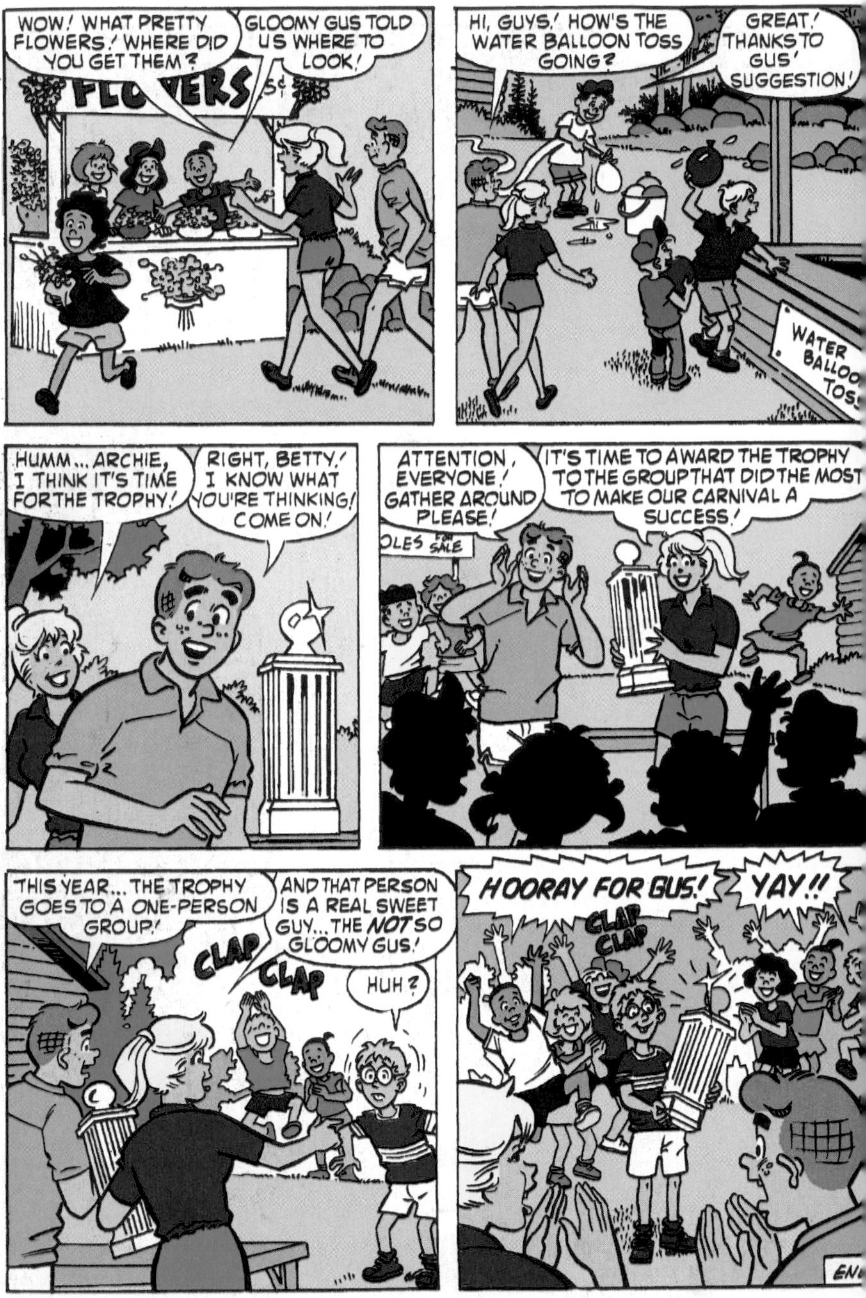

WOW! WHAT PRETTY FLOWERS! WHERE DID YOU GET THEM?
GLOOMY GUS TOLD US WHERE TO LOOK!
FLOWERS 5¢
HI, GUYS! HOW'S THE WATER BALLOON TOSS GOING?
GREAT! THANKS TO GUS' SUGGESTION!
WATER BALLOO TOS
HUMM... ARCHIE, I THINK IT'S TIME FOR THE TROPHY!
RIGHT, BETTY! I KNOW WHAT YOU'RE THINKING! COME ON!
ATTENTION, EVERYONE! GATHER AROUND PLEASE!
IT'S TIME TO AWARD THE TROPHY TO THE GROUP THAT DID THE MOST TO MAKE OUR CARNIVAL A SUCCESS!
OLES FOR SALE
THIS YEAR... THE TROPHY GOES TO A ONE-PERSON GROUP!
AND THAT PERSON IS A REAL SWEET GUY... THE NOT SO GLOOMY GUS!
CLAP CLAP
HUH?
HOORAY FOR GUS!
YAY!!
CLAP CLAP
EN

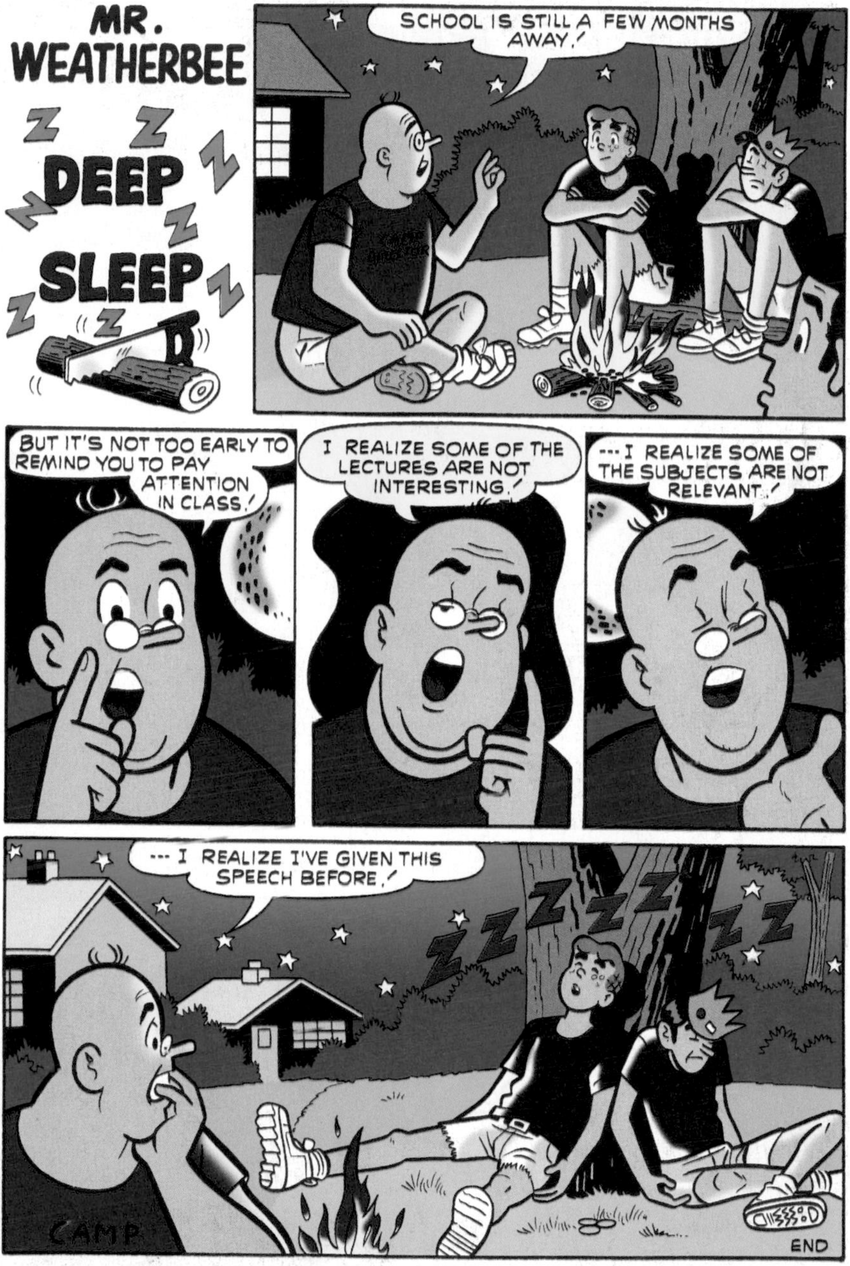
MR. WEATHERBEE
DEEP SLEEP
SCHOOL IS STILL A FEW MONTHS AWAY.!
BUT IT'S NOT TOO EARLY TO REMIND YOU TO PAY ATTENTION IN CLASS.!
I REALIZE SOME OF THE LECTURES ARE NOT INTERESTING.!
---I REALIZE SOME OF THE SUBJECTS ARE NOT RELEVANT.!
--- I REALIZE I'VE GIVEN THIS SPEECH BEFORE.!
CAMP
END

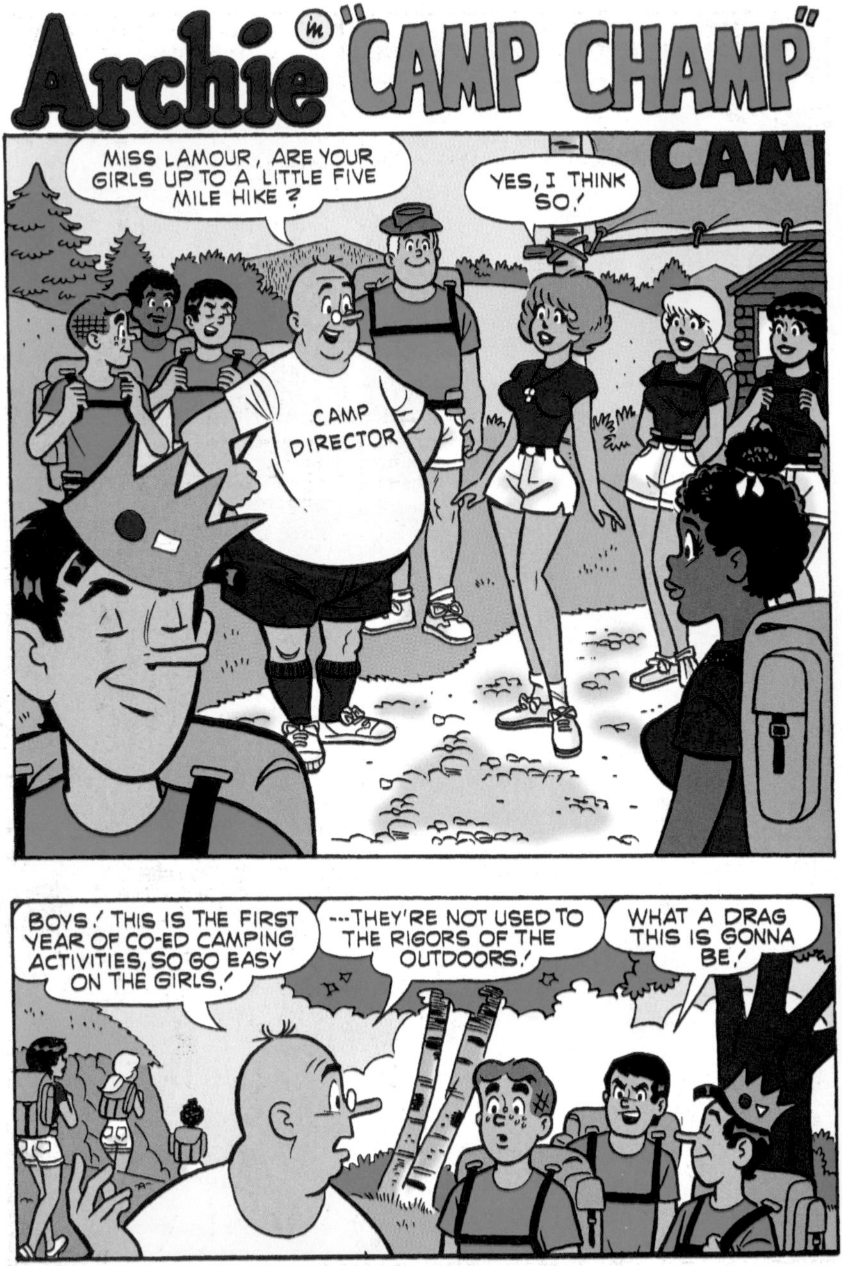
Archie in "CAMP CHAMP"
CAM
MISS LAMOUR, ARE YOUR GIRLS UP TO A LITTLE FIVE MILE HIKE ?
YES, I THINK SO!
CAMP DIRECTOR
BOYS! THIS IS THE FIRST YEAR OF CO-ED CAMPING ACTIVITIES, SO GO EASY ON THE GIRLS!
---THEY'RE NOT USED TO THE RIGORS OF THE OUTDOORS!
WHAT A DRAG THIS IS GONNA BE!

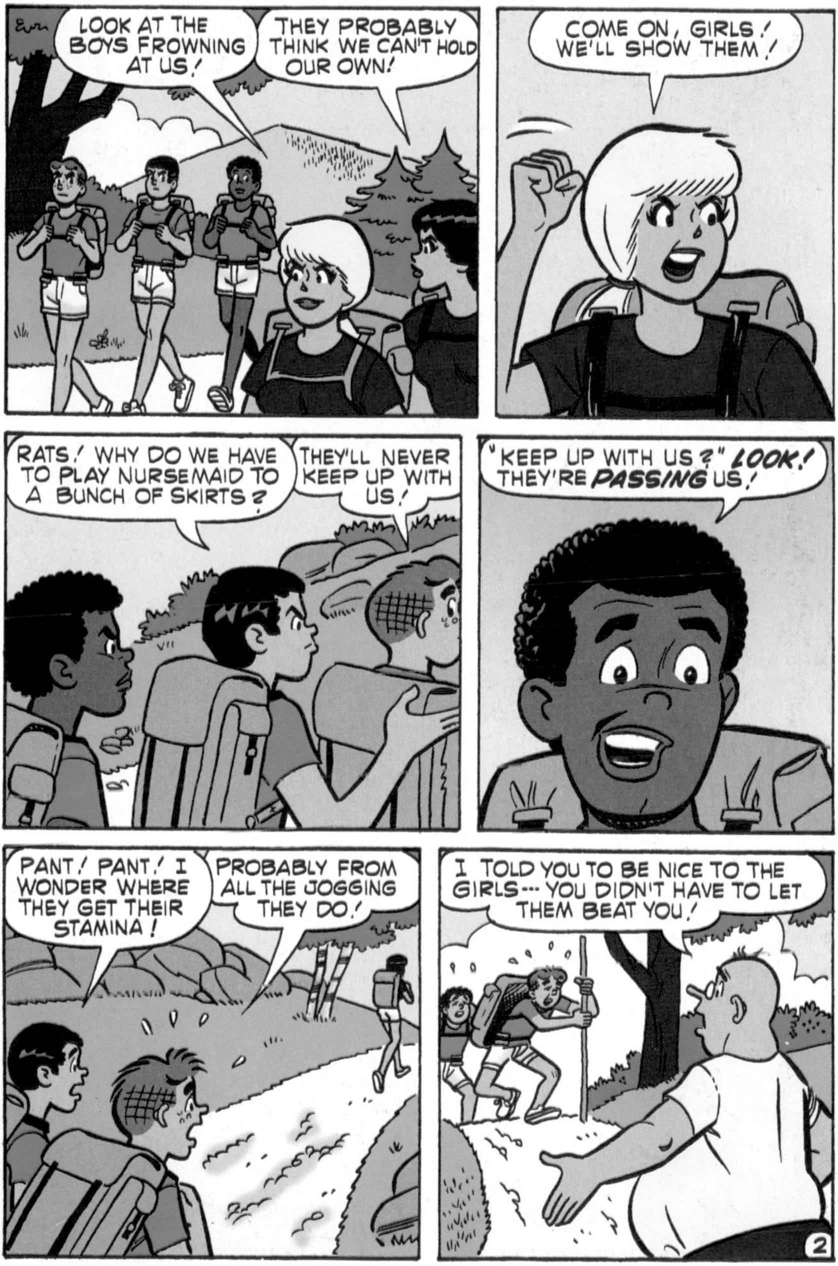
LOOK AT THE BOYS FROWNING AT US!
THEY PROBABLY THINK WE CAN'T HOLD OUR OWN!
COME ON, GIRLS! WE'LL SHOW THEM!
RATS! WHY DO WE HAVE TO PLAY NURSEMAID TO A BUNCH OF SKIRTS?
THEY'LL NEVER KEEP UP WITH US!
"KEEP UP WITH US?" LOOK! THEY'RE PASSING US!
PANT! PANT! I WONDER WHERE THEY GET THEIR STAMINA!
PROBABLY FROM ALL THE JOGGING THEY DO!
I TOLD YOU TO BE NICE TO THE GIRLS--- YOU DIDN'T HAVE TO LET THEM BEAT YOU!
2

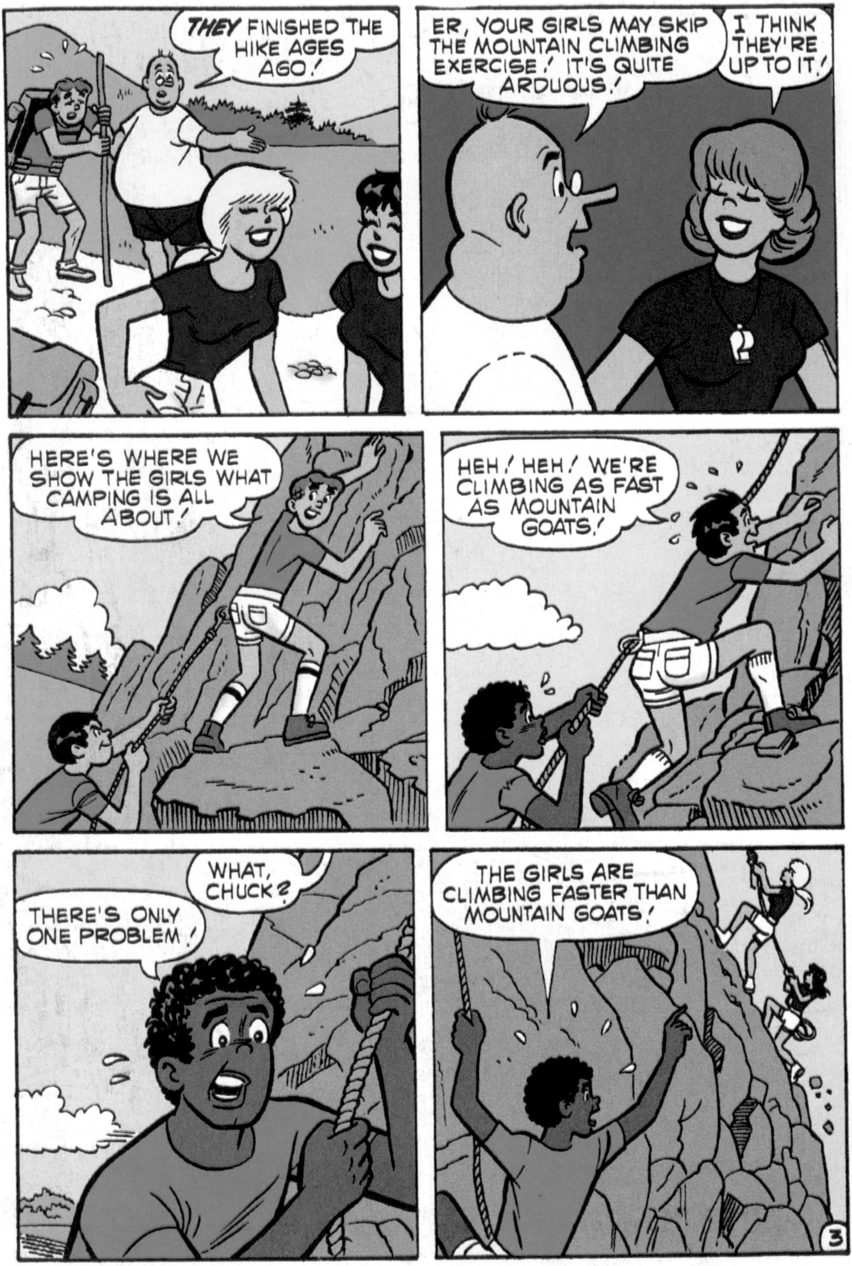
THEY FINISHED THE HIKE AGES AGO!
ER, YOUR GIRLS MAY SKIP THE MOUNTAIN CLIMBING EXERCISE! IT'S QUITE ARDUOUS!
I THINK THEY'RE UP TO IT!
HERE'S WHERE WE SHOW THE GIRLS WHAT CAMPING IS ALL ABOUT!
HEH! HEH! WE'RE CLIMBING AS FAST AS MOUNTAIN GOATS!
THERE'S ONLY ONE PROBLEM!
WHAT, CHUCK?
THE GIRLS ARE CLIMBING FASTER THAN MOUNTAIN GOATS!
3

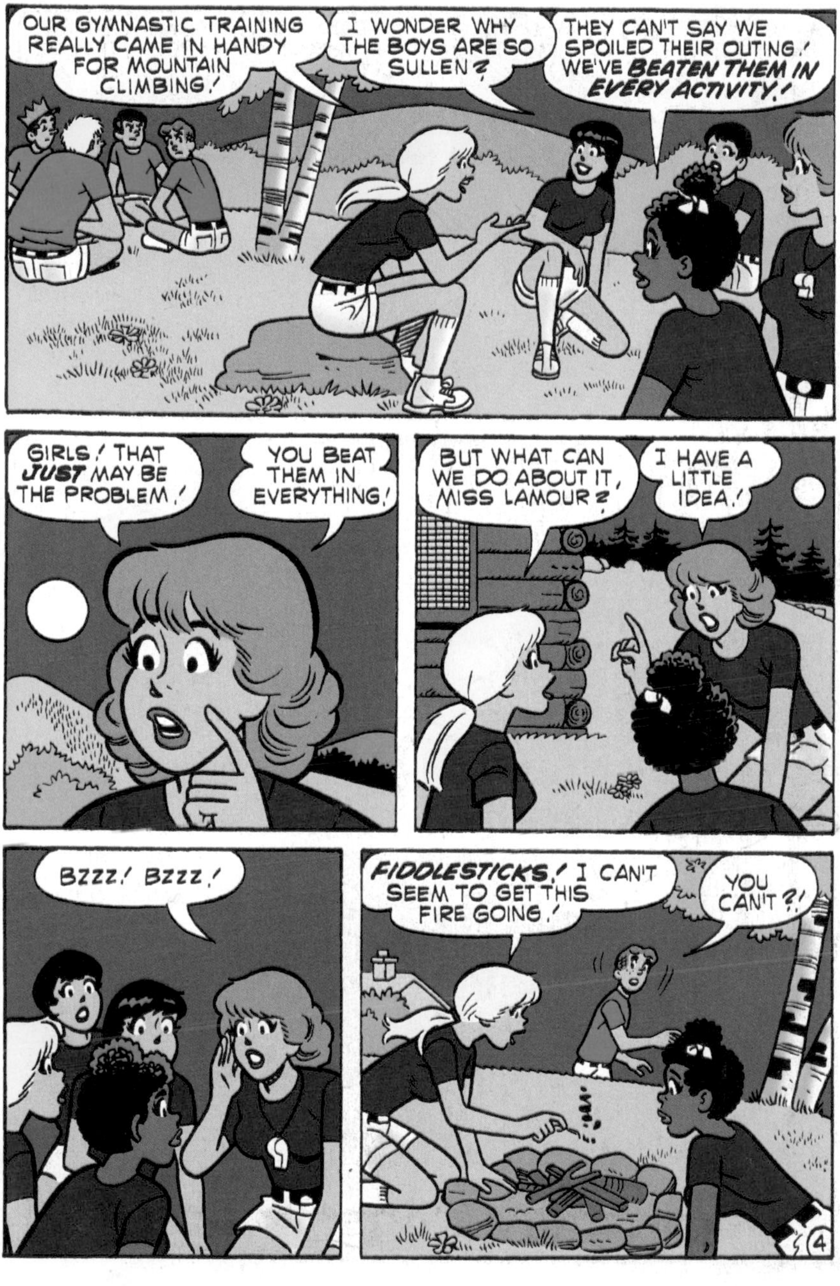
OUR GYMNASTIC TRAINING REALLY CAME IN HANDY FOR MOUNTAIN CLIMBING!
I WONDER WHY THE BOYS ARE SO SULLEN?
THEY CAN'T SAY WE SPOILED THEIR OUTING! WE'VE BEATEN THEM IN EVERY ACTIVITY!
GIRLS! THAT JUST MAY BE THE PROBLEM!
YOU BEAT THEM IN EVERYTHING!
BUT WHAT CAN WE DO ABOUT IT, MISS LAMOUR?
I HAVE A LITTLE IDEA!
BZZZ! BZZZ!
FIDDLESTICKS! I CAN'T SEEM TO GET THIS FIRE GOING!
YOU CAN'T?!
4

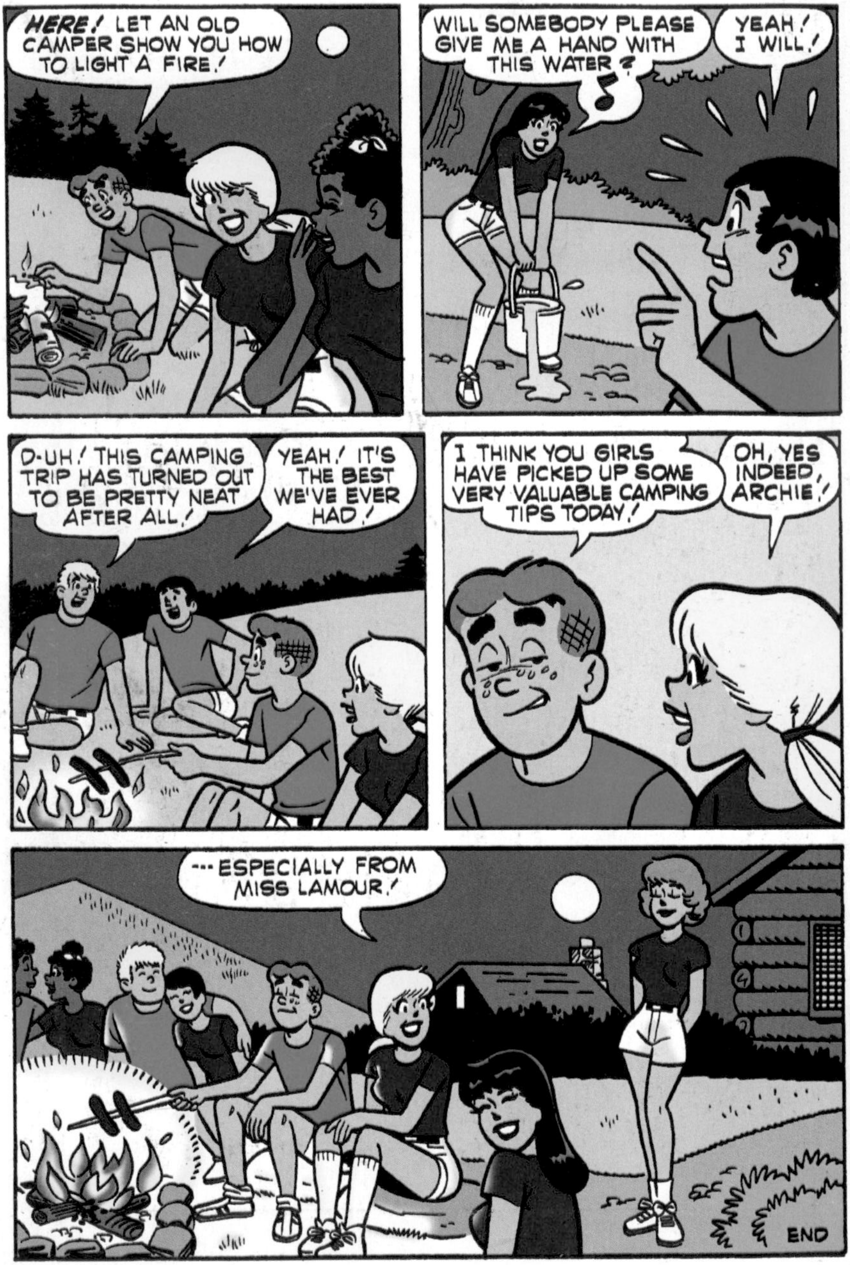
HERE! LET AN OLD CAMPER SHOW YOU HOW TO LIGHT A FIRE!
WILL SOMEBODY PLEASE GIVE ME A HAND WITH THIS WATER?
YEAH! I WILL!
D-UH! THIS CAMPING TRIP HAS TURNED OUT TO BE PRETTY NEAT AFTER ALL!
YEAH! IT'S THE BEST WE'VE EVER HAD!
I THINK YOU GIRLS HAVE PICKED UP SOME VERY VALUABLE CAMPING TIPS TODAY!
OH, YES INDEED, ARCHIE!
---ESPECIALLY FROM MISS LAMOUR!
END